THE LAST DAYS OF
DEMOCRACY

THE LAST DAYS OF
DEMOCRACY

HOW BIG MEDIA
AND
POWER-HUNGRY GOVERNMENT
ARE TURNING
AMERICA INTO A DICTATORSHIP

ELLIOT D. COHEN & BRUCE W. FRASER

Prometheus Books
59 John Glenn Drive
Amherst, New York 14228–2197

Published 2007 by Prometheus Books

Inquiries should be addressed to
Prometheus Books
59 John Glenn Drive
Amherst, New York 14228–2197
VOICE: 716–691–0133, ext. 207
FAX: 716–564–2711
WWW.PROMETHEUSBOOKS.COM

11 10 09 08 07   5 4 3 2 1

Library of Congress Cataloging-in-Publication Data

Cohen, Elliot D.
    The last days of democracy : how big media and power-hungry government are turning America into a dictatorship / Elliot D. Cohen, Bruce W. Fraser.
        p. cm.
    Includes bibliographical references.
    ISBN 978–1–59102–504–7 (alk. paper)
    1. Mass media—Political aspects—United States. 2. United States—Politics and government—2001– 3. Democracy—United States. I. Fraser, Bruce W. II. Title.

P95.82.U6C64 2007
302.230973—dc22

                                                            2007001609

Printed in the United States of America on acid-free paper

CONTENTS

8 **CONTENTS**

INTRODUCTION

by Peter Phillips
Director, Project Censored

The Bush administration is paltering to the American public with exaggerated misconceptions of world-wide terrorism to frighten us into supporting a global police state, and the US corporate media serves as the handmaid of this deception. With seven hundred military bases and a budget bigger than that of the rest of the world combined, the US military and its corporate media partners have become the new supreme-power force, repressing "terrorism" with full-spectrum dominance and cognitive ideological control.

The twenty-four-hour news shows on MSNBC, Fox, and CNN are closely interconnected with various governmental and corporate sources of news. Maintenance of continuous news shows requires a constant feed and an ever-entertaining supply of stimulating events and breaking news bites. Advertisement for mass consumption drives the system, and prepackaged sources of news are vital within this global news process. The preparation for and following of ongoing wars and terrorism fits well into the visual kaleidoscope of preplanned news. Government public relations specialists and media experts from private commercial interests provide ongoing news feeds to the national media distribution systems. The result is an emerging macro-symbiotic relationship between news dispensers and news suppliers. Perfect examples of this relationship are the press pools organized by the Pentagon, both in the Middle East and in Washington, DC, which give prescheduled reports on the war in Iraq to selected groups of news collectors (journalists) for distribution through their individual media organizations.

According to *PR Watch*, a publication of the Center for Media and Democracy, although the number of media formats and outlets has exploded in recent years, television remains the dominant news source in the United States. More than three-quarters of US adults rely on local TV news, and more than 70 percent turn to network TV or cable news on a daily or near-daily basis, according to a January 2006 Harris Poll.

Building on the format of prepackaged news, the public relations industry has experienced phenomenal growth since 2001. There are three publicly traded mega-corporations; in order of largesse: Omnicom, WPP, and Interpublic Group. Together, these firms employ 163,932 people in over 170 countries. Not only do these monstrous firms control a massive amount of wealth, they possess a network of connections in powerful international institutions with direct connections to governments, multinational corporations, and global-dominance group policy-making bodies. The Pentagon alone spent $1.1 billion on public relations and advertising in a thirty-month period starting in 2002.

Omnicom maintains an enormous group of subsidiaries, affiliates, and quasi-independent agencies such as BBDO Worldwide, DDB Worldwide, TBWA Worldwide, GSD&M, Merkley + Partners, and Zimmerman and Partners along with more than one hundred sixty firms through Diversified Agency Services division, including Fleishman-Hillard, Integer, and Rapp Collins.

WPP, a UK-based conglomerate, also touts an impressive list of subsidiaries such as Young & Rubicam, Burson-Marsteller, Ogilvy & Mather Worldwide, and Hill and Knowlton, along with numerous other PR, advertising, and crisis management firms.

Before the first Gulf War, a propaganda spectacle took place courtesy of Hill and Knowlton. This company helped create a national outrage against Iraq by recounting horrifying events supposedly caused by Iraqi soldiers in Kuwait. A young woman named Nayirah claimed in congressional testimony and before a national audience that she saw "Iraqi soldiers come into the [Kuwait] hospital with guns, and go into the room where 15 babies were in incubators. They took the babies out of the incubators, and left the babies on the cold floor to die." What the public was not told was that Nayirah was the daughter of Sheikh Sand Nasir al-Sabah, Kuwait's ambassador to the United States. The public also wasn't told that her performance was coordinated by the White House and choreographed by the US public relations firm Hill and Knowlton on behalf of the Kuwait government.

The big PR firms are closely interconnected with corporate media. Four members of the WPP group sit on the Council on

Foreign Relations. An Omnicom board member holds a position at Time Warner, one of the largest US media conglomerates; another holds a lifetime trustee position at PBS.

The public relations company Rendon Group is one of the firms hired for the PR management of America's preemptive wars. In the 1980s, the Rendon Group helped form American sentiment regarding the ousting of President Manuel Noriega in Panama. The company shaped international support for the first Gulf War, and in the 1990s created the Iraqi National Congress from image to marketing to the handpicking of Ahmed Chalabi. The Rendon Group created the images that have shaped support for a permanent war on terror including the toppling of the statue of Saddam Hussein, Private Jessica Lynch's heroic rescue, and dramatic tales of weapons of mass destruction.

The public relations industry continues its rapid consolidation of power and influence due in part to the contracts associated with the wars in Iraq and Afghanistan and the contentious relations between the United States and Iran, Russia, China, and Latin America.

At the end of President Bill Clinton's administration, global dominance advocates founded the Project for the New American Century (PNAC). Among the PNAC founders were eight people affiliated with the number one defense contractor, Lockheed Martin. Seven others were associated with the number three defense contractor Northrop Grumman. Of the twenty-five founders of PNAC, thirteen were later appointed to high-level positions in the George W. Bush administration.

In September 2000, PNAC produced a seventy-six-page report titled "Rebuilding America's Defenses: Strategy,

Forces and Resources for a New Century." The report, similar to the 1992 "Defense Policy Guidance" report, called for the protection of the American homeland, the ability to wage simultaneous theater wars, the right to perform global constabulary roles, and the control of space and cyberspace. It claimed that the 1990s were a decade of defense neglect and that the United States must increase military spending to preserve American geopolitical leadership as the world's superpower. The report also recognized that "the process of transformation . . . is likely to be a long one, absent some catastrophic and catalyzing event such as a new Pearl Harbor." The events of September 11, 2001, presented exactly the catastrophe that the authors of *Rebuilding America's Defenses* theorized were needed to accelerate a global dominance agenda. The resulting permanent war on terror has led to massive government defense spending, the invasions of two countries—and the threatening of three others, and the rapid acceleration of the US plans for military control of the world.

Three years ago, I met a Dutch journalist, Willem Oltman, at the International Campaign Against US Aggression on Iraq in Cairo, Egypt. Oltman described his teen years during World War II in the Dutch resistance movement. "The Nazi's called us terrorists," he exclaimed. "Now as the US invades and occupies other countries you do the same thing," he added.

Maintaining a US military global police force enriches defense contractors and inflames resistance. There is no worldwide terrorism threat other than the one we create when we make war on other peoples. Nor is there a media system that gives us the substance of the global empire's injustices.

A military global-dominance partnership with corporate media includes penetration into the actual boardrooms of media in the United States. A research team at Sonoma State University recently finished conducting a network analysis of the boards of directors of the ten big media organizations in the United States. The team determined that only 118 people compose the membership on the boards of directors of the ten big media giants. These 118 individuals in turn sit on the corporate boards of 288 national and international corporations. Four of the top ten media corporations in the United States have military DOD contractors on their boards of directors, including:

William Kennard: *New York Times*, Carlyle Group
Douglas Warner III: GE (NBC), Bechtel
John Bryson: Disney (ABC), Boeing
Alwyn Lewis: Disney (ABC), Halliburton
Douglas McCorkindale: Gannett, Lockheed Martin

The media elite, a key component of the policy elite in the United States, acts as the watchdog of acceptable ideological messages, the controller of news and information content, and the focus of decision making regarding media resources.

The corporate media in the United States has also shown an expanding dependency on global-dominance spokespersons as sources for news. Not only are former military generals often commentators on US talk shows, there is increasing use of global dominance think tanks as expert sources on TV news stories. For example, from 2000 to 2005, there was an 80 percent increase in the number of expert sources the

New York Times used from the American Enterprise Institute; and there was a 144 percent increase in the number it used from the Center for Strategic and International Studies.

Embedded reporters (news collectors) working directly with military units in the field must maintain cooperative working relationships with unit commanders as they feed breaking news back to the US public. Cooperative reporting is vital both to continued access to government news sources and to cognitive ideological control of the public. Therefore, rows of news story reviewers back at corporate media headquarters rewrite, soften, or spike news stories from the field that threaten the symbiotics of global news management.

For example, the *New York Times* published an article on April 20, 2005, reporting how seventeen innocent Afghans had been recently freed from Guantánamo prison after three and a half years. "Several of the Afghans said in interviews that they had been told by American officers that they were being freed because they were innocent of any crime," the article reported. "The men would be given new clothes, turbans and travel money and allowed to go home," the paper disclosed.

Prior to the release of the Guantánamo prisoners, Seymour Hersh had exposed the United States's worldwide abuse of power and violation of human rights in the *Guardian* and the *New Yorker*. Hersh documented that Secretary of Defense Donald Rumsfeld, with approval from the White House, had authorized a special-access program (SAP) to go on global manhunts for terrorists. It was deemed acceptable to kidnap suspected terrorists and take them to countries that would get tough on (torture) them during interrogations. Several hundred people captured wholesale in Afghanistan and transported to Cuba were deemed "unlawful enemy combatants" without rights of due process or coverage under the Geneva Convention.

The *New York Times*'s story covered the release of the internees without Hersh's historical context of high-level official approval. Additionally, the *New York Times* story failed to address how, in a country that supports due process and human rights, our military could take such tragic action violating the rights of these men and their families. Instead the story implies that the kidnapping of these Afghans was justified in that undoubtedly some of the prisoners were guilty. Failure to publish the full truth regarding the release of the Afghan prisoners and document torture is a strong indication that the *New York Times* and corporate media groups in general are unable and unwilling to fully address human rights violations by our own government.

Challenging the US military's global-dominance agenda is but one part of rebuilding democracy in the United States. Also needed is media reform from the bottom up by funding a diversity of independent media operations to challenge the corporate media's top-down propaganda. Needed also is the passage of laws that make it illegal for PR firms to create false news stories.

This book is one step in this agenda. Exposing the media lies and biases is an ongoing battle necessary for American democracy. Having a free press that addresses world poverty, sickness, and environmental issues will go much further in preventing single acts of terrorism inside the United States than any military actions we can muster. It is time to challenge the global-dominance agenda and stand up for human rights and the traditional American values of grassroots democracy, due process, governmental transparency, and a free-active media.

CHAPTER 1

THE NEW AMERICAN DICTATORSHIP

LONDON BRIDGE IS FALLING DOWN

On May 1, 2005, the *London Times* reported the contents of a leaked memo recording the minutes of a July 23, 2002, meeting between Tony Blair and his inner circle of advisers seven months before the US-led invasion of Iraq. The memo reported that "Bush wanted to remove Saddam, through military action, justified by the conjunction of terrorism and WMD [weapons of mass destruction]. But the intelligence and facts were being fixed around the policy." The memo also stated, "It seemed clear that Bush had made up his mind to take military action, even if the timing was not yet decided. But the case was thin. Saddam was not threatening his neighbours, and his WMD capability was less than that of Libya, North Korea or Iran." Nevertheless, "If the political context were right, people would support regime change," explained Blair. And, according to the *London Times*, "a separate secret briefing for the meeting said Britain and America had to 'create' conditions to justify a war."

This was surely the story of the century, the kind of stuff they make movies out of. It's the tail wagging the dog with a vengeance: "creating" the conditions of war; making the facts "fit" the policy. And, to top this, the memo states that "there was little discussion in Washington of the aftermath after military action." It was the scheming, lying manipulation of a nation into a war that would cost thousands of innocent lives, for bogus reasons, and without a carefully conceived exit plan.

This chilling theme is one that has been repeated in history. Listen to these words:

> Why of course the people don't want war. But, after all, it is the leaders of the country who determine the policy and it is always a simple matter to drag the people along, whether it is a democracy, or a fascist dictatorship, or a parliament, or a communist dictatorship. Voice or no voice, the people can always be brought to the bidding of the leaders. That is easy. All you have to do is tell them they are being attacked, and denounce the peacemakers for lack of patriotism and exposing the country to danger. It works the same in any country.

These are the words of Hermann Goering, the Reich Marshall of Adolf Hitler.[1] But they might as well have been the words reported by the *London Times* in 2005. The disgusting truth is that history does repeat itself and people do forget. But the plot thickens still.

The story of the century, "The Most Powerful Nation on Earth Duped into Going to War," received scant coverage by the mainstream media (MSM). There was a virtual media blackout. While Michael Jackson and the Runaway Bride were being beat to death on Fox, CNN, NBC, CBS, and ABC, Internet bloggers and the foreign press buzzed with the story of the century.

When the Internet buzz finally exploded, the MSM could no longer ignore it, at least not entirely. Accordingly, it gave lip service to the memo, dismissing it with the unqualified, official line that it was "nothing new," while news shows like NBC's "Chris Matthews Show" played "softball" about whether the United States had an adequate exit plan in place before it invaded Iraq. The central issue, whether the Bush administration betrayed Congress and the American people, received scant attention. There is little doubt why mainstream corporate media didn't report this story initially and then soft-pedaled it afterward. This was no mere oversight, nor was it a simple case of shoddy reporting. It was part of a systematic takeover of a formerly free nation by a politico-corporate machine that speaks only in empty rhetoric about freedom and democracy. What this colossal machine really cares about is money, money, and more money. The only checks and balances it respects come with dollar signs.

In a free, democratic nation, the media serves as a Fourth Estate, a fourth branch of government that protects the people against abuses of power. It is supposed to expose government corruption and send it packing by keeping voters in the loop. This is why the Founding Fathers drafted the First Amendment to the US Constitution, which states, "Congress shall make no law . . . abridging the freedom of speech, or of the press." In fact, Thomas Jefferson thought the press more important than government. So spoke this sage: "The basis of our government being the opinion of the people, the very first object should be to keep that right; and were it left to me to decide whether we should have a government without newspapers, or newspapers without a government, I should not hesitate a moment to prefer the latter."[2]

The media was conceived from the start to be an adversary of government, to serve as a watchdog of the people, but this noble guardian of democracy has lost its teeth and has now become a docile lapdog of government. White House press conferences have become coffee klatches with prestaged questions and even fake journalists infiltrating the press corps to advocate for government. The press secretary himself has become a parrot for the government, not an impartial liaison. Mainstream corporate media routinely wine and dine politicians and take them on vacations just to make headway with corporate lobbies. Official government spokespersons become the final arbiters of the truth as budgets for investigative reporting are scrapped and infotainment replaces hard news. Stories are killed, "edited," buried, or otherwise sanitized to conceal important details. Editorials slanted to the beat of government policy are passed off as "breaking news." Prepackaged "news" produced for the government by public relations firms has been seamlessly knitted into the nightly news of local network affiliates and passed off as "real news."[3]

Why did so many Americans erroneously believe there was a connection between Saddam Hussein and Osama bin Laden? Association psychology worked like a charm when

"Dubya" mentioned these names in the same breath. But the media did nothing to dispel the myth. Worse, it helped to propagate it by repeating official government sources—like Dick Cheney—instead of doing its own investigative reporting. It was more "cost-effective" to parrot official sources than to spend money to probe and investigate.

When CNN, "the most trusted name in news," presented the story of the Abu Ghraib prison abuses, it reported that Bush was "concerned" about the abuses, not that he said he was concerned. If the abuses were ordered from the top, he would surely have been concerned, but primarily about protecting himself. The press didn't look into that, either.

In the aftermath of the outing of "Deep Throat" (AKA former FBI agent Mark Felt), the mainstream news networks have had the audacity to ask whether Felt was a hero or a traitor to his nation. In this, the lesson learned from Watergate, that not even the president of the United States can be placed above suspicion, has been lost in banter about whether anonymous sources should be used and whether an FBI agent who blows the whistle on illegal government activities should be considered a criminal. The intimidation here is less than subtle, and the media message is clear: Trust your government unconditionally, for it can do no wrong. And the sorry truth is that this media messenger is supposed to be the vanguard of democracy entrusted with protecting Americans against governmental abuse of power!

Yes, the scent of Nixon is in the air with the leak that the Bush administration has an "enemies list" with over ten thousand names on it, from left-leaning, nonmainstream reporters like Joe Conason to Democratic senator Barbara Boxer; and, of course, how could they leave out Michael

Moore! Digging deep into the personal lives of these "Enemies of State," this brainchild of "Bush's Brain" (AKA Karl Rove) has afforded a self-serving use for the USA PATRIOT Act in digging up dirt. According to a White House aid, Rove is very frank about the purpose of the list: "Karl operates under the rule that if you fuck with us, we'll fuck you over." And all you need to do in order to "fuck" with them is to disagree with their policies. This would have made even Nixon blush! But this story has not made it to the mainstream to date.

And speaking of abuses of the USA PATRIOT Act, imagine what the Feds could do with their spying activities if they didn't have to get a warrant from a court before invading the privacy of American citizens! On December 16, 2005, the *New York Times* broke the story "Bush Lets U.S. Spy on Callers without Courts." I use the word "broke" somewhat loosely, since, by its own admission, the *Times* held off publishing the story at the request of the Bush administration for more than a year. According to the article, the president had secretly authorized the National Security Agency (NSA) to engage in mass, warrantless wiretapping of phone and e-mail messages of thousands of American citizens for four years on the grounds that this was necessary in fighting its war on terror. After meeting with the Bush administration, the *Times* agreed not to divulge the story, allegedly in order not to alert terrorism suspects that they were being spied on.

Was the *Times* covering up criminal activities by the government? On January 16, 2006, former vice president Al Gore delivered a powerful speech in Constitution Hall in Washington, DC, blasting the Bush administration for dangerous breaches of US citizens' constitutional right against unlawful searches and declaring the need for special counsel "to pursue the criminal issues raised by warrantless wiretapping of Americans by the President." Gore pointed out that "during the period when this eavesdropping was still secret, the President went out of his way to reassure the American people on more than one occasion that, of course, judicial permission is required for any government spying on American citizens and that, of course, these constitutional safeguards were still in place."4 In other words, Bush lied to us, the American people.

When Clinton attempted to deceive us about his private sex life, the press was all over it like a sleazy soap opera, and every gruesome detail of Clinton's sex life (as graphically articulated in the Starr Report) was eventually plastered all over the newspapers. Yet, despite the seriousness of the allegations, Gore's speech didn't see the light of day on mainstream network news. Not even the *New York Times* dignified it, even though, the day after Gore's speech, it did do a follow-up story on the still ongoing Bush wiretappings. Did the boys in Washington pay the *Times* another visit?

Just in case you are wondering what's so urgent about media vigilance in getting the word out on Bush's domestic spying activities, it's useful to recall the words of the Fourth Amendment of the United States Constitution.

> The right of the people to be secure in their persons, houses, papers, and effects, against unreasonable searches and seizures, shall not be violated, and no warrants shall issue, but upon probable cause, supported by oath or affirmation, and particularly describing the place to be searched, and the persons or things to be seized.

Lest our Constitution not be worth the paper it's written on, we Americans deserve no less than relentless, single-minded, objective media coverage of Bush's systematic invasion of Americans' privacy in all of its Gore-y details!

And, just in case you are thinking that they haven't gotten around to warrantless *physical* searches, guess again. On March 27, 2006, *U.S. News & World Report* revealed that, in a little-noticed white paper submitted to Congress on January 19 by Attorney General Alberto Gonzales, the Justice Department has claimed that "the president has inherent authority to conduct warrantless physical searches for foreign intelligence purposes." The article went on to report at least one instance of an American citizen (a defense attorney who was representing a subject of a terrorism investigation) having allegedly been the target of warrantless covert searches by the FBI in both his home and office. With the exception of Keith Olbermann's "Countdown," on MSNBC, the story received virtually no mainstream coverage. Yet, for all of us who value our Fourth Amendment rights—or what's left of them—this story was of monumental importance. A vigilant, responsible media in a democratic society would have sounded the alarm, putting every American citizen on alert. It would have strained every ounce of its investigative powers to expose such illegal, clandestine, government activities and to see that such egregious claims to absolute authority were subjected to the court of popular opinion. Instead, the MSM acted like the handmaiden to dictatorship. Yes, dictatorship! The media buried its head in the sand while the government it had been charged to scrutinize organized yet a further assault on our freedom.

There is also a distinction to be made between the

overzealous but still earnest attempt to protect a nation against terrorists through the exercise of such unconstrained executive power (no matter how misguided and illegal such an exercise of power might be) and the appeal to the threat of terrorism in order to frighten the American people into giving up their civil liberties. As will become clear in chapter 7, there is good reason to believe that the government is guilty of the latter form of treachery. Yet the specter of such a heinous possibility is scarcely raised in the MSM, not even by the *New York Times*.

A government that was *merely* concerned about protecting its citizens against another terrorist attack would have no practical need to resort to unlawful surveillance. It hardly makes sense to engage in warrantless wiretapping and physical searches when these same activities could be conducted with the permission of a court. The Foreign Intelligence Surveillance Act (FISA) courts that have been set up for these very purposes have rarely turned down a request. Moreover, the law provides up to seventy-two hours after the search has been conducted to obtain court approval. No, it is more rational to think that the government is up to hanky-panky than to suppose that there is a necessity for bypassing the courts.

Here's such an example of hanky-panky as reported by Mark Crispin Miller in his recent book *Fooled Again*. According to Miller, sometime late on the night of Friday, July 2, 2003, or in the early morning hours of Saturday, the offices of Burges and Burges, an Akron consulting firm employed by the Ohio Democratic Party working for the election of John Kerry, were burglarized. The only things stolen were two computers containing sensitive, campaign-related information.

Several similar burglaries occurred in Ohio in which the targets were consistently computers containing highly sensitive information—including e-mails discussing strategies for countering anticipated attempts to turn voters away from the polls. As you might expect, none of these events received MSM coverage.

Obviously, no court would have signed off on such illicit activities. Yet these facts offer insight into why a government that would stoop to such illicit activities for personal gain might prefer to sidestep getting a court warrant.

In August 2006 a federal judge ruled that Bush's NSA spying program was unconstitutional; and in January 2006 a civil law suit was also filed by the ACLU. In January 2007 the Bush administration surprised its critics by claiming that it would seek warrants from the FISA Court for domestic spying. However, while the MSM carried this announcement, it failed to mention that the warrants in question would apparently include standing orders from the court; in other words, blank checks. At the time of this writing, the exact nature of such court oversight is not clear. According to four anonymous congressional officials who have been briefed by the Justice Department, the oversight is a mixed bag of individual and general warrants. The Bush administration has predictably refused to release these secret orders to the public on grounds of "national security." In a letter to two high-ranking members of the Senate Judiciary Committee, Attorney General Alberto Gonzales stated of these orders that "they are innovative, they are complex, and it took considerable time and work for the Government to develop the approach that was proposed to the Court and for the judge on the FISC to consider and approve these orders." So at most what we know is that we can be "innovatively" spied on based on a "complex" set of directives devised by the Bush administration (not the FISA Court) that include some individual warrants but also some standing warrants that can be applied at the discretion of the Bush administration.

The Bush administration appears to have favored this "compromise" proposal over at least one other that had been proposed in the form of congressional legislation—the so-called Terrorist Surveillance Act of 2006—which would allow the Bush administration forty-five days to get an individual warrant. Given the Bush administration's predilection for secrecy and its distain for oversight, it is not unreasonable to suspect that the compromise proposal gives it greater power and authority to invade the privacy of American citizens than any alternative proposal it previously considered. What does this say about the constitutionality of this new spying program? There are some, even in Congress, who worry that the Bush administration may have merely traded one set of black bags for another.

But striking up "innovative" and secret compromise agreements with the FISA Court to sidestep individual warrants for eavesdropping on Americans might be just the tip of the iceberg. In April 2006 a former AT&T employee, Mark Klein, has disclosed another secret NSA program for wholesale, warrantless monitoring of millions of domestic and foreign e-mail messages nationally on a daily basis. According to Klein, at the request of the government, AT&T has installed e-mail parsing equipment in a secret room hidden deep inside AT&T's San Francisco office, and the cables carrying incoming electronic messages have been spliced and routed to this room. According to Klein, access to the room requires

NSA clearance. And Klein, who is presently in the process of filing a class action law suit, has hard data to prove the existence of this NSA spying operation. He has internal company documents and even personal photos. Moreover, Klein learned from a coworker that there are at least six other locations where secret rooms have been installed, including Atlanta, San Diego, Los Angeles, Palo Alto, San Jose, and Seattle.

What this means is that every American who sends an e-mail message through the AT&T system, not just terrorism suspects, is being spied on. (And, it would not come as a surprise to find that the NSA had similar outposts at other major Internet service providers.) According to Criminal Defense Lawyer Nancy Hollander, who represents several Muslim Americans, "I've personally never been afraid of my government until now. And now I feel personally afraid that I could be locked up tomorrow." Beware of what you might put into your e-mail messages. This is no wild conspiracy theory. It's the ugly reality of what our free nation has become in the last six years.[5]

And it gets even worse when you learn that the Pentagon and the CIA have also gotten involved in spying on American citizens. The FBI is supposed to be the main agency for domestic counterterrorism, and the CIA is supposed to stick to overseas espionage activities. However, this is no longer the case. Under Bush, the CIA and the Pentagon have been actively issuing "national security letters" to credit card companies, banks, and other financial agencies to turn over the records of hundreds of American citizens. Here then is the true state of the union—a burgeoning police state.

Yet the MSM has ghoulishly preferred to play down or ignore such stories, since, under the Bush administration, media organizations that step out of line pay a price. For example, when *Newsweek* in its May 9, 2005, issue published a report claiming that interrogators at the US military prison at Guantánamo Bay, Cuba, desecrated copies of the Quran, the Muslim holy book, the White House did more than disavow the claim. It also blamed the magazine for deaths occurring during riots in Afghanistan and demanded a "full retraction" of the story. *Newsweek* obediently retracted by saying that its senior government source had backed away from his initial story. White House press secretary Scott McClellan threw *Newsweek* a bone for taking "a good first step" but admonished that it now had a further responsibility to spread the word throughout the Muslim world that US interrogators "treat the Quran with great care and respect." Does the editor in chief of *Newsweek* reside at 1600 Pennsylvania Avenue?

Of course, when the Pentagon released a statement dismissing the allegations as lacking credibility, CNN, Fox, NBC, CBS, and ABC obediently reported it, thereby putting an end to naughty *Newsweek*'s limp attempt to act like a real news outlet.

Yet the *London Sun* got away with publishing a prison photo of Saddam Hussein in his underwear under the headline "Tyrants in his Pants" along with such quotes as "It's over, guys. The evil days of Saddam's Baath Party are never coming back—and here's the proof." The *London Sun*, which is owned by Rupert Murdoch, the owner of Fox News Channel and a close ally of the Bush administration, did not have to apologize to anyone, because it did just what the Bush administration wanted it to do: helped to quell the opposition in Iraq by diminishing the image of its leader.

When a mysterious bulge appeared on the back of

George W. Bush's jacket during the first presidential debate of the 2004 election, Salon.com published a careful investigation along with a picture revealing the mysterious bulge. Salon cited expert testimony asserting that the bulge was probably a receiver. Salon also reported that government agents had been checking journalists to see what frequency their cameras were operating at.

Did the MSM cover the story? Well, sort of. For example, the *New York Times* published a short piece that quoted a Bush spokesperson who called the suspicions "nonsense," and that was the last word from the *Times* on the subject. Curiously, the *Times* had been visited by a high government official just prior to publishing this article dismissing the allegations.

These and countless other examples make it clear that the corporate MSM is failing at its charge of keeping Americans informed. Censorship, government propaganda, parroting of official government sources, media manipulation, and government intimidation have replaced careful investigative reporting as the norm.

And things continue to worsen as the government finds ways (some more subtle than others) to relax media ownership rules to let fewer and fewer media giants control more and more markets. This trend toward government deregulation of corporate media ownership violates constitutional safeguards on diversity, public interest, and the capacity to self-govern. The popular rebuttal that we now have more stations and, therefore, more diversity, is a glaring fallacy. When these bountiful stations have but a few owners, a few very wealthy ones, it's not hard to see what side of the political divide they'll land on.

There is, of course, the Internet, the last bastion of free speech. But corporate media presence on the Net is expanding, and, as you will see, the dismantling of the free-access architecture of the Internet has already commenced. Unbeknownst to most Americans, who rely on the MSM for information, corporate media has been given the green light by the FCC, acting with authority from the US Supreme Court, to commandeer the cables and phone lines that carry information, throw out independent service providers, and, effectively, turn the Internet into just another tentacle of the mainstream corporate media. Unless corporate media is stopped, this last bastion of democracy will soon topple.

As will be discussed in chapter 4, we now inhabit a matrix where freedom is largely an illusion. In choosing between brands of toothpaste, we have the sense that freedom is still ours for the taking. But the reality of freedom in America is waning. The minds of Americans are now being polluted and programmed with propaganda and disinformation. We have entered a brave new world that rewards conformity to the status quo and punishes divergence; a world where freedom has secretly been redefined as conformity to authority. We are embarking on a new era where technology will make it easy for government to monitor what we read, where we go, what we see, what we think, and, ultimately, who we are.

The defense of freedom has become a pretext to acquire our freedom. The good name of freedom is exploited in patriotic callings to arms, but these are just empty slogans used by government to keep us as pawns in its own pursuit of power and control. What has fighting a war in Iraq to do with defending American soil against terrorists when those who attacked us on September 11, 2001, were not even Iraqis? Such pretentious appeals to freedom only keep us *thinking* that we are free.

In 1981, when the Soviet Union marched into Poland and declared martial law, I (EC) was a young journal editor who had published an inaugural issue of a philosophy journal containing an article "Political Free Speech Ought to Be an Absolute." At the same time, I received a request from a professor in Poland for the journal issue. I paused to think what it would mean to send literature that would surely have been viewed as "subversive." In those early days, I counted myself fortunate to live in a democratic society that thrived on free speech, especially the political sort. It is chilling to think that there is now afoot in America the very same oppressive trends that seemed so utterly alien to me as a young writer.

This is why media is so fundamental to freedom. Without a functional media, there is no stopping government from divesting us of our freedom, imperceptibly and incrementally stealing off with it; all along reminding us that freedom is not free, never mentioning that our freedom itself is the very price to be paid. The media may be our only salvation, but it is now functionally inept.

THE EMPEROR IS NAKED

It is useful to be reminded of the perennial wisdom of the United States Declaration of Independence:

> We hold these truths to be self-evident, that all men are created equal, that they are endowed by their Creator with

certain unalienable Rights, that among these are Life, Liberty and the pursuit of Happiness. —That to secure these rights, Governments are instituted among Men, deriving their just powers from the consent of the governed . . .

Now read this carefully: **the government derives its just power *from* the consent of the citizens, and it exists in furtherance of *our* fundamental rights to life, liberty, and the pursuit of happiness.**

These rights are trespassed every time Americans pay taxes believing that their money is for a purpose that has been falsely represented. They are violated every time a young person is sent overseas to fight a war the reasons for which have not been honestly represented—such as when the "facts are fixed" around the policy.

In a democracy, it is the citizens who are the ultimate decision makers. Politicians are representatives of the people and are entrusted to act according to the will of the people. This will is disabled when it is uninformed or, worse, misinformed. This is why we need a functional press to make sure that the will of the people remains informed. Otherwise we cannot even pretend to have a working democracy. Otherwise we cannot even begin to strip away the veil of lies and deceit that keeps a naked emperor in clothes.

Totalitarian, antidemocratic governments have historically divested the governed of the knowledge needed to collectively participate in a democratic process. They have sought to keep citizens in ignorance because people in such a condition are more dependent on others to make decisions for them.

Dictators have routinely sought control of the media in

order to ensure that the truth does not filter down to the people. For example, *Pravda* of the former Soviet Union fed communist propaganda to the people and kept them ignorant of what was happening in other parts of the world. Conversely, dictators have pathologically sought to keep *themselves* informed and to utilize covert activities to police their own citizens—for example, the KGB in the former Soviet Union.

So, two clear signs that democracy is in trouble are that the press is aligned with government in not adequately keeping the people informed—especially about government activities, and, second, the government is itself pathologically preoccupied with policing its own citizens—invariably for some "legitimate" reason related to "national security."

On three separate occasions, President George W. Bush quipped that dictatorship would be a lot easier than democracy, and on one occasion he added, "Just as long as I'm the dictator." Coming from the leader of the free world, these comments may rightly be taken as a bad joke, but was Bush *just* joking? The present erosion of fundamental constitutional rights in America gives this question import with cause for much concern.

For example, Section 213 of the PATRIOT Act, the controversial antiterrorism measure instituted shortly after the attacks of September 11, 2001, authorizes issuance of "sneak and peek" warrants to search the homes of anyone suspected of a federal crime, even a misdemeanor having nothing to do with terrorism, without the person's knowledge. The Fourth Amendment of the Constitution affirms that "the right of the people to be secure in their persons, houses, papers, and effects, against unreasonable searches and seizures, shall not be violated, and no Warrants shall issue, but upon probable cause . . ." Unfortunately this provision does not require "probable cause." Without adequate judicial safeguards, how secure are we in our persons, houses, papers, and effects?

Section 215 of this same act allows the federal government to "make an application for an order requiring the production of any tangible things (including books, records, papers, documents, and other items) for an investigation to protect against international terrorism or clandestine intelligence activities." However, since the act does not say what constitutes "international terrorism," the Pandora's box is opened for appropriation of anything personal the government might deem to be subversive of its own authority.

There have also been clear instances of KGB-like activities undertaken to control "subversive" activities for purported purposes of "national security." For example, in February of 2004, the Austin police department sent undercover agents to spy on antiwar protesters during organizing meetings. And similar undercover operations have occurred throughout the nation to infiltrate antiwar organizations. Such acts as these smack of a police state in which the First Amendment right to freedom of speech is given just lip service.

And since the inception of the war in Iraq, peaceful antiwar protesters exercising their First Amendment right of assembly have been arrested. For example, on March 19, 2005, to mark the second anniversary of the Iraq invasion, simultaneous protests were held in Times Square, Brooklyn, and the Bronx outside military recruiting stations. There were twenty-four arrested in Times Square during a die-in and another eight in Brooklyn outside recruiting stations on Flatbush Avenue. Whatever happened to those immortal

First Amendment words, "Congress shall make no law respecting . . . the right of the people peaceably to assemble"?

The MSM has also consistently failed to give adequate coverage of the antiwar movement. On CNN's "Reliable Sources," in an interview about whether the media have provided just coverage of protests against the war in Iraq, witness what Dan Rather guardedly stated, "[W]e've tried on the 'CBS Evening News,' for which I'm responsible . . . to give the coverage we think is merited, but I'm open to the criticism. The White House and the administration power is able to control the images to a very large degree. It has been growing over the years. And that's the context in which we talk about, well, how much coverage does the anti-war movement merit? And I think it's a valid criticism it's been underreported."[6] The White House is "**able to control the images to a very large degree**"? This is CBS, not *Pravda*; this is the United States, not the Soviet Union; and the White House is not the Kremlin! The good citizens of this nation with whom the political franchise is vested see and hear largely only what the government deems suitable for their eyes and ears. This is not democracy; and this is not freedom.

The tendency of the current administration to control images adverse to its interests has prompted even the most heartrending deception. One example is the story of Patrick Tillman, a former NFL football player who gave up a three-year 3.5 million-dollar contract with the Arizona Cardinals to serve his nation in the military shortly after the attacks of September 11, 2001. In the immortal words of US military spokesman Lt. Col. Matthew Beevers, "In today's world of instant gratification and selfishness, here is a man that was defined by words like loyalty, honor, passion, courage, strength and nobility. He is a modern-day hero."[7]

Sadly, this national hero was gunned down in Afghanistan by friendly fire, but the Pentagon covered this fact up and reported that he was killed by *enemy* fire. The military burned Tillman's uniform and protective armor as part of a cover-up, and not even his brother (also enlisted) and his parents were informed of the circumstances of his death. It was one month after Tillman's burial that the truth finally surfaced. Tillman's mother, Mary Tillman, stated, "I'm disgusted by things that have happened with the Pentagon since my son's death. I don't trust them one bit." And Tillman's father stated, "The investigation is a lie. It's insulting to Pat."[8] However, the image of a great American athlete heroically giving up his life to fight the enemy was good for the war effort, whereas the image of friendly fire would have worked against it.

The mainstream corporate media is complicit in such deception every time it passively reports what it hears from officialdom as though it were the truth. CNN reported that President Bush was concerned about the prison abuses at Abu Ghraib, not that he *said* he was concerned. If the commander in chief had approved the treatment under question, he would certainly have been concerned, but not necessarily about the violation of the *victims'* rights. After the presidential election of 2004, when the exit polls largely contradicted the election outcome, the *New York Times* dismissed the possibility of voter fraud with an official denial from a White House spokesperson.

Prior to the invasion of Iraq, the *New York Times* was, by its own admission, guilty of substituting official reports for hard fact in its coverage of whether there were weapons of mass destruction (WMD) in Iraq. In a brief editorial (albeit not on its front page), the paper guardedly stated, "But we do fault ourselves for failing to deconstruct the W.M.D. issue with the kind of thoroughness we directed at the question of a link between Iraq and Al Qaeda, or even tax cuts in time of war. We did not listen carefully to the people who disagreed with us. Our certainty flowed from the fact that such an overwhelming majority of government officials, past and present, top intelligence officials and other experts were sure that the weapons were there. We had a groupthink of our own."[9] This admission followed a previous editor's note to the same effect. Still, this belated and guarded admission may have merely been an attempt to save face in light of the obvious faux pas of having supported a preemptive war based on faulty intelligence at best and the perpetration of fraud at worst. Guarded admissions of wrongdoing by wrongdoers caught with their pants down are never noble and are even more regrettable when the wrongdoer is a well-respected newspaper such as the *New York Times*.

Thorough investigative reporting does not hang its hat on a denial by the very individuals under investigation. Instead, it vigorously pursues and follows up on any story portending important consequences for the public. Now, what would you say if a judge passed a verdict of "not guilty" because the accused denied the allegation? "No, your Honor, I did not break and enter" says the accused. "Not guilty," says the judge. Would this not be an affront to the American system of jurisprudence? The case is the same when the mainstream corporate media attempts to turn official statements into facts without putting them on trial. This is a kangaroo press!

A sad example of the MSM's lack of such fortitude was in its coverage of the serious potential for voter fraud in the 2004 presidential election (see chapter 10). Years prior, there had been reasonable concern that the security of electronic touch-screen voting machines might be breached. Experts in computer programming pointed to the ease at which malicious code could be installed into the thousands of lines of "spaghetti" code composing an electronic voting program. And, after the election, when several credible studies emerged with evidence that the exit polls could not have been so far off, the MSM summarily dismissed the possibility of election fraud. In contrast, when the Ukraine came up with such skewed election results, the election was declared invalid and a new one was conducted.

How does this bode for democracy in America? If we cannot cast our votes with the confidence that they will count, count equally, and that no other votes will be counted; and if there is no reliable Fourth Estate to expose possible fraud and to restore our trust in the system, then democracy in America is indeed in jeopardy.

The news hounds should have been hot on the trail! Given the enormity of the stakes for a democratic society, and given the debacle of 2000 in Florida, media had a duty to scrupulously investigate and keep Americans fully informed about anything that had potential to compromise their right to vote.

Sadly, mainstream corporate media substituted their usual parroting of official government and corporate officials, and the question was relegated to an occasional editorial.[10] So what stories *were*, in fact, making the front pages? Scott Peterson, Kobe Bryant, and Michael Jackson.

"How many viewers think Michael Jackson is a pedophile?" was substituted for "How many viewers still have the vote?" And here's another question that never made headlines: "How many viewers were being duped and treated like dimwits?"

Americans have become fodder for systematic politico-corporate deception. The MSM is now the mouthpiece for government deception and manipulation of reality to advance its own agenda. The true victims are the American people whose trust is exploited and whose constitutional rights are denied. '

But the problem doesn't end there. The current administration has also challenged the separation of government powers in America. On one occasion, President Bush said, "The legislature's job is to write law. It's the executive branch's job to interpret law." This is a good recipe for tyranny. In a democracy, the courts, not the executive branch, interpret the law! This lack of knowledge is an affront to the basic infrastructure of our system of government.

Article 1, Section 9, Clause 2 of the US Constitution states that the writ of habeas corpus shall not be suspended "unless when in cases of rebellion or invasion the public safety may require it." This means that it is unconstitutional to detain someone indefinitely without having a court determine whether lawful grounds exist for the detention. But when more than six hundred suspected "enemy combatants" were "disappeared" and brought to Guantanamo Bay, Cuba, they were deprived of the writ of habeas corpus.

The Bush administration maintained that the president was exercising his constitutional powers in a time of war, but in *Hamdi v. Rumsfeld* (April 2004), the Supreme Court denied that Bush had constitutional authority to detain enemy combatants without the protection of the courts. Wrote Justice Sandra Day O'Connor, "Whatever power the United States Constitution envisions for the Executive in its exchanges with other nations or with enemy organizations in times of conflict, it most assuredly envisions a role for all three branches when individual liberties are at stake."

Nevertheless, the Court's words fell on deaf ears when Congress walked lockstep with the Bush Administration to pass the Military Commissions Act of 2006. This act denied the writ of habeas corpus to any "alien" (non-US citizen) determined to be an "unlawful enemy combatant." What is even more alarming is the vague manner in which the act defined "unlawful enemy combatant."

According to this act, an "unlawful enemy combatant" is "an individual engaged in hostilities against the United States who is not a lawful enemy combatant." Basically, this means that if a person is not a soldier in the service of a foreign government, but is nevertheless engaging in "hostilities" against the United States, then this person is an unlawful enemy combatant. Notice that this definition does not require that such a person be an "alien," which accordingly leaves open the possibility that this designation could also be applied to an American citizen. Nor does it require that one be part of or affiliated with al Qaeda, the Taliban, or any other terrorist organization. Nor does one's "hostile" act have to be done to aid such a force. Nor does one have to have supported such acts. Nor does one have to be in violation of the "law of war." Nor is there anywhere in the act where the term "hostilities" is defined. For example, is an anti-war activist an unlawful enemy combatant? What about an American journalist who publishes leaked information damaging to the Bush administration? What about an anti-Bush blogger? In short, the definition is vague enough to include any American citizen who is acting in a way the president deems "hostile" to the United States. As such, it is difficult to imagine a single piece of legislation with greater potential to undermine freedom and democracy in America.

The act also deprives "unlawful enemy combatants" the protection of the Geneva Conventions if they happen to be "aliens" (even Canadians!). According to the act, "no alien enemy unlawful combatant subject to trial by military commission . . . may invoke the Geneva Conventions as a source of rights at his trial by military commission." As for who interprets the meaning and application of Article 3 of the Geneva Conventions, concerning whether or not a prisoner has been tortured, "the President has the authority for the United States to determine the meaning and application of the Geneva Conventions and to promulgate higher standards and administrative regulations for violation of treaty regulations which are not grave breaches of the Geneva Conventions."

While a list of "grave breaches" is provided in the legislation, the bill enjoins that no foreign or international law shall be used by any US court of law to interpret these breaches. This means that it is up to the president to decide whether or not someone is guilty of torture or other cruel and inhumane violations of the Geneva Conventions. For example, according to this act, the president has the authority to stipulate a patently cruel and inhumane form of torture like "waterboarding" (the simulation of drowning) to be just and legal treatment. It also means that the president has the authority to decide whether he himself is guilty of having tortured anyone. And, of course, the act's provisions regarding torture have been conveniently made retroactive so that they take effect as of November 26, 1997.

This president has, in fact, eviscerated the constitutionally delegated power of Congress in another, even more pervasive manner. Bush has used "signing statements" as a way of summarily dismissing laws passed by Congress. For example, in signing the ban on torture, as well as other national security laws passed by both houses of Congress, Bush has issued statements granting himself the right to disregard these laws at his discretion.

This means of overriding or "vetoing" Congress is patently illegal. If the president simply vetoes a bill passed by both houses of Congress, Congress can still override the presidential veto by a two-thirds majority of both houses as provided by Article 1, Section 7 of the Constitution. On the other hand, signing statements constitute a form of "line item veto" (picking and choosing what provisions of a bill to accept or reject). By any reasonable interpretation of the Constitution, this is unlawful. For one, in 1998 the Supreme Court ruled that presidential line item vetoes are unconstitutional. Second, whereas line item vetoes would still be subject to congressional override, signing statements are immune from congressional override. Put bluntly, setting aside the checks and balances established by the United States Constitution, Bush has delegated himself the discretionary power to bypass Congress to decree the law of the land. And what do you think this is called? You guessed it. **It's called dictatorship!**

And the dictatorial powers of the "president" keep on increasing ad nauseam. In January 2007 Bush issued an executive order establishing a "gatekeeper" inside every federal agency. This is an individual appointed by the White House who will make these agencies carry out the president's mandates. In this way, the president now has direct control over the rules and policies government develops to protect civil rights, privacy, public health, safety, and the environment. In effect, this trumps congressional authority since the authority of federal agencies derives from laws enacted by Congress. Now, however, these agencies get their orders directly from the president! So, while policies such as those created by the Environmental Agency and the Occupational Safety and Health Administration could previously have been independently shaped by civil servants and scientists, these individuals are now under careful watch and scrutiny by the White House.

From the start, the Bush administration asserted its dictatorial sway over Congress. Article 1, Section 7, Clause 11 of the United States Constitution delegates the power to declare war to Congress, but, prior to his invasion of Iraq, Bush successfully persuaded Congress to relinquish its congressional power to him. The point is not that the outcome proved catastrophic, which it did. The point is rather that this was an assault on the system of checks and balances put into our Constitution by our nation's Founding Fathers. The declaration of war is too complex a task for only one man to bear, even an intelligent one. That's why the Constitution does not place this power in the hands of the president alone. In American democracy, we rely upon the sound judgment of a majority, not the dictates of a single ruler. The latter is not democracy.

Unfortunately, the midterm elections of November 2006 have not stemmed the progressive decay of congressional power; and, thus far, the new Democratic Congress has done nothing substantial to restore checks and balances. While congresspersons, both Republican and Democrat, have decried the beating of the Bush war drum—in particular the escalation of the war in Iraq—they have to date been compliant with the chief executive; and while talk of impeachment has pre-dated the November 2006 elections, this talk has proven to be pre-election rhetoric giving only the appearance that real change was in the offing. Such glimmers of hope that democracy would soon be restored in America with the incoming Congress have all but faded away.

The power grab by the White House in the last six years has been so blatant, so egregious that even the conservative Cato Institute has identified Bush's attack on the US Constitution as a threat to our way of life. In a review and critique of Bush's constitutional record, editor Gene Healy and Timothy Lynch, director of the Project on Criminal Justice, note the following:

> [F]ar from defending the Constitution, President Bush has repeatedly sought to strip out the limits the document places on federal power. In its official legal briefs and public actions, the Bush administration has advanced a view of federal power that is astonishingly broad, a view that includes
>
> - a federal government empowered to regulate core political speech—and restrict it greatly when it counts the most: in the days before a federal election;
> - A president who cannot be restrained, through validly enacted statues, from pursuing any tactic he believes to be effective in the war on terror;

- A president who has the inherent constitutional authority to designate American citizens suspected of terrorist activity as "enemy combatants," strip them of any constitutional protection, and lock them up without charges for the duration of the war on terror—in other words, perhaps forever; and
- A federal government with the power to supervise virtually every aspect of American life, from kindergarten, to marriage, to the grave.[11]

The authors conclude, "President Bush's constitutional vision is, in short, sharply at odds with the text, history, and structure of our Constitution, which authorizes a government of limited powers."[12]

The Bush administration has effectively taken control of the United States of America. "The president appears to believe that he is the ultimate arbiter of what's legal and what's illegal . . ." states the Cato Institute, noting in addition that "[u]nder this sweeping theory of executive power, the liberty of every American rests on nothing more than the grace of the White House."[13] While such reflections may be reassuring to those who have been seduced by the administration's propaganda about terrorism, the reality is that the Bush administration has demonstrated a record of coercion, political backstabbing, and vengeful behavior that should make every American cringe at the thought of leaving our rights in their hands. Do you want to speak out about the tyranny of W? Better watch out! You might well be branded a terrorist.

In defending dictatorship, the seventeenth-century British philosopher Thomas Hobbes held that whatever the dictator commands is law and therefore he can never do anything unlawful. According to Hobbes, we the people should relinquish our freedom to a single man or an assembly of men for the sake of security. For Hobbes, without a common absolute power to keep us "in awe," we would be in a perpetual state of danger and "war of all against all" wherefore life would be "solitary, poor, nasty, brutish and short." Hobbes, like Bush, maintained that the chief executive has absolute, unchecked authority "to do *whatever* he shall think necessary to be done, both beforehand, for the preserving of peace and security by prevention of discord at home and hostility from abroad . . ."[14]

Hobbes made no bones about it. According to him, there shouldn't be any checks and balances on the sovereign power, which was unconditional and absolute. The executive authority had the right to do anything in the name of national security, no questions asked. When you strip away the façade of freedom and democracy, this is also Bush's political philosophy. This is the classical view of dictatorship, the opposite of democracy.

BUSH'S "CULTURE OF LIFE" IS REALLY A CULTURE OF OPPRESSION

In 2005, when the nightly news buzzed about the Terry Schiavo case, the central focus was on whether Michael Schiavo, Terry's husband, had the right to have her feeding tube removed. This forty-one-year-old woman from St. Petersburg, Florida, had been diagnosed as being in a persistent vegetative state for over a decade, and her husband had been working through the courts to have her feeding tube removed, maintaining that this would have been her wish. However, Terry's parents opposed removing the tube, maintaining that she was not truly in a persistent vegetative state and that she had the ability to interact in rudimentary ways with her family (for example, smiling at them).

The MSM exploited the pathos of this case from both sides. Everyone in America had nightly incursions into the lives of this family torn apart over tragedy. The nation was in the grips of this highly publicized case as Terry's vacant smile was indelibly engraved on anyone who watched TV news.

It was this face that became a symbol of George W. Bush's "culture of life." For the Bush administration, this poor woman's tragedy became a welcome diversion from the somber rhythm of the casualty reports coming out of Iraq. And the administration did its best at sucking out whatever life was left in this case for its own self-aggrandizing purposes—so much so that Bush even interrupted his Easter break in Texas to fly back in the middle of the night to sign a law taking the case to federal court after the Florida courts consistently ruled in favor of permitting withdrawal of the feeding tube. Said Bush, "I urge all those who honor Terri Schiavo to continue to work to build a culture of life where all Americans are welcomed and valued and protected, especially those who live at the mercy of others."15

But the ugly truth was that Terri Schiavo was in a persistent vegetative state, her cerebral cortex was liquefied, and the Florida courts had gotten it right according to Florida law. The other half of this ugly truth not discussed by the MSM was that the Bush administration was violating the separation of powers when it attempted to intrude on a state matter. The fact was that the Schiavo case was no different than torrents of other tragic cases of this sort. These are deeply personal matters that can and should be settled by the families working in concert with primary care teams and hospital ethics committees. And where these avenues fail, such cases should be settled in the state courts. When the president of the United States tries to impose his will on matters so deeply personal as these and intrudes on what is lawfully the domain of the state courts, it's time to look carefully at what's happening to us as a free nation.

But it gets even worse. Not only did the president attempt to dictate the outcome of this case, so did his brother, then Florida governor Jeb Bush, who had earlier passed a law to reinsert Schiavo's feeding tube. This law was subsequently found unconstitutional by the Florida Supreme Court, which ruled that it violated "the fundamental constitutional tenet of separation of powers."

After the president's attempt to strong-arm a federal appeals judge into overturning the state court's decision failed, Jeb Bush spoke to his fellow Floridians and to the nation with assurance that he would accept the rule of law. This pledge received national MSM coverage. However, what didn't get mainstream coverage was what happened on the morning Schiavo had her feeding tube removed.

Just hours after the federal judge ordered Schiavo's feeding tube removed, Governor Bush, on the basis of a legal technicality, directed a team of state police to seize Schiavo from her hospice in Pinellas Park, Florida, and to have the tube reinserted. However, the state police were met with the local police, who had been ordered by the judge to protect Schiavo. In the end, the state police backed down, and Schiavo was permitted to die.

This story of how Jeb Bush sent in the troops, even after the attempt to resuscitate the case in federal court had failed, was broken by the *Miami Herald*, and the local news tracked it.[16] (We know, because we're Floridians!) But it was played down nationally by the MSM. In a real democracy, it would have been headline news on CNN!

To the bitter end, the Bushes were vigilant in attempting to impose their will and in the process they used this poor woman as a pawn in a political game. But even after all this had played out, Bush's army didn't relent. Egged on by the president, who repeatedly condemned "activist judges," former House majority leader Tom Delay (a name that will live in infamy!) gave all judges who had refused to fall in line an ominous warning: "We will look at an arrogant, out of control, unaccountable judiciary that thumbed their nose at the Congress and president when given jurisdiction to hear this case anew and look at all the facts. . . . The time will come for the men responsible for this to answer for their behavior, but not today."[17]

It's not America when judges must fear reprisal from the president or his foot soldiers for not deciding according to their dictates. Unequivocally, this is dictatorship. Referring implicitly to Delay's threatening of the judges in the Schiavo case as well as other similar threats, former Supreme Court Justice Sandra Day O'Connor remarked that "we must be ever-vigilant against those who would strongarm the judiciary into adopting their preferred policies. It takes a lot of degeneration before a country falls into dictatorship, but we should avoid these ends by avoiding these beginnings."[18] Since O'Connor uttered these words, there have been an increasing number of assaults on the separation of powers, and it is likely that they will continue to increase as long as this problem goes unaddressed. Unfortunately, it has systematically been dusted under the rug by big media.

Recall those immortal words of the Declaration of Independence: "Governments are instituted among Men, deriving their just powers from the consent of the governed." That should mean that the will of the majority of Americans should be taken seriously by our leader. But that would be true only if we are really still a democracy.

Bush's recent handling of the issue of stem cell research provides another instructive example of how far this president will go in order to impose his will on the American people. In July 2006, both the Senate and House of Representatives, including a number of Republicans, joined in passing legislation providing for government support of stem cell research. Seventy-five percent of Americans are now in favor of such research aimed at unlocking cures for Alzheimer's, Parkinson's, paralysis, and many other diseases that crush the lives of hundreds of thousands of Americans each year. However, despite the fact that the collective voice of Congress had spoken in concert with the will of the American people, the president vetoed the legislation. Unfortunately, there were still many in Congress who voted lockstep with the president. As a consequence, Congress was unable to muster the required two-thirds majority in both houses to override the presidential veto.

In the aftermath of this veto, the MSM spun its wheels speculating about why the president would have taken a stance so unpopular among Americans. "Was this a wise political move for the president?" queried the talk show hosts. And they called in their usual arsenal of political "experts" to speculate.

This was business as usual. Not surprisingly, no one in the MSM pointed to the blatant, arrogant disregard this president showed for the will of the majority of Americans. No red flag went up signaling that the president was *dictating* to the American people, imposing his own moral value on a majority of Americans. There is no requirement under the Constitution that a president sign a bill with which he disagrees. Had Bush refused to sign this bill as a matter of *personal* conscience, it would have become law *without his approval*. Instead, he chose to *veto the will of the American people*.

No one in the MSM pointed out that this was a president who made a mockery out of the "culture of life" by sending faithful Americans off to war on false pretenses. No one pointed out the blatant hypocrisy. Instead there was spineless, gutless banter about how politically expedient it was for the president to take an unpopular stance. What is now needed more than ever before in the history of this nation is a media with balls, not one that has been castrated by government.

NOTES

1. Hermann Goering, conversation with psychologist Gustave Gilbert, April 18, 1946, http://www.quotationspage.com/quote31446.html (accessed August 4, 2006).

2. Thomas Jefferson, letter to Edward Carrington Parris, January 16, 1787, http://odur.let.rug.nl/~usa/P/tj3/writings/brf/jef152.htm (accessed August 4, 2006).

3. Recently there was a proposal in Congress to require government to identify the government as the source of this news, but

the measure didn't pass. The FCC has, however, passed a rule requiring that the networks identify the government sponsor. Whether and to what extent the MSM will comply remains to be seen.

4. "Transcript: Al Gore on the Limits of Executive Power," http://www.algore.org/index.php?option=com_content&task=view&id=325&Itemid=292 (accessed January 29, 2007).

5. "For Your Eyes Only," *NOW with David Brancaccio*, PBS, February 16, 2007, http://www.pbs.org/now/shows/307/index.html (accessed February 18, 2007).

6. CNN, *Reliable Sources*, March 9, 2003.

7. Associated Press, "Tillman Killed While Serving as Army Ranger," ESPN, April 30, 2004, http://sports.espn.go.com/nfl/news/story?id=1788232 (accessed January 29, 2007).

8. David Zucchino, "Account of Tillman's Killing Is Challenged," *Los Angeles Times*, December 6, 2004, http://www.forums.yellowworld.org/showthread.php?t=20520 (accessed January 29, 2007).

9. "A Pause for Hindsight," *New York Times*, July 16, 2004, http://www.commondreams.org/views04/0716-15.htm (accessed November 28, 2004).

10. Paul Krugman, "Hack the Vote," *New York Times*, December 2, 2003, http://www.nytimes.com/2003/12/02/opinion/02KRUG.html (accessed November 5, 2004).

11. Gene Healy and Timothy Lynch, "Power Surge: The Constitutional Record of George W. Bush," Cato Institute, 2006, p. 1.

12. Ibid.

13. Ibid., pp. 13–14.

14. Thomas Hobbes, *Leviathan*, chap. 18; my italics.

15. "President Discusses Schiavo, WMD Commission Report," White House, http://www.whitehouse.gov/news/releases/2005/03/20050331.html (accessed January 29, 2007).

16. Carol Marbin Miller, "Police Showdown over Schiavo Averted," *Miami Herald*, http://www.yuricareport.com/Bush

SecondTerm/PoliceShowdownOverSchiavoAverted.html (accessed March 26, 2005).

17. "Republican Leader Warns Judges: You Will Answer for This," *Toronto Star*, April 1, 2005, http://www.commondreams .org/cgi-bin/print.cgi?file=/headlines05/0401-04.htm (accessed August 4, 2006).

18. "Retired Supreme Court Justice Hits Attacks on Courts and Warns of Dictatorship," http://www.rawstory.com/news/2006/ Retired_Supreme_Court_Justice_hits_attacks_0310.html (accessed August 4, 2006).

CHAPTER 2

THE FOX
IS GUARDING
THE HENHOUSE

The corporate media behemoths are in the pocket of the Bush administration. These giant corporations routinely spin off an intricate, seamless politico-corporate media web of deception. As a result, the mainstay of the daily American news diet is quite literally a paid political announcement. Instead of protecting against abuses of government power by keeping us adequately informed, these companies have become complicit in destabilizing and undermining our freedom and democracy. They have sold out the public trust to turn a profit. No longer can Americans trust the MSM to keep a watchful eye on government.

WHO'S IN BED WITH WHOM?

With so many TV and radio stations in the mainstream, it might seem as if we Americans now enjoy more access to news and information than ever before. Unfortunately, quantity alone does not ensure quality, nor does it ensure that a sufficient diversity of perspectives have been included to compose a democratic forum. In fact, there are presently only a handful of ever-dwindling corporate media giants that own the MSM. This means that you can see and hear only what these few companies want you to see and hear.

Here is a list of the top five media companies in broadcast TV, radio, and cable/satellite TV:[1]

Figure 2.1

Ranking	Broadcast TV	Radio	Cable/Satellite TV
1	Fox/News Corp	Clear Channel	Comcast
2	CBS/Viacom	Infinity/Viacom	DirecTV/News Corp
3	NBC/General Electric	Entercom	Time Warner
4	Tribune Company	Cox	EchoStar
5	ABC/Disney	ABC/Disney	Charter

All of these companies are enmeshed by partnerships, joint ventures, and contractual relations in an elaborate, government-driven military-industrial complex. These corporate media giants rely on government for lucrative contracts, tax breaks, government subsidies, access to White House officials for cost-effective news coverage (quoting these sources instead of doing costly investigations), industry deregulation, and other perks. In this context of favor trading and quid pro quo, the costs of lobbying in Washington, wining and dining congressional staff, and making political contributions are simply costs of doing business.

For example, General Electric supplies jet engines to Lockheed Martin, which is a major weapons contractor for nuclear weapons and ballistic missile defenses including components of the Strategic Defense Initiative ("Star Wars"), which was scrapped during the Clinton administration but revived by the Bush administration. GE and Lockheed Martin have joint ventures including a joint research center. In 2005, Lockheed awarded GE a $50 million contract for presidential helicopter engines. General Electric has spent more than any other top broadcast company on lobbying and has also made the most political contributions. Between 2000 and 2004, it spent around $3 million in sponsoring trips for congressional staff.[2]

In 2000, Microsoft, which co-owns the cable news channel MSNBC with General Electric, created its government division, which has as its main purpose the procurement of government contracts, especially lucrative ones such as those afforded by the US Department of Defense. And Microsoft has a history of government defense contract partnerships with such major defense contractors as General Dynamics.[3] So, it is easy to see how GE/NBC lacked independence of judgment in reporting the case for going to war with Iraq. Under these politico-corporate pressures, journalists like Tim Russert and Chris Matthews became model GE employees.

As you can see from figure 2.1, the three top media companies for the respective media are News Corp, Clear Channel, and Comcast. These three companies also have cooperative relations. In 2004, News Corp contracted with Clear Channel to provide news for Clear Channel stations in several major markets, which, in this five-year deal, can bring Fox News to more than five hundred affiliates, giving Fox a substantial radio presence. And Fox Cable Network also partners with Comcast.[4]

In 2004, News Corp also acquired DirecTV/Hughes Electronics, a General Motors Company, making it (along with EchoStar) one of the two major direct satellite TV providers in the world. In 2005 the company also partnered with XM Satellite Radio, giving it a substantial stake in XM radio. As a satellite TV provider, News Corp has contractual relations with Boeing, one of the world's largest military defense contractors. It is not hard to do the logic. DirecTV/News Corp depends on Boeing to provide it with satellites; Boeing depends on the US government for its defense contracts. Given these dependencies, what do you think would happen if News Corp's "news" division spoke honestly about military matters such as the war in Iraq? For example, what would happen if it had exposed Bush's lack of justification for waging a war in Iraq? Well, Boeing wouldn't have been a very happy camper; nor would the Bush administration. Given this complex media-military-government network, it is no easy matter to tell the truth when the truth means lost revenues for one of the contractors in the network.

With the exception of Fox, a common charge typically launched from the Right against the MSM is that it is too "liberal." This charge is not so much false as it is unintelligible. Mega-corps like News Corp, GE, and Time Warner don't have an intrinsic commitment to increasing individual autonomy and freedom of American citizens; they don't care about social, religious, or political reform *unless* such changes translate to maximization of profit. These companies have no qualms against making campaign contributions to anyone—Republican or Democrat—who will help them to further their bottom line. Corporate logic, which is the logic that largely governs the MSM, is definitely not liberal.

Nor is this logic inherently "conservative" in the sense that it is driven by an intrinsic commitment to traditional "family values" or any other substantive social or religious perspective. Even Rupert Murdoch, the ultra-conservative head of News Corp, rises and declines with the tide of the bottom line. Bruce Page, author of *The Murdoch Archipelago*, has described Murdoch's opportunistic character as "fluid nothingness at the core."[5]

What truly unites behemoth corporations with the political Right is the latter's willingness to feed corporate avarice in exchange for attaining greater power and dominance over the lives of Americans. Insofar as conservative regimes like the Bush administration place big business above grassroots social reform, they are the party of choice for these giant corporations. This is not because of a corporate commitment to a certain ideological vision of society, but simply because supporting such a regime portends profit. Giant media corporations are political chameleons and fair-weather friends, to be sure. If the neocons continued to lose power in Congress and could no longer control the Federal Commerce Commission (FCC), the Pentagon, the Supreme Court, and other federal institutions bearing on corporate prosperity, most of these giant media corporations would likely look elsewhere for bedfellows.

This isn't to say that there aren't any dyed-in-the-wool political affiliations among corporate heads. For example, Fox CEO Roger Ailes has been a long-standing Republican Party

operative dating back to the Nixon administration. Nevertheless, when a Democrat seems open to serving a corporation's
bottom line interests, its officers are usually prepared to play
ball. This is why corporate leaders make it their business to
have deep financial ties to political power brokers.

A good example of such cronyism is Thomas Hicks,
former vice chair of the Clear Channel radio empire, and its
current chair, Lowry Mays. These men have had well-known
financial and political ties to the Bush administration. Under
their auspices, in 2003, Clear Channel sponsored nationwide
rallies (Rally for America) aimed at supporting the war in
Iraq. It also engaged in censoring certain songs it deemed to
be subversive of the war effort. At the helm of organizing
these rallies was MSNBC talk show host and Bush administration cheerleader Glenn Beck. The lesson here is that there
can be a bright future in the MSM spotlight for those prepared to be foot soldiers of the federal government.

Until recently, Hicks was the chair and CEO of the pow-
erhouse corporate buyout firm, Hicks, Muse, Tate, & Furst
(now called Hicks Muse under the chairmanship of Muse). In
this capacity, he enjoyed long-standing business ties to
George W. Bush. When Bush became governor of Texas in
1995, he approved legislation establishing the University of
Texas Investment Management Company (UTIMCO), a private firm that controlled the university's public fund. Hicks,
who had had his eye on the school's $13 billion endowment,
was subsequently named chair. In this capacity, Hicks handed
out many lucrative contracts to corporate cronies of both
himself and Bush, including the Carlyle Group, to which the
Bushes (not to mention the bin Ladens) belonged. Lowry
Mays, a fellow Texan, oilman, and supporter of Bush was

also on the board of UTIMCO and succeeded Hicks as its chair.

In 1999, Hicks purchased the Texas Rangers from George W. Bush in a deal that included a new stadium financed by taxpayers on private land Bush acquired below market value by having the city of Arlington, Texas, condemn it.

In 2000, Hicks, Muse, Tate, & Furst contributed more than half a million dollars to Bush's presidential campaign. In 2003 the Bush-controlled FCC attempted to relax media ownership rules that would allow Clear Channel to increase its holdings.

This is how it works. "You scratch my back and I'll scratch yours." Never mind the public interest. Nor is such politico-corporate cronyism and conflict of interest unique to the likes of Clear Channel. Even the Public Broadcasting Corporation has been infiltrated by the Bush White House. In March 2005, the Republican chair of this corporation, Kenneth Tomlinson, hired the director of the White House Office of Global Communications as a senior staff member. While this government officer was still on the White House staff, she helped draft guidelines that could have bearing on the content of public radio and television broadcasts. In fact, the chairman had previously contracted with a consultant to keep track of the guests' political leanings on the progressive PBS show *NOW with Bill Moyers*.

And, there have even been blood ties as when John Ellis, working for Fox, called Florida in the 2000 presidential election for his first cousin, George W. Bush. And still these corporations boast of their objectivity in news reporting. CNN calls itself "the Most Trusted Name in News" while Fox self-praises, "Fair and Balanced."

Unfortunately, the Fox is guarding the henhouse! Without a reliable MSM that keeps us adequately informed of government activities, we, the voting public, are not free when we attempt to voice our opinions and vote our consciences.[6] We are instead the pawns of a politico-corporate media machine that has betrayed the American trust in order to amass power and wealth. The price of this betrayal is nothing less than the eventual demise of democracy in America.

THE SOCIO-PATHOLOGY OF CORPORATE MEDIA GIANTS

This tendency of media corporations to put profit above democracy is to a large extent dictated by several related factors: the corporation's size, overall mission, and the status of the newsroom within the corporate culture. The larger the corporation looms, the more focused it will be on dividends over democracy. The larger the company, the more easy it gets to treat consumers as nameless, faceless numbers to be tallied. In a small business, there is still the possibility of human interaction between the customer and the business owner. As the business grows in size, walls of bureaucracy are erected between customers and owners and the prospect for human interaction between the two becomes impossible. The human dimension is thereby factored out, and flesh-and-blood human beings with names and faces become figures on a balance sheet.

Quite clearly, it is much easier to make decisions that undermine human welfare when the decision maker does not personalize those whose welfare is compromised. When the corporate executives of Ford Motor Company decided to forego installing an inexpensive protective part on the gas tank of its Pinto, it did so knowing full well that there would be casualties. The cost of paying for these casualties was simply balanced against the cost of installing the part in all of its cars. Since it appeared more cost-effective on balance not to install the protective part, the decision was made not to install it. The decision didn't factor in human beings with names and faces; instead, it proceeded exclusively in terms of bottom-line logic.

After the fact, Ford Motor Company did indeed have to face its victims, whose mangled and deformed bodies then became more than just ciphers. And, in its cold calculation, it had failed to factor in the damage caused to its own public image and the prospective toll on its future car sales.

Corporate MSM logic tends to be blind in a similar way. It fails to account for the cost of democracy lost in failing to serve its vital role as Fourth Estate. From a narrow business perspective, this cost is not so easily quantified and does not show up on the balance sheet. But it is a real cost that is borne by all of us when the corporate media is in business with a megalomaniac government.

In gigantic conglomerates such as General Electric, news reporting is considered just one of the many goods and services the corporation sells. From jet engines to home appliances, GE is in business to make money, and the newsroom is similarly expected to justify its existence by turning a profit, no less than any other division of the company. Unfortunately, this expectation overlooks the newsroom's unique status. The news business is special because it is vital to democracy. That is why our Founding Fathers protected it in the First Amendment. When blind bottom-line corporate logic dictates the terms of the news, this protection is placed in jeopardy. It is only when there is some distance between the governing corporate culture and the newsroom that freedom of the press is able to flourish. Otherwise it runs the risk of being prostituted. This is exactly what is happening!

LESS UNSCRUPULOUS MEDIA CORPORATIONS

There are companies, however, such as the New York Times Company, that can be favorably contrasted with companies like General Electric. As the mission statement on GE's Web site clearly shows, the news room is just one more part of the corporate culture: "From jet engines to power generation; financial services to plastics, and medical imaging to news and information, GE people are dedicated to turning imaginative ideas into leading products and services that help solve some of the world's toughest problems."[7]

In contrast, the "core purpose" of the New York Times Company is to "enhance society by creating, collecting, and distributing high-quality news, information, and entertainment."[8] While this company owns nine local television stations and two New York radio stations, 90 percent of its revenues come from its newspaper business, which includes the *New York Times*, *International Herald Tribune*, *Boston Globe*, and fifteen other daily newspapers.[9] Having staked its good name and reputation on providing quality journalism ("All the News That's Fit to Print"), it is understandable how failure to provide high-quality journalism to its patrons (many of whom are non–New Yorkers) could mean dwindling subscriptions and lost revenues. The *Times* is an heirloom of the Sulzberger family and has remained under its control since 1896. The family's guiding philosophy that brought this paper to prominence is that quality journalism will pay in the long run, and the paper has relied on this philosophy to get it through hard times in the past. However, like many news agencies after the 9/11 attacks, the *Times* substituted deference to the Bush administration for quality journalism. As discussed in chapter 1, the paper became unduly reliant on official government spokespersons for coverage of such issues as the events leading up to the US invasion of Iraq and voter fraud during the 2004 presidential election. And, as discussed by Peter Phillips in the introduction to this book, the *Times* has also failed in its coverage of the Bush administration's torture of innocents branded "unlawful enemy combatants." Now, facing hard financial times, with declining stock values and its future uncertain, it has more recently begun to display some vital signs of a living, breathing Fourth Estate and of living up to its journalistic credo.

For one, it brought to light the Bush administration's by now infamous *warrantless* National Security Agency (NSA) domestic spying program. It also sounded the alarm on the constitutionally dubious SWIFT (Society for Worldwide Interbank Financial Telecommunication) program, which allows the Bush administration to sift through thousands of Americans' bank records without congressional or judicial oversight. The *Times* ran the story despite the urging of the Bush administration not to publish it.

Never mind whether or not these efforts by the *Times* to

resuscitate itself as a watchdog of democracy have been attempts to rescue its bottom line or to live up to its core purpose. They are probably both.[10] The more important point is that you are *more* likely to get (although by no means assured of getting) the news from a smaller news-oriented and news-focused corporation like the Times Company than you are from a multipurpose behemoth like GE. This is because the Times' newsroom is not part of some grander corporate culture that fails to recognize the value and uniqueness of news reporting in a democratic society. Unlike GE, which is a conglomerate of desperate businesses, the *Times*'s main focus is on the news. In a very real sense, if democracy fails, then so does the *Times*. Its core mission is to "enhance society" through reporting the news, which in the very least includes apprising us of whether the government is abusing its powers. Insofar as it fails to expose abuses of power by government, it acquiesces in its own demise. In a dictatorship, there is no need for the likes of the *Times*.

In fact, the ire the *Times* recently evoked in the Bush administration by exposing its *unauthorized, wholesale, warrantless* examination of the banking records of thousands of Americans is a good indication of how dangerously close we are to the end of democracy in America.[11] This program, which was begun weeks after the attacks of September 11, 2001, had as its official goal the tracking of wire transfers overseas by American citizens as well as noncitizens believed to be associated with al Qaeda. The program, however, was hardly a secret, because public documents posted to the Internet discussed it. For example, the United Nations recommended tracking wire transfers and posted its committee report on its Web site. In addition, the president signed an executive order on September 23, 2001 (Executive Order 13224), for "Blocking Property and Prohibiting Transactions with Persons Who Commit, Threaten to Commit, or Support Terrorism." This document, which was posted to the White House Web site, explicitly stated that "a need exists for further consultation and cooperation with, and sharing of information by, United States and foreign financial institutions as an additional tool to enable the United States to combat the financing of terrorism." Quite obviously, the targeted financial institutions included the Brussels-based banking consortium known as SWIFT (mentioned previously) from which the Bush administration obtained thousands of Americans' banking records.

The *Times* did not consider it breaking news that the SWIFT program actually existed. This was already an established fact. Nor did it contend that it was wrong for the government to inspect the bank records of persons who were believed to be associated with known terrorist organizations. Rather, the real news for the *Times* was the Bush administration's abuse of power. In an editorial defending its decision to publish the story, the *Times* stated, "From our side of the news-opinion wall, the Swift story looks like part of an alarming pattern. Ever since Sept. 11, the Bush administration has taken the necessity of heightened vigilance against terrorism and turned it into a rationale for an extraordinarily powerful executive branch, exempt from the normal checks and balances of our system of government. It has created powerful new tools of surveillance and refused, almost as a matter of principle, to use normal procedures that would acknowledge that either Congress or the courts have an oversight role."[12]

When the story broke, George W. Bush called it "disgraceful" and Dick Cheney accused the *Times* of making it "more difficult" to defend against terrorism. The then-Republican-dominated House followed suit by passing a resolution to condemn the paper for printing the story, and some members even went so far as to accuse the paper of treason.

Not only this. Two other papers had followed the *Times* in printing the story—the *Wall Street Journal* (*WSJ*) and the *Los Angeles Times*. The *Los Angeles Times* defended its choice to publish the story. However, after the Bush administration attacked the *Times*, the conservative *WSJ*, known for its Republican slant, rolled over. Curiously, although the *WSJ* published the same information as the *New York Times*, it jumped on the government bandwagon by lambasting the *Times*. In an editorial, the *WSJ* accused the *Times* of irresponsibly helping the terrorists by "wrapping itself in the First Amendment," and trying bogusly to portray the *WSJ* as its "ideological wingman." Attempting to drive a wedge between its own reasons and those of the *Times* for deciding to cover the story, the *WSJ* defensively stated, "Treasury officials did not tell our editors they had urged the Times not to publish. What Journal editors did know is that they had senior government officials providing news they didn't mind seeing in print. If this was a 'leak,' it was entirely authorized. . . ."[13]

The Bush administration "entirely authorized" the *WSJ* to publish what it urged the *Times* not to publish? A double standard if there ever was one, this reeked with the stench of a government setup.[14] After all, the *Times* had already incurred the wrath of Bush when it broke the NSA domestic spying program. As long as the *Times* walked lockstep with the administration, the government left it alone. As soon as it attempted to assert its constitutional charge as a member of the Fourth Estate, it was ambushed.

As for the *WSJ*, it is not hard to determine its real motivation for backpedaling. Like the *Times*, it had recently encountered bad times with declining subscriptions and stock values. However, unlike the *Times*, it preferred to taste boot wax than to "wrap itself in the First Amendment." Unfortunately, in its attempt to quell the fire and appease a megalomaniac government, the *WSJ* performed much like its larger corporate brethren, emerging as yet another pawn in a blind struggle for money and power. It sold out.

Companies like GE, Time Warner, and other giant media conglomerates are more likely to adapt to a dictatorship than to sacrifice their existence in opposing it. This is because these companies are not essentially *news* companies. For example, the company name "News Corp" is a misnomer. This corporation is really an *entertainment* business, and reporting news is just part of show time. Its allegiance to the truth is comparable to that of a writer of historical fiction at best. Seeing the words "News Corporation" appearing on the Twentieth Century Fox logo at the beginning of one of its flicks speaks volumes. It should rather read, "Entertainment Corporation." This company delivers infotainment, not news. Its professed reverence for truth and democracy is largely a cover for politico-corporate quid pro quo aimed at amassing power and money.

Democracy is not a contest to see which political ideology can most successfully silence another. Everyone in a democracy is entitled to express his or her political perspective. The problem is not simply that Fox or any other "news" organization chooses to air right-wing conservative (or left-wing liberal) views; the problem is far more complex than this. First, and most obvious, news media have a duty to be truthful. In the words of the Code of Ethics of the Society of Professional Journalists, "public enlightenment is the fore-runner of justice and the foundation of democracy. The duty of the journalist is to further those ends by seeking truth and providing a fair and comprehensive account of events and issues.[15] Unfortunately, for giant media conglomerates like GE/NBC and News Corp, the facts are just commodities that can be crafted ("cooked") to turn a profit.

For example, in attempting to bolster President George W. Bush's push for privatization of the social security system, Fox News reporter Brit Hume recently stated, "It turns out that FDR himself planned to include private investment accounts in the Social Security program when he proposed it. In a written statement to Congress in 1935, Roosevelt said that any Social Security plan should include, 'Voluntary contributory annuities, by which individual initiative can increase the annual amounts received in old age,' adding that government funding, 'ought to ultimately be supplanted by self-supporting annuity plans.'"[16] Unfortunately, the statement was lifted out of context from FDR's actual statement, which was not talking at all about privatization and investment in corporate annuities but instead was referring to the system of Social Security as we now know it; one in which employees and employers both contribute to the Social Security fund.

Such deceit is part of the News Corp game plan. It is precisely what Fox News CEO Roger Ailes expects of his "journalists." Former employees of Fox have consistently complained of management "sticking their fingers in the writing and editing of stories to cook the facts to make a story more palatable to right-of-center tastes." [17] This sort of corporate-sponsored deception is in contrast to that of the infamous former *New York Times* reporter Jayson Blair, who, without editorial authority, fabricated dozens of stories. When this fraud was exposed, the *Times* admitted its culpability and suffered a credibility crisis. The more subtle deception built into the fabric of Fox News goes unacknowledged by the network and is in fact systematically denied through empty, robotic repetition of the words "fair and balanced."

News media have an ethical duty to "clearly label opinion and commentary," thereby distinguishing them from "news reporting."[18] Unfortunately, TV news has often managed to confuse the two, smuggling political commentary into its news reporting by framing it in emotively active language. For example, since 1997, Sinclair Broadcasting Group, an independent group owner of stations covering 25 percent of the nation's television audience, had donated more than $200,000 to Republican candidates. Inserting its own "news" into its programming, it has referred to peace activists as "wack-jobs," the French as "cheese-eating surrender monkeys," progressives as the "loony left," and the liberal media as the "hate-America crowd."[19] Patterning itself after Fox, Sinclair also attempted to promote its own right-wing political agenda by requiring its affiliates to air an anti-Kerry documentary just two weeks prior to the 2004 presidential election.[20] Under pressure from its affiliates, shareholders, and advertisers, Sinclair backed down.[21]

Media also have an ethical duty to "present a *diversity* of expressions, opinions, and ideas in context."[22] However, the corporate MSM has hijacked the public airwaves to further its own narrow commercial interests. This is nowhere more apparent than in talk radio. With few exceptions, such as the Air America and Pacifica networks, this has invariably been radically conservative. For example, government chair leaders such as Rush Limbaugh, Shawn Hannity, Michael Savage, and Bill O'Reilly, to name just a few, dominate the AM dial. And should becoming a mindless Limbaugh "dittohead" turn your stomach, don't expect to find asylum in National Public Radio (NPR). Consider, for example, Kenneth Tomlinson's recent attempts to stamp out any glimmers of "liberal bias" in the public media.[23]

FILM CENSORSHIP: COMING SOON TO A THEATER NEAR YOU

The ways in which corporate cronyism and quid quo pro restrict what we Americans see and hear form an intricate web that goes beyond TV and radio. These restrictions are even reflected in the movies we see. This is the case in part because movie production companies are owned by the same giant media corporations that control TV and radio. For example, News Corp (parent company of Fox News) owns 20th Century Fox, and Time Warner (parent company of CNN) owns Warner Brothers. These behemoths typically give viewers a great deal of "bang" for their buck—lots of sex and violence—but not much food for serious social and political thought. A now classic example is the tremendous obstacles Michael Moore faced in attempting to find a distribution company to underwrite his Bush-criticizing documentary *Fahrenheit 9/11*, after Disney (parent company of ABC) refused to permit Miramax Films, another Disney company, from distributing the film. Coming to blows with their Disney parent, co-chairs of Miramax Bob and Harvey Weinstein resolved to purchase the rights to the movie for $6 million of their own money; they ended up distributing the film through several independent companies including their own company, Fellowship Adventure. In hindsight, the film turned out to be a box office smash, but, unlike most first-run movies, *Fahrenheit 9/11* was first shown in only a relatively small number of selected theaters throughout the nation.

According to Moore, Michael Eisner, then CEO of Disney, told his agent that "he would never let Disney be the one to get the movie into the theaters because he didn't want to anger Florida Gov. Jeb Bush and complicate Disney's situation, with millions of tax breaks and other incentives at stake."[24] Once again, this was quid pro quo and intimidation in lieu of tolerance and concern for diversity, democracy, and the public good. It was narrow, profit-defined corporate logic as usual. This logic dictates that you don't offend the government if you want to expand your bottom line. So Eisner's Disney chose to fall in line. His concern was not whether Moore's film was in the best interest of the public, whether America would have been the better for it being accessible to the public, or whether Americans had the right to see and judge for themselves; his chief concern was instead whether it would be in the best financial interest of Disney to show the film. Eisner's personal political ideology—whether or not he had one—never even came into play.

A more recent example is Al Gore's award-winning documentary *An Inconvenient Truth*, about the global warming crisis. While there is probably no single subject more serious than the threat global warming poses to our planet, this documentary played on less than a hundred screens nationally when it opened over the 2006 Memorial Day weekend. Despite this fact, it was a top-ten box office hit in its first week. According to *Variety* magazine, it has had the "biggest-ever opening for a documentary—despite it being Memorial Day weekend and the release of *X-men*)." Unlike Moore's *Fahrenheit 9/11*, *An Inconvenient Truth* was distributed by a major distributor, Paramount Pictures under its Paramount Classics division.

So you might imagine that it would have received greater exposure. In fact, through his company National Amusements, media mogul Sumner Redstone owns controlling interests in Paramount and its mother company, Viacom. This fact is significant because National Amusements is itself a movie theater company with most of its theaters located in the northeast. Yet relatively few of these theaters even carried the documentary. As of June 26, 2006, only one out of fifteen of its theaters in the state of New York carried it.

The largest movie theater company in the world is Regal Entertainment Group, which includes United Artist theaters; the second-largest is AMC Entertainment, which includes Loews. In New York, only two Regal theaters showed *An Inconvenient Truth*, and only one out of its eleven theaters in Manhattan showed it. In Manhattan, only two AMC theaters out of eleven showed it. In this progressive hub, one might have expected the interest level to be high enough to support more opportunities for potential viewers. It is worth noting that when *Fahrenheit* opened in June 2004, it played on just 4 of Regal's 108 movie screens in Philadelphia and its suburbs.[25]

The film's synopsis on Fandango, the nation's largest ticketing service—whose partners include Regal and AMC—reads as follows: "Filmmaker Davis Guggenheim follows Al Gore on the lecture circuit, as the former presidential candidate campaigns to raise public awareness of the dangers of global warming and calls for immediate action to curb its destructive effects on the environment." The use of the words "former presidential candidate" is significant. Presidential candidates are many and sundry and they often fade into oblivion, but vice presidents are relatively few and they have recently played an important role in American policy.

This play down is not surprising once you see who owns Regal! Recall the discussion earlier in this chapter regarding Hicks Muse and its intimate business ties to George W. Bush. Well, in 1998, Hicks Muse teamed up with another corporate buyout company, Kohlberg Kravis Roberts, in a $1.5 billion takeover of Regal Cinemas. Henry Kravis, the founding partner of this company had also been a major benefactor of the Republican Party. He was in fact also financial co-chair of George Herbert Walker's re-election campaign in 1992.

The current chairman of the board, CEO, and president of AMC is Peter C. Brown. Brown is also the chairman of the board of Embarq, a division of Sprint and the nation's fifth-largest local phone service provider. As you will see in chapter 8 (which covers the politico-corporate takeover of the Internet), the giant telecoms, including Sprint, are neck-deep in cooperative efforts with the Bush administration. In fact, Sprint is among the telecoms that recently handed over its private customer phone records to the Bush administration at its request. Dan Hesse, the CEO of Embarq and former AT&T executive, makes it quite clear that Embarq is against government regulation of the Internet, a service his company also provides. The giant telecoms, including Sprint, are presently lobbying Congress for the green light to set up tollbooths on the Net, thereby enabling these companies to assess higher fees to content providers that use more bandwidth. Said Hesse, "The notion is: Can you sell first class seats? Because if you don't the whole thing is going to go down to the lowest common denominator."[26] But in order to sell "first class seats" on the Internet, he needs a government pass. So the plot thickens as it becomes evident that the officer making the decisions for AMC Entertainment directs the board of a giant telecom that is beholden to the Bush administration.

And what has Bush himself said about Gore's film? When asked if he planned on seeing it, he replied, "Probably not." While Gore has spent thirty years studying the problem, Bush did not care to dignify the study.

And there are obvious reasons why this movie would be censored or played down by the Bush administration, which has tried to keep the global warming problem under wraps for some time. Recently, the administration sought to silence NASA's chief climate scientist, James Hansen, who said he was receiving threats from NASA officials. According to Hansen, the space agency's backlash was part of the Bush administration effort to downplay climate change. There have been, in fact, over the past year, an increasing number of climatologists who have complained about the federal government's efforts to silence them or to alter their findings or otherwise discourage them from speaking out.[27]

And why on God's green earth would the Bush administration want to do a thing like that? Well, the answer once again harkens back to big business. Presently the Bush administration does not require companies to cut greenhouse gas emissions. Here is the mother of all quid pro quos: favor trading away the earth itself!

Recently, ten corporations—Alcoa, BP America, Caterpillar, Duke Energy, DuPont, FPL Group, General Electric, Lehman Brothers, PG&E, and PNM Resources—have formed an alliance to slow global warming. These companies have proposed a mandatory, market-driven approach to climate protection. According to this program, companies would be given a fixed amount of credits on greenhouse emissions and would be able to sell or trade their remaining credits to other companies that have depleted their existing credits.

Whether such a plan would work to slow global warming is not clear; however, it is significant that these companies have not proposed a simple mandatory capping of emissions without the ability to buy more opportunities for destabilizing the environment. To companies driven by bottom-line interests, it is not likely that such a flat proposal would fly.

The future survival of our planet thus depends largely on what is likely to prove cost effective for large corporations. If more of these corporate giants than not oppose mandatory caps on greenhouse emissions—which presently appears to be the case—then government will predictably continue to downplay the problem, enlisting the media to help it.

Unfortunately, instead of working to expose the serious threat of global warming, the corporate media have cooperated with the Bush administration in concealing it. As will become clear in the chapters ahead, the government's systematic attempt at controlling the content of media programming never was the unavoidable consequence of successfully fighting a global war on terror. To the contrary, it is an ongoing government program of indoctrination, manipulation, intimidation, and the dumbing down of Americans, all for the purpose of amassing tremendous power and wealth and ultimately world domination. This was never about spreading democracy here and abroad or about peace, security, and human welfare; it was always about power and control. And, in an effort to fatten their wallets and ensure their own prosperity, the giant media corporations have been complicit.

NOTES

1. Based on estimated revenues for 2004. Compiled by the Center for Public Integrity, http://www.publicintegrity.org/telecom/industry.aspx?act=paytv (accessed February 19, 2007).

2. "Well Connected: Tracking the Broadcast, Cable, and Telecommunications Industry," Center for Public Integrity, http://www.publicintegrity.org/telecom/itview.aspx?act=contribs&sub=broadcast (accessed February 19, 2007).

3. Pat Kearney, "Microsoft Does Business with the Department of Defense," TheStranger.com, vol. 10, September 27, 2000, http://www.thestranger.com/2000-09-21/city5.html (accessed February 19, 2007).

4. Fox Cable Network/Comcast, http://comcast.foxcable.com/map.html (accessed February 19, 2007).

5. Tina Brown, "Rupert Murdoch: Bending with the Wind," *Washington Post*, September 15, 2005, http://www.washington

post.com/wp-dyn/content/article/2005/09/14/AR2005091402628.html (accessed February 19, 2007).

6. And this is assuming the vote is not rigged, an assumption that is disputed later in this book.

7. General Electric, "Our Company," http://www.ge.com/en/company/ (accessed February 19, 2007).

8. New York Times Company, "Mission and Values," http://www.nytco.com/mission.html (accessed February 19, 2007).

9. "The Future of the New York Times," *Business Week Online*, January 17, 2005, http://www.businessweek.com/magazine/content/05_03/b3916001_mz001.htm (accessed February 19, 2007).

10. The credo of the *Times* is that quality journalism pays, so increasing its bottom line is still, after all, its ultimate standard of performance.

11. Eric Lichtblau and James Risen, "Bank Data Is Sifted by US in Secret to Block Terror," *New York Times*, June 23, 2006.

12. "Patriotism and the Press," *New York Times*, June 28, 2006.

13. "Fit and Unfit to Print: What Are the Obligations of the Press in Wartime?" *Wall Street Journal*, http://www.opinionjournal.com/editorial/feature.html?id=110008585 (accessed February 19, 2007).

14. Buzzflash, "Hideous WSJ Editorial Board Inadvertently Proves NYT Set Up for Bushevik Red Meat Attack," July 1, 2006, http://www.buzzflash.com/analysis/06/07/ana06054.html (accessed February 19, 2007).

15. Society of Professional Journalists, Code of Ethics, preamble, http://www.spj.org/ethics_code.asp (accessed February 11, 2007).

16. Brit Hume, "Dems Invoke FDR," Foxnews.com, February 4, 2005, http://www.foxnews.com/story/0,2933,146409,00.html (accessed February 19, 2007).

17. Seth Ackerman, "The Most Biased Name in News: Fox News Channel's Extraordinary Right-Wing Tilt," *Fairness and Accuracy in Reporting*, July/August 2001, http://www.fair.org/index.php?page=1067 (accessed February 19, 2007).

18. Radio-Television News Directors Association, Code of Ethics.

19. Paul Schmeizer, "The Death of Local News," AlterNet.org, April 23, 2003, http://www.alternet.org/story.html?StoryID=15718 (accessed April 30, 2004).

20. "TV Group to Show Anti-Kerry Film on 62 Stations," *New York Times*, October 11, 2004.

21. "Sinclair Won't Air Full Anti-Kerry Film," *Morning Edition*, NPR, October 20, 2004.

22. Radio-Television News Directors Association, Code of Ethics, my italics.

23. Fortunately, Tomlinson is no longer chair of the National Corporation for Broadcasting.

24. "Lifeline for 'Fahrenheit 9/11': Miramax Chiefs Will Buy Michael Moore's Film and Get It Distributed," CBS News, May 13, 2004, http://www.cbsnews.com/stories/2004/05/13/entertainment/main617158.shtml (accessed February 19, 2007).

25. Tom Flocco, "Fahrenheit 9-11 Censored in PA Republican Stronghold?" TomFlocco.com, June 26, 2004, http://www.tomflocco.com/fs/Fahrenheit911.htm (accessed February 19, 2007).

26. Charlie Anderson, "Toll Fight: Tech, Telecom Firms Hurtle toward a Collision on Internet Fees," *Kansas City Business Journal*, June 2, 2006, http://www.bizjournals.com/kansascity/stories/2006/06/05/focus1.html (accessed February 19, 2007).

27. "Top NASA Scientist Says He's Being Censored on Global Warming," ABC News, January 29, 2006, http://www.abcnews.go.com/WNT/story?id=1555183 (accessed February 19, 2007).

Chapter 3

LOOK WHO'S *NOT* LOOKING OUT FOR YOU

In the last chapter, we soaked up the culture of corporate media and saw how the newsrooms of gigantic conglomerates are expected to turn a profit just like any other division of the corporation. It is the bottom line, not the public's need to know, that ultimately determines what's newsworthy. As you will see, this view of journalism practice flatly contradicts the ethics codes of journalism practice. Unfortunately, it is this view that governs individual journalists who work within the confines of these colossal media empires.

THE HIGH-PRICED HOOKERS OF MEDIAVILLE

With very few exceptions, the front men and women of the MSM—the radio and TV talk show hosts and pundits—are company employees who are willing to toe the corporate line in order to keep their jobs. As this book has shown, the net result of such media line toeing is the mass dissemination of government propaganda and deception—all to the beat of what's in the company's best financial interest. Yet not all media deceit is created equal, and there are some media hosts who are more convincing than others.

One of the most notorious spin masters on TV today is Bill O'Reilly, host of Fox's *O'Reilly Factor*. Among right-wing conservative talk show hosts, he is among the most widely criticized, especially by progressives. Nevertheless, the worst kind of media deceit does *not* come from the likes of Bill O'Reilly.[1]

Nobody could reasonably deny that O'Reilly takes things to the extreme. Taking seriously *The O'Reilly Factor* is like taking seriously the Jerry Springer TV show or professional wrestling. There is a persistent element of incredulity in much of what he says. Fox keeps the *Factor* because it attracts viewers and makes money for the company. But that is also why Springer's TV show has managed to stay on the air.[2] As mentioned earlier in this book, News Corp (parent company of Fox News, which carries *The O'Reilly Factor*) is not really a *news* organization after all; it's an *entertainment* company, and O'Reilly can indeed be entertaining—just not credible.

The most salient journalistic transgression (and there are many) of O'Reilly's editorializing is not his political tilt to the far right; in America, extremists also have a right to be heard. It is rather his propensity to misstate the facts in order to maintain his views. David Letterman summed this up well when O'Reilly was a guest on his late-night talk show.

Without a hint of jest, Letterman quipped, "I have the feeling that about 60 percent of what you say is crap." From falsehood about the existence of a political movement to steal Christmas to bogus statistics about how many Americans oppose military force in Iraq, evidence for Letterman's incredulity is not hard to find.[3]

Nor is the *Factor* "fair and balanced." However, the emptiness of this slogan is not specific to O'Reilly, since it's emblematic of Fox programming in general. For example, just consider Alan Colmes, the limp token "liberal" on the *Hannity & Colmes* TV show. Once asked by *USA Today* about his political ideology, this "liberal" responded, "I'm quite moderate." Lacking charisma and unwilling to stand his ground, Colmes is a Fox setup. Epitomizing the proverbial liberal straw man, summarily blown over by the dynamic, ultraconservative Hannity, the show would, paradoxically, be more "fair and balanced" if Colmes retired.

The coverage of a newsworthy item can aptly be called "balanced" only when the diversity of perspectives on the matter are equally represented. It is "fair" only when neither side uses intimidation, fear, fraud, misstatement of fact, or other nonevidentiary, nonrational tactics to gain an undue advantage over others espousing alternative perspectives.

O'Reilly's condescension and bullying of guests who disagree with him is evident even to those who watch the show from an objective, impartial perspective. I can recall watching the normally steady hands of *New York Times* columnist Paul Krugman begin to tremble on the March 29, 2005, show as O'Reilly, a relatively large man, leaned forward and told him how he didn't "like" him. This host stands tall for narrow-mindedness, intolerance, and hostility.

In a democracy, everybody has a right to his or her political views. Political free speech is the closest thing there is to an absolute right. But even in a democracy, there are limits, such as when espousing a view in a public place creates a clear and imminent danger to the lives of others. Still, there are some views that, even though a person has a right to hold them, are blatantly immoral and defy basic moral principles of social existence.

Perhaps the most reprehensible remark O'Reilly has ever made in this category came in response to a ballot measure passed by 60 percent of San Franciscans opposing military recruitment at public colleges and high schools. Said O'Reilly, "[I]f Al Qaeda comes in here and blows you up, we're not going to do anything about it. We're going to say, look, every other place in America is off-limits to you, except San Francisco. . . . You want to blow up the Coit Tower? Go ahead." The morally base, vindictive, and intolerant nature of this remark speaks for itself.[4] And there is also the by now classic threat O'Reilly made on his syndicated radio show (*The Radio Factor*) to get "Fox security" after a guest who "erred" by making favorable mention of MSNBC's *Countdown* host, Keith Olbermann. Whatever else you might make of this, it oozes with venomous intolerance.

And, as if these cases aren't enough to prove the point, consider O'Reilly's recent rant about a fifteen-year-old boy who was allegedly abducted at the age of eleven and sexually molested for four years by his abductor: "The situation here for this kid looks to me to be a lot more fun than what he had under his old parents. . . . There was an element here that this kid liked about his circumstance." Sadly, these are the words of a man whose mantra has been "looking out for the folks."

Such hypocrisy, hate mongering, and callous disregard for others is certainly not unique to O'Reilly. Ann Coulter, "the queen of mean," is an excellent example. In her recent liberal-bashing book titled *Godless: The Church of Liberalism*, Coulter attacks a group of widows who lost their husbands in the 9/11 attacks and who have been critical of Bush's handling of terrorism. Coulter says, "These broads are millionaires, lionized on TV and in articles about them, reveling in their status as celebrities and stalked by grief-arazzis. I've never seen people enjoying their husbands' deaths so much."

This blatant lack of empathy and scornfulness toward the victims of such a horrendous tragedy reflects an attitude so callous that it's pathological. In his recent book *Conservatives without Conscience*, John Dean, former counsel for the Nixon administration, has suggested that there is a disturbing trend in media and politics toward "conservatism without conscience." According to Dean, conservatives without consciences (not to be confused with conservatives *with* consciences) are mean-spirited, malicious, disrespectful of codes of civility, intolerant, prejudiced, dishonest, dogmatic, hypocritical, and fierce. They also define themselves negatively in terms of their hatred for liberals, which can be anyone with whom they disagree.

Coulter and O'Reilly clearly fit Dean's characterization of "conservatives without conscience." In keeping with the above descriptions, they are mean-spirited individuals bent on venting their hostility on anyone they oppose, even at the expense of blatant incivility. For John Dean, it is this same callous and conscienceless attitude among neoconservatives in politics and media that is feeding America's steady decline in democracy toward fascism. One reason for this, he thinks, is the ability of these individuals to submit blindly to authority and do things that a person of conscience—conservative and liberal alike—would not do.

It is in this sense that outspoken liberal bashers like Coulter and O'Reilly make excellent foot soldiers for the Bush administration. They are willing and able to put a favorable spin on things that most people with a conscience could not advocate. But there's also a sense in which such pundits make *poor* foot soldiers. This is because they are often so *obviously* biased and contemptuous that they aren't taken seriously by people who do have consciences—which is most of us. In this way, they are less dangerous than they would be if they were more subtle and insidious.

This isn't to say these hate-mongering spin doctors aren't able to draw followings, even substantial ones. Unfortunately, there are always going to be like-minded "ditto-heads" (Limbaugh worshipers included) who lack the ability to think for themselves and are looking for a common enemy upon which to vent their hostilities. But most Americans are not hate mongers in search of a common enemy. The average American does not believe that women who were widowed by the 9/11 attacks enjoy the attention brought about by the deaths of their husbands. Nor does the average American think that the residents of San Francisco deserve to be attacked by terrorists. This kind of in-your-face hate mongering is unlikely to appeal to most Americans. Nor do they think children, in some way, "like" to be abducted and raped.

These hateful hosts and pundits lose considerable credibility simply by being hypocritical. For example, as Dean points out, Coulter has little trouble bashing "liberals," but she gets upset (walks off the stage and even cries) when she thinks she's been treated unfairly.[5] And, while O'Reilly has had little trouble personally attacking people—for example, he called Hillary Clinton "a left wing nut"; Ralph Nader a "loon"; Bill Moyers a "secular far left fanatic"; John Kerry a "sissy"; and Barbara Boxer a "nut"—he will not tolerate being personally attacked.[6] For example, on his show *Countdown with Keith Olbermann*, Olbermann has made a habit of putting O'Reilly on his list of "Worst Persons in the World," and O'Reilly in turn has attempted to have Olbermann fired.

Rush Limbaugh deserves honorable mention here. While Limbaugh has been quite aggressive in attacking drug addicts, he (as well as his followers) thought it quite unfair when his drug addiction to Oxycontin was reported, as well as the allegation that he had illicitly obtained the drug to support his habit.[7]

Unfortunately, not all TV and radio "conservatives without conscience" are as in-your-face as Bill O'Reilly and Ann Coulter. There are some who put up a facade of democracy and are therefore more apt to deceive the public. In December 2003, when MSNBC's Chris Matthews played *Hardball* with then Democratic presidential candidate Howard Dean, Matthews asked Dean the *leading* question, "If we elect you, when will the geyser go off?" implying that Dean had a bad temper.[8] By attempting to answer this question, Dean would have effectively admitted that he had a bad temper. While such a tactic might be dismissed as merely a journalistic device to uncover the truth, this explanation becomes exceedingly less credible when it is realized that the interlocutor works for a company that was already "playing ball" with an administration that sought a second term in the White House.

Unfortunately, it's routine to see Matthews announce he's playing hardball while tiptoeing around guests like California governor Arnold Schwarzenegger and Republican house majority whip Tom DeLay and defaming guests like Howard Dean.

For example, although DeLay was guilty of accepting travel expenses from Washington lobbyist Jack Abramoff to play golf in Scotland, Matthews put him on the air on his January 30, 2006, show and coached him through his lies and deceit:[9]

> **Matthews:** So that picture of you—that picture we keep seeing of St. Andrews—I'm not much of a golfer but, you're a better golfer obviously—but do you think that's unfair to say that you went over there on a junket?
>
> **DeLay:** It's incredibly unfair.
>
> **Matthews:** Why? Who paid for the trip?
>
> **DeLay:** A legitimate conservative organization.
>
> **Matthews:** But wasn't there a pass through?
>
> **DeLay:** No, there was no pass through.
>
> **Matthews:** They came up with the money themselves.
>
> **DeLay:** That's exactly right. They raised their money themselves.
>
> **Matthews:** That public policy group . . .

DeLay: That's exactly right.

Matthews: So you don't have any problem with that trip?

DeLay: Not at all.

And then Matthews sealed his support with this glowing compliment: "I mean everybody knows that you're a tough Republican, conservative, who gives his life for the cause. You're not in it for the money or the lifestyle." Matthews, who used to write speeches for Democratic House Speaker Tip O'Neil, is everything but a Democrat. He has admitted being "more conservative than people think"; he has spoken candidly about his having voted for George W. Bush and about his affections for him. He once remarked, "Bush glimmers with a sunny nobility" and "Everybody sort of likes the president except for the real whack-jobs."[10] So if you don't like the president because you think he is leading the nation down the wrong road, that makes you a "whack-job"? While it is one thing to express your own likes or dislikes, it is quite another to poison the well against anyone who might share a contrary opinion. This doesn't mean that, as a journalist, Matthews hasn't a right to his own political views and party affiliation. However, these views are not supposed to determine how hard he pitches his balls to the batter up. He masquerades as a champion of democracy—getting at the truth through rigorous, unbiased interrogation—while all along he is a foot soldier for the government.

Moreover, Matthew's guest list has been blatantly skewed to the right. For example, in January 2006, Republican/conservative guests outnumbered Democrats/progressives 55 to 38 (59 percent to 41 percent); and in February this ratio increased to 55 to 34 (62 percent to 38 percent). In addition, during these months, there were significantly more elected Republican/conservative government officials than there were Democratic/progressive ones—a ratio of 22 to 18; and there were vastly more conservative journalists/pundits to progressive ones—a ratio of 42 to 13.[11]

Matthews's willingness to prostitute his views is evident from his recent back peddling on the Iraq war. Amid the rising tide of opposition to the war, Matthews has preferred to try to save face rather than to fess up. For example, as a guest on MSNBC's *Imus in the the Morning*, on September 21, 2006, Matthews proclaimed, "I have been a voice out there against this bullshit war from the beginning." Yet here is what he said of Bush's proclamation of "mission accomplished" on May 1, 2003:

> He won the war. He was an effective commander. Everybody recognizes that, I believe, except a few critics. . . . He looks for real. . . . [H]e didn't fight in a war, but he looks like he does. . . . We're proud of our president. . . . Women like a guy who's president. Check it out. The women like this war. I think we like having a hero as our president.

And, on the July 31, 2005, airing of *Hardball*, Matthews maintained that, inasmuch as Democratic critics recognize that Bush made a "smart decision" to invade Iraq, Bush "deserves to have a place in history" because "[y]ou can't say he did the right thing but he didn't quite do it right." And prior to Bush's November 30, 2005, speech on strategies to end the Iraq war, Matthews praised the president and derided democratic critics as "carpers and complainers."[12] When these facts are taken in the context of the colossal, revenue-driven corporation that employs Matthews (General Electric), it's not hard to see why he has enjoyed a lucrative, uninterrupted career with MSNBC. Despite his democratic roots, he has been willing to insert himself into the corporate culture that cares more about yielding dividends to shareholders than it does about the welfare of a nation on the verge of dictatorship. Like a high-priced hooker, Matthews has prostituted himself for his corporate pimp in exchange for his lavish existence.

Media codes of ethics typically instruct journalists to avoid conflicts of interest, real or perceived.[13] Yet, if the companies by whom individual journalists are employed ignore such fundamental ethics, then there is an obvious strain placed upon individual journalists to practice within the strictures of professional ethics. It is this challenge that is likely to separate the truly noble journalists from the likes of Bill O'Reilly and Chris Matthews.

When the First Amendment of the United States Constitution states that Congress shall make no law abridging freedom of speech, or of the press, it aims at a separation of the press from governmental control. It is no accident that such a separation was foremost in the minds of the Founding Fathers, for it is a fundamental condition of a democratic nation. Democracy implies autonomous rule by the people. People cannot decide freely if they are not adequately informed. They cannot decide freely if government controls the flow of information they receive. We depend on the media to check for and expose abuses in the judicial, legislative, and executive branches. To the extent that the media satisfactorily serves this function, it is democratic; to the extent that this function is impaired, it is *un*democratic.[14]

With few exceptions, talk show hosts and news anchors

of the major broadcast TV, cable TV, and radio networks resemble high-priced hookers. For their millions, they have sold out their journalistic integrity—if they ever had any. These journalists lack the moral fiber we need from the press to sustain our democracy. They do not deserve the celebrity status they receive. No, they deserve instead to be given their (street) walking papers!

This problem is not limited to a relatively small number of national journalists who work for the major networks. All journalists, local and national, are under similar pressures from corporate headquarters. For example, a study of 206 journalists and 81 news executives (150 from local news outlets and 137 from national news organizations) revealed three related reasons why journalists censor stories. Eight in ten (77 percent) of the sample surveyed said that stories that are important but dull are avoided. A majority (52 percent) said that complex stories are at least sometimes avoided. More than one-third (35 percent) said that news that might hurt the financial interests of the news organization are not reported, and 29 percent said stories that could hurt the financial interests of advertisers are not reported. In each case, the bottom line is that the bottom line determines whether and how a story is run. The corporate game plan is unequivocally to make money, not to serve the welfare of the citizens by keeping them informed.

This study also polled investigative journalists who are members of Investigative Reporters and Editors (IRE). Half of those polled said that newsworthy stories are often or sometimes ignored because they conflict with the financial interests of the news organization. About six in ten (61 percent) of this group of IRE members said that corporate owners exert significant influence in determining which stories get covered.[15]

This doesn't mean that investigative reporters are not going out (some even putting their lives on the line) to get stories that never see the light of day. In some cases, however, the facts are cooked even before the story is written. This is clearly the case with the "embedded" journalists covering the present Iraq war. These journalists must sign a contract giving the military complete control over what gets reported. In addition, some of these embeds are actually military propagandists posing as civilian journalists.[16] Nothing could be further from the Fourth Estate's watchdog function than this system. The government is given a blank check to write its own reports about how and what it is doing. This turns the media into a wingman of the government, not a watchdog of democracy.

JOURNALISTS WITH CHUTZPAH

Journalists who permit themselves to be used in spreading government propaganda and lies do more harm than good by putting a credible face on a farce. In 2003, CNN's top war correspondent, Christiane Amanpour, displayed the characteristics of a journalist true to her cause when she broke ranks and reported that the press was being muzzled during the Iraq war. She made clear that CNN had allowed itself to be "intimidated" by the Bush administration and its foot soldiers at Fox News, who instilled "a climate of fear and self-censorship."[17] It takes courage—chutzpah—such as this for an American journalist to truly be a vanguard of the Fourth Estate.

Journalists like Amanpour embody qualities that are intrinsic to being a competent journalist. A look at the different journalism codes of ethics can give you an idea of what some of these qualities are. For example, Article 1 of the Statement of Principles of the American Society of Newspaper Editors, titled "Responsibility," says:

> The primary purpose of gathering and distributing news and opinion is to serve the general welfare by informing the people and enabling them to make judgments on the issues of the time. The newspapermen and women who abuse the power of their professional role for selfish motives or unworthy purposes are faithless to that public trust. The American press was made free not just to inform or just to serve as a forum for debate but also to bring an independent scrutiny to bear on the forces of power in the society, including the conduct of official power at all levels of government.[18]

According to the Code of Ethics of the Society of Professional Journalists, under "Seek Truth and Report it," "[j]ournalists should be honest, fair and courageous in gathering, reporting, and interpreting information."[19] And they "should be free of obligation to any interest other than the public's right to know."

According to the Code of Ethics of the Radio-Television News Directors Association, radio and television journalists should not "accept gifts, favors, or compensation from those who might seek to influence coverage"; they should "present the news fairly and impartially, placing primary value on significance and relevance."

In sum, journalists true to their cause must be *respon-*

sible, *loyal*, *fair*, *impartial*, *honest*, and *courageous* in reporting the news. This is what is required to be a *competent* journalist. Competence in journalism cannot be separated from its ethical foundations. As Beauchamp and Klaidman point out in their book *The Virtuous Journalist*, "Tape can be edited accurately, fairly, and objectively, or it can fail to meet these criteria. The editing cannot justifiably be called competent unless they are satisfied, which suggests that moral criteria are embedded in our very conception of competent journalistic practice."[20]

An editor or newsroom director who works as a foot soldier for the Bush administration cannot be a competent journalist because such an individual cannot be accurate, fair, and objective. As discussed earlier (chapter 2), newsrooms like CNN that are part of gigantic conglomerates (like Time Warner) are least likely of all news organizations to be accurate, fair, and objective because of their immersion in a corporate culture that views the newsroom not as a special entity but as just another division of the corporation. And as such, it is expected to toe the corporate line. When CNN rolled over for Bush in reporting on the war in Iraq, it did so because, on its cost-benefit analysis, it determined that cooperating with the government would be, on balance, more cost-effective than not cooperating. When the corporate bottom line rather than public interest serves as the standard of what gets reported and how it gets reported, news organizations fail to provide competent journalism—journalism that is accurate, fair, and objective. The true victims of such incompetence are you and me—the American people.

Unfortunately, in the present environment in which the news is being influenced by deals struck between government and corporate media, competence has been severed from its moral roots and journalistic virtue has become an empty aspiration to which many journalists merely pay lip service. Under the direction of its corporate and government masters, the press's seeming participation in the façade of democratic charter may be among its greatest breaches of public trust. As journalist Norman Solomon remarked, "[D]eceptive propaganda can only succeed to the extent that journalists are gullible—or believe that they must pretend to be—while encouraging the public to go along with the charade."[21] Putting on the façade of conducting business as usual, while delivering half the news or disseminating government propaganda, is neither honest, courageous, responsible, nor fair. Nor, in the end, is it likely to be in the best interest of the public.

The great philosopher Aristotle said that a truly brave person "feels and acts according to the merits of the case and in whatever way the rule directs," even if this involves great personal sacrifice.[22] The professional codes of ethics of American journalists instruct them to avoid conflicts of interest and to remain loyal to the American people who rely on them to stay informed. This means that journalists must speak out against those powers working to undermine the public trust even if this means speaking out against their corporate employers (just as Christiane Amanpour did with CNN). This is what being a journalist in a democratic society means. This is nonnegotiable and comes with the territory. It's not only cowardly to remain silent, it's incompetent!

The French philosopher Jean-Paul Sartre said that "to choose to be this or that, is to affirm at the same time the value of what we choose."[23] When a journalist chooses to work for a corporation that is violating the public trust, he or she cannot avoid responsibility for whatever evils are perpetrated by that corporation. The old saw "I only work here" is no excuse, because the journalist can choose to quit. For Sartre, the journalist who works for a news organization that engages in deceptive practices but refuses to accept culpability for the deception is just a coward.[24]

When CBS news anchor Dan Rather appeared on the *Late Show with David Letterman* six days after the September 11 attack, he stated, "George Bush is the president, he makes the decisions," and "Wherever he wants me to line up, just tell me where. And he'll make the call." Eight months after the 9/11 tragedy, in a BBC television interview, Rather admitted that he and other journalists had been intimidated about "asking the toughest of the tough questions" for fear of being branded unpatriotic.[25]

On CNN's *Reliable Sources*, in an interview about whether the media had provided just coverage of protests against the war in Iraq, Rather guardedly stated, "[W]e've tried on the 'CBS Evening News,' for which I'm responsible . . . to give the coverage we think is merited, but I'm open to the criticism. The White House and the administration power is able to control the images to a very large degree. It has been growing over the years. And that's the context in which we talk about, well, how much coverage does the anti-war movement merit? And I think it's a valid criticism it's been underreported."[26]

It's too bad that Rather's admissions were not voiced consistently and unequivocally before the American public. His willingness to continue as an anchor for CBS (until he was retired by the network), despite these admissions, spoke to his readiness to "line up" wherever he was told. Rather betrayed the public trust that he, as a journalist, was supposed to uphold. Courage in this situation would have meant standing on principle—those principles of honesty, responsibility, fairness, and loyalty to the journalistic faith—instead of allowing himself to be intimidated, even if this meant personal sacrifice. In the end, Rather tried to redeem himself by trying to prove that Bush did not faithfully serve in the Air National Guard. But failure to verify his source only made him look incompetent. Too bad he was at first so willing to walk lockstep. He might have left CBS with dignity and professionalism. What is more, he might have set an example for other journalists.

In stark contrast is journalist Edward R. Murrow, who put his job at CBS on the line to stand up to corporate and sponsorship pressures in order to expose the scaremongering, witch-hunting lies and tactics of Senator Joseph McCarthy in the 1950s. Murrow clearly showed how national TV could be used as a remarkably effective vehicle for exposing abuses of power. He put public welfare above his own personal job security and now stands as a symbol of the courage and dignity that is lacking today in corporate journalism. It is unfortunate, although not shocking (given its current corporate climate), that CBS has not produced a dynamic figure such as Murrow at a time in American history that so sorely needs one.

Another example of a journalist willing to put public welfare above personal job security is NPR's Daniel Schorr, who, in 1976, was fired by CBS News for sending a secret congressional intelligence report to the *Village Voice* when CBS refused to cover the story. According to Schorr, the network had struck a deal with the White House to go easy on the administration.

Schorr placed the democratic mission of the press on a higher plane than his career. In the words of the Society of Professional Journalists, a journalist should be "vigilant and courageous about holding those with power accountable."[27] This appears to be what Schorr attempted to accomplish, and he was fired for the undertaking.

Arthur Kent (aka "the Scud Stud"), well known for his heroic coverage of the first Gulf War, effectively ended his career with NBC when he publicly derided *Dateline* for its manipulation and reediting of stories.[28] Kent's dedication to truth and his courage to stand his ground have been earmarks of his long and celebrated career in journalism. Five months prior to the US invasion of Iraq in 2003, when journalists like Dan Rather and Chris Matthews were "lining up" with the Bush administration, Kent prophetically warned, "if the administration is failing in Afghanistan, why should anyone accept that there's a clear, winning strategy in place for war in the Gulf?" And just ten days into the war Kent complained, "each broadcast day is dominated by official lines. The spin on the story coming from the Bush administration, the White House, the Pentagon . . . why are there not tougher questions?" And just three weeks into the war, and about three weeks before Bush declared "mission accomplished," he prophesized, "we're going to have a very long Vietnam moment, where U.S. forces and the U.S. administration face an implacable enemy." A journalist with a keen sense of reality, I (EC) have come to know and respect Kent for his journalistic integrity and unwavering commitment to truth.

On January 30, 2003, and again on January 31, 2003, Paul Begala, the Democratic proponent of CNN's *Crossfire* (now off the air) boldly denounced the news media for its politically biased and shoddy coverage of news surrounding the Bush administration.

> Last night I reported to you on the breath-taking hypocrisy of President Bush, praising the work of the Boys and Girls Clubs, calling them "little beacons of light," then cutting off their electricity by reducing their budget $10 million. I suggested that none of the major media would have the guts to report President Bush's brazen bad faith. I was wrong a little. One reporter, Mike Allen, at one newspaper, "The Washington Post," wrote one sentence about it. Nothing in "The New York Times," nothing on the AP, nothing on CNN, except here on CROSSFIRE, or any of the other so-called news networks. The lesson, you can bask in the glow of a wonderful group even if you've cut its budget, because the press corps is so cowed by the Bush White House, you can almost hear them moo. President Bush, of course, could not be reached for comment. He was too busy laughing his ass off.[29]

The show was cancelled in 2005, although one of Begala's conservative Bush-supporting counterparts, Tucker Carlson, went on to host his own show on prime-time CNN. The Bush administration had in fact tried to remove Begala as well as James Carville from *Crossfire* during the 2004 presidential race on the grounds that they were both working (as volunteers) for the Kerry campaign. This was a lame reason for CNN to remove them, since both expressly identified themselves on the show as partisans—"from the left." A more likely reason was that the Bush administration didn't want the likes of Begala and Carville on the air because they were speaking out against Bush. Neither Begala nor Carville currently have their own shows.

When Stephen Colbert of Comedy Central's *The Colbert Report* roasted the president at the White House correspondents' dinner, he used humor to cut to the chase. Looking Bush squarely in the eyes, he said, "I believe in this president. Now, I know there are some polls out there saying that this man has a 32 percent approval rating. But guys like us, we don't pay attention to the polls. We know that polls are just a collection of statistics that reflect what people are thinking in 'reality.' And reality has a well-known liberal bias."

Later he quipped, "I believe the government that governs best is the government that governs least. And by these standards, we have set up a fabulous government in Iraq." This was gutsy humor; granted, the speech didn't waste time on social amenities, but it did take nerve. It is this nerve that goes to the heart of what the press is *supposed* to be. The press is not supposed to be a bedfellow of the media; it is supposed to be an *adversary*!

In 2000, Walter Cronkite, world renowned for his forthrightness and unwavering commitment to a democratic press, helped to launch Mediachannel.org, an online news organization devoted to the exploration of media concerns. He stated:

> As you know, I've been increasingly and publicly critical of the direction that journalism has taken of late, and of the impact on democratic discourse and principles. Like you, I'm deeply concerned about the merger mania that has swept our industry, diluting standards, dumbing down the news, and making the bottom line sometimes seem like the only line. It isn't and it shouldn't be. . . . Pressure to go

along, to get along, or to place the needs of advertisers or companies above the public's need for reliable information distort a free press and threaten democracy itself. . . .

We're always ready to speak out when journalists are at risk. But today we must speak out because journalism *itself* is at risk.[30]

Edward R. Murrow, Daniel Schorr, Arthur Kent, and other journalists of their ilk who have taken the journalistic high road of *speaking out* against corporate and government corruption and collusion, despite personal risk and sacrifice, are more appropriate models of journalistic excellence than the likes of Bill O'Reilly and Chris Matthews, who have earned their fame by being good politico-corporate lapdogs. If the watchdog of democracy is *really* to have teeth—if this isn't to be just another sham—then those who carry the torch must not allow fear and intimidation tactics strategically advanced by the politico-corporate establishment for self-serving reasons to distract them from their primary mission. Journalists who place the public trust above their own self-aggrandizement must carry this torch.

There is a cumulative effect of good journalism. While especially brave and gifted journalists such as those mentioned can and should set an example for others to follow, a functional Fourth Estate is a community effort. Many competent journalists who work together, each doing his or her respective part, can equal a functional news media. There are presently a number of good journalists at work trying to do their part. The ones who work for big media often become increasingly disenchanted with the politico-corporate culture and, sooner or later, butt heads with their corporate bosses and eventually quit or are fired. A good example is

Kristina Borjesson, who, after twenty years as a MSM insider, was excommunicated by CBS when she challenged government claims about TWA Flight 800. The experience did not destroy her determination, however. It simply inspired her to expose the corruption of the politico-corporate media establishment.[31]

Many of these good journalists work for independent media organizations. Let me mention just a few. On radio: Air America hosts Randi Rhodes (*Randi Rhodes Show*), Janeane Garofalo and Sam Sedar (*Majority Report*), Mike Papantonio and Robert F. Kennedy Jr (*Ring of Fire*); Pacifica Radio host Amy Goodman (*Democracy Now*). Investigative reporters/media researchers: Greg Palast (independent journalist), James Fallows (*Atlantic Monthly*), Norman Solomon (Institute for Public Accuracy), Charles Lewis (Center for Public Integrity), Mark Crispin Miller (New York University). Online: Mark Karlin (Buzzflash), Jeff Chester (Center for Digital Democracy). Media activists: Robert McChesney (Free Press), Jeff Cohen (FAIR), Pete Tridish (Prometheus Radio Project), Peter Phillips (Project Censored), Robert Greenwald (film and documentary producer).

Are all or most of these journalists likely to be called "liberal" by the politico-corporate establishment? Yes, indeed, but that simply means that they stand for what this establishment—especially its "conservatives without conscience"—despise. In this context, *liberal* is a dirty word. The establishment might as well call them assholes or fools or some other "O'Reillian" term of chastisement! The term *liberal* as it is used by the politico-corporate establishment is pejorative and expresses deep hostility, but it is devoid of cognitive import.

Some of the above-mentioned journalists are better known than others, but most readers are not likely to recognize many of them. They are not household names like Bill O'Reilly, for example. However, collectively, they are a force with which to be reckoned. The Bush administration would like nothing better than to see these voices silenced and is getting closer and closer to this goal. If and when that happens, our democracy will have effectively ended.

However, independent media alone are not likely to stop the decline of democracy in America. The MSM also needs to do its part. Unfortunately, in its current state, it cannot be part of the solution when it is itself largely part of the problem. The middle name of democracy is freedom—freedom of speech and of action. These individualistic modes of being are precisely what are in decline as the MSM, under the auspices of its corporate and political parents, fashions reality to the beat of its insatiable appetite for profit. In perceiving, thinking, and acting exactly the way the media want us to—for its own self-aggrandizing purposes—democracy evaporates along with our freedom.

NOTES

1. I here include other kindred fabricators, notably Rush Limbaugh and Ann Coulter.

2. I am not referring here to Springer's radio show on Air America, which is surprisingly quite edifying.

3. "In Letterman Appearance, O'Reilly Repeated False Claim That School Changed 'Silent Night' Lyrics," Media Matters, January 4, 2006, http://www.mediamatters.org/items/2006 01040009 (accessed February 11, 2007).

4. "O'Reilly to San Francisco," Media Matters, November 10, 2005.

5. John Dean, *Conservatives without Conscience* (New York: Viking, 2006), p. 26.

6. "O'Reilly: 'I Don't Do Personal Attacks Here,'" Media Matters, February 27, 2006, http://www.mediamatters.org/items/200602270001 (accessed February 11, 2007).

7. Dean, *Conservatives without Conscience*, p. 26.

8. Miranda Daniloff Mancusi, "Hardball with Chris Matthews and Former Vermont Governor Howard Dean," New Stories, Kennedy School of Government, Harvard University, http://www.ksg.harvard.edu/news/news/2003/hardball_dean_120103.htm (accessed April 29, 2004).

9. "Tom DeLay Stays Focused on Re-election Bid: Hardball Talks Exclusively with the Embattled House Representative," *Hardball with Chris Matthews*, MSNBC, http://www.msnbc.msn.com/id/11099862/ (accessed February 11, 2007).

10. "Hardball for the Left, Softball for the Right: Conservatives Dominate on Hardball," Media Matters, March 8, 2006, http://www.mediamatters.org/items/200603080005 (accessed February 11, 2007).

11. Ibid.

12. See "Matthews Claimed He Has Opposed Iraq War 'From the Beginning,' That Media Coverage of War 'Sucks'—But He Has Frequently Contributed to Problematic War Reporting," Media Matters, September 21, 2006, http://mediamatters.org/items/200609210010 (accessed February 11, 2007).

13. See Deni Elliott, "Conflicts of Interest," in *Journalism Ethics*, ed. Elliot D. Cohen and Deni Elliott (Santa Barbara, CA: ABC-CLIO, 1997), pp. 91–96.

14. "I would go so far as to say that media reform is not an issue that is best cast along left-right lines. It is better thought of as elementary to democracy. . . . It is a cannon of liberal democ-

racy, not socialist theory . . . that a democracy cannot exist without a press system that provides a rigorous accounting of people in power and the presentation of a wide range of informed opinions on the important issues of the day and age. Without such a media system, the promise of democracy becomes very hollow very quickly." Robert W. McChesney, *Rich Media, Poor Democracy: Communication Politics in Dubious Times* (Urbana: University of Illinois Press, 1999), p. xxviii.

15. "Self Censorship: How Often and Why. Journalists Avoiding the News," Pew Research Center for the People and the Press, April 30, 2000, http://www.people-press.org/reports/display.php3?ReportID=39 (accessed February 11, 2007).

16. "Embedded," Source Watch: A Project of the Center for Media and Democracy, January 6, 2006, http://www.sourcewatch.org/index.php?title=Embedded (accessed February 11, 2007).

17. Peter Johnson, "Amanpour: CNN Practiced Self-Censorship," *USA Today*, September 14, 2003, http://www.usatoday.com/life/columnist/mediamix/2003-09-14-media-mix_x.htm (accessed February 11, 2007).

18. American Society of Newspaper Editors, Statement of Principles, http://www.asne.org/kiosk/archive/principl.htm (accessed February 11, 2007).

19. Society of Professional Journalists, Code of Ethics, https://www.spj.org/ethics_code.asp (accessed February 11, 2007).

20. Stephen Klaidman and Tom L. Beauchamp, "The Virtuous Journalist: Morality in Journalism," in *Philosophical Issues in Journalism*, ed. Elliot D. Cohen (New York: Oxford University Press, 1992), p. 45.

21. Norman Solomon, "Media War and the Rigors of Self-Censorship," in *Censored 2003*, ed. Peter Phillips (New York: Seven Stories Press, 2002), p. 248.

22. Aristotle, *Nicomachean Ethics*, book 3, chap. 7, in *The*

Basic Works of Aristotle, ed. Richard Mckeon (New York: Random House, 1941).

23. Jean-Paul Sartre, "Existentialism," in *Philosophers at Work: Issues and Practice of Philosophy*, ed. Elliot D. Cohen (Ft. Worth, TX: Harcourt, 2000), p. 246.

24. "Those who hide their complete freedom from themselves out of a spirit of seriousness or by means of deterministic excuses, I shall call cowards." Sartre, "Existentialism," p. 448.

25. Solomon, "Media War and the Rigors of Self-Censorship," pp. 241–42.

26. CNN, *Reliable Sources*, March 9, 2003.

27. Society of Professional Journalists, Code of Ethics.

28. Ibid.

29. *Crossfire*, transcripts, January 31, 2003, http://www.cnn.com/TRANSCRIPTS/0301/31/cf.00.html.

30. Walter Cronkite, MediaChannel.org, February 2000, http://www.mediachannel.org/originals/cronkite.shtml.

31. Michelle Goldberg, "Flexing the Power of the Press," AlterNet, April 23, 2002, http://www.alternet.org/story/12941/.

Chapter 4
THE MEDIA MATRIX

Americans value their freedom not only because it is inherently satisfying to be able to choose freely, but also because the goals we set for ourselves reflect who we are—our values, aspirations, and dreams. When our actions are controlled or influenced by others, whether it is our government, corporate America, or the media, we are deprived of the opportunity to live as individuals; we are deprived of the opportunity to express our values through our actions, to communicate those values to our children, and to live free, independent lives. We are, in other words, deprived of the American dream. Freedom is essential to that dream because it is through our freedom that self-expression, self-reliance, and self-worth become possible.

THE UN-AMERICAN DREAM

The American dream means different things to different people, of course. For some it means access to economic opportunities, while for others the American dream is synonymous with the concept of self-governance and civil liberties. But in the diversity of perspectives on the American dream there is a common thread: the dignity of the person. Democracy is the political system that makes this dignity possible as a political ideal; in America, this ideal is evident in the Bill of Rights to the Constitution. At the heart of the American dream lies a profound respect for the sovereignty of the person, but also for the importance of self-reliance, moral character, and personal responsibility.

One of the great tragedies of the hostile takeover of the media by the monoliths of corporate America is that this dream is being quietly transformed into an American nightmare. Like the women in Ira Levin's famous novel *The Stepford Wives*, Americans are being reprogrammed by the media to be utterly complacent as their dignity is siphoned off and they are forced into a form of psychological slavery. What makes this transformation so frightening is the degree to which the majority of Americans willingly give over the control of their lives as a result of the subtle influences of the media on their beliefs, thinking, and behavior. Rather than worrying about our eroding civil liberties, we are fixated on celebrity scandal and keeping up with the Joneses, with the possibility of a bird flu pandemic or of a terrorist attack in our local shopping mall. Our judgments about truth, reality, and the core values of the American dream have been manipulated and distorted to the point that we are a shadow of our former selves. We are, as it were, caught in a matrix of deception that blinds us to the emerging tyranny of American government and the end of the American experiment in democracy. As one concerned citizen recently noted while reflecting on the shortcomings of the Bush administration:

> We are a nation devolving to tribalism . . . , and this nurturing of the worst side of human nature has allowed us to accept policies that were unthinkable a mere six years ago: We can torture people, because they are foreign and different. We can wiretap anyone, because we are a nation bursting at the seams with people harboring different ideas. We can calmly discuss in the halls of Congress slapping a felony on Samaritans who give water to human beings dying of thirst in the desert, if the dying are foreign and different. We can draw up plans to use nuclear weapons on people who are foreign and different. And so on. . . . This is not just empire building or corporate hegemony or a natural outcome of capitalism. This is war against the fundamental idea of America itself.[1]

THE ILLUSION OF FREEDOM

The situation in which Americans now find themselves is remarkably like that described by Plato, the well-known Greek philosopher, in his work of political philosophy titled *Republic*. Like the majority of great thinkers, Plato was interested in the impact of illusion and propaganda on the citizenry and on the role of popular mythology in shaping our psyches. In this famous work, Plato describes human beings born into bondage at the bottom of a cavern deep below the earth's surface. Chained to benches and restrained in such a way that they can only look in the direction of the back of the cave, the inhabitants of this underground world witness a panoply of shadows moving across the back wall, projected like images in a cinema from higher up in the cave. The shadows are constructed and controlled by a small group of people who dwell near the light of a fire and spend their time orchestrating the operatic dance of shadows that are mistaken for reality by the slaves below. Plato has his readers contemplate the view of reality these slaves would inevitably embrace, as well as the possibility of their release and ascent to the surface. It is a chilling account both for its political and its psychological implications: reality and the inner world of thought are controlled by the masters of this subterranean society. In such a world, there is no such thing as freedom.

Plato's metaphorical account of propaganda and thought control has exercised the imagination of thinkers for twenty-five hundred years. Closest to our own era, the rise of fascism in the first half of the twentieth century spawned social critiques very similar to that of Plato's, including such widely read works as Aldous Huxley's *Brave New World* and George Orwell's *1984*. With the emergence of the Information Age in the latter part of that century, the image of mind control has become interwoven with concerns about the power of technology to transform communication, concerns captured in popular works such as the film *The Matrix*. Fundamental to these accounts of the struggle to preserve human dignity and freedom is the question of how liberty and knowledge are related—how the ability to make meaningful choices depends on access to the truth. After all, if some outside force controls what we think—if our world-view is like the shadows on the back of Plato's cave—then our choices are also controlled. You might think a choice between CNN and Fox News is meaningful, but in reality you're choosing between equally faint and deceiving representations of the truth.

To make this connection between truth and freedom clear, imagine that a rogue scientist discovers a way to control your thoughts by implanting electrodes inside your brain and manipulating the mechanisms that determine what you think and feel. Suppose also that these electrodes are implanted without your knowledge during a minor surgery and that the scientist takes full control over your thoughts just as you awake. Now imagine that after opening your eyes and bringing the world back into focus it suddenly occurs to you that you are dissatisfied with your life, that you need to reevaluate things. You feel as though you are not making a difference in the world and that if you don't change things now you will end up a disgruntled pensioner who grumbles over the cost of gasoline and spends his afternoons napping during the *Dr. Phil* show. Your greatest fear is that you will die in utter obscurity and that your life will not have mattered one iota. And it is our rogue scientist who is making you think so.

So, intent on changing your life, you decide that when you recover from your surgery you will join the armed forces and defend your country against the Muslim hoards threatening from the East (of course, this threat is also the creation of our rogue scientist). The idea of defending freedom and achieving the recognition that comes with service to your country cheers you up considerably. Feeling better, you take a deep breath, straighten yourself up in the hospital bed, and look out over the austere, antiseptic décor of the room you share with a man in the last throes of emphysema. Beyond these walls lies a great future, a future of gods and heroes.

Ah, the freedom of choice—the freedom to change your life through self-determination. But there is no freedom here; free choice is an illusion in this scenario. The dissatisfaction with your personal life, the idea about old age and obscurity, and the idea of the Great Enemy of the Nation are all implanted by our rogue scientist. And although it was you who made the final choice as to what to do with your life, that choice was the product of the images and beliefs that occupy your mind. To the extent that those beliefs are controlled, so, too, is your capacity to make real choices, and hence your freedom is as much an illusion as the false beliefs on which your choice is based.

In the case of an imaginary scientist controlling your brain waves, it is easy to see that freedom is an illusion. But what's the difference if the mechanism of control is inside your head or outside in your environment? What's the difference if your thoughts are controlled by use of embedded electrodes or remotely by the use of propaganda? In Plato's cave, the minds of the prisoners are controlled through the construction of images outside the head rather than inside, but the result is the same. The difference between our rogue scientist and Plato's image makers is a matter of geography—the location of the source of control. Whether your thinking is controlled through the media, through psychological manipulation, or through some other mechanism makes no difference with respect to the outcome: in each case, genuine choice is eliminated. The lesson is that *genuine choice depends on access to the truth* (or at least the freedom from manipulation). In his classic work *Public Opinion*, journalist Walter Lippmann summed up this idea: "[W]hat each man does is based not on direct and certain knowledge, but on the pictures made by himself or given to him. If his atlas tells him that the world is flat he will not sail near what he believes to be the edge of our planet for fear of falling off."[2]

Deception is a tricky thing; it depends on more than just telling people what you want them to believe. A lie has to be plausible; it has to be supported in some way by what a person experiences. In other words, mind control depends not only on implanting or shaping our ideas but on creating a reality—an outside world—that mirrors those ideas. The thought experiment about the rogue scientist makes this idea plain: the idea that you need to change your life and fight off the Muslim hoards wouldn't be an effective mechanism for controlling your behavior if you left the hospital room and discovered that no one else was talking about this Great Threat. Ideas and reality have to intersect, and so mind control requires the creation of ideas *and* the engineering of reality. Again, Lippmann astutely expresses the point: "Without some form of censorship, propaganda in the strict sense of the word is impossible. In order to conduct a propaganda there must be some barrier between the public and the event. Access to the real environment must be limited, before anyone can create a pseudo-environment that he thinks wise or desirable. For while people who have direct access [to the truth] can misconceive what they see, no one else can decide how they shall misconceive it, unless he can decide where they shall look, and at what."[3]

One of the most pernicious illusions that has been created for popular consumption, and an illusion that makes it all the more difficult to seé the deception that permeates our lives, is the idea that Americans are *radically free*, that we are *always* free to make a meaningful choice regardless of the "information" we receive. Contrary to the idea that real freedom depends on truth, this view is based on the idea that nothing can interfere with our ability to choose freely, and hence that claims about corporate influence or political propaganda are empty. We hear this myth in the rhetoric of privatization, whether the issue is Social Security, education, or outsourcing of military contracts; we here it from the smut peddlers who take refuge behind the First Amendment.

And we hear it routinely in the rhetoric of the president. In his 2003 State of the Union address, George W. Bush *told* us we're free: "Americans are a free people, who know that freedom is the right of every person and the future of every nation. The liberty we prize is not America's gift to the world, it is God's gift to humanity" (applause). In his 2005 speech, he used the words "free" or "freedom" twenty-seven times. Americans are a free people. You must *always*, no matter what, think of yourself as free. That way you will never know it when you're not! This is subtle mind control aimed at eliminating the question "Am I really free?" and replacing it with the *assumption* of being unconditionally, entirely free.

The myth of radical freedom is seductive because it gives people a sense of being empowered, of having control over their own lives, of being free agents. The myth also resonates with our moral intuitions about the importance of people taking responsibility for themselves and their actions, an idea that can be supported only if human beings are truly free. The myth thus appears to square with a core feature of the American dream itself, and it seduces us into thinking that all is right with the world.

The lie of radical freedom is palatable because it capitalizes on the fact that people *feel* that their choices are beyond the control of the media and the government, just as the choice made by the person whose mind is controlled by the rogue scientist *feels* free to make his choice. The most sinister aspect of this lie is that it tells us there is no lie, and so it creates the illusion that we have control over our lives at the very moment that control is being stripped away. It is this lie that is at the very heart of the program to control our thinking and our choices, as it prevents us from questioning the legitimacy of the power wielded over us by the politico-corporate establishment. It is at its core the manipulation of the American dream in an effort to reinforce a politics of privilege for the ruling class in this country.

"Okay," you say, "but where's the beef? How does all this connect up with reality?" If you're feeling like this account is somehow divorced from the real world, here's a reality check. In *reality*, our nation's most powerful institutions, the mega-corporations, constantly engage in this kind of engineering, in shaping our thought processes and in shaping our world through the introduction of new products. In *reality*, these institutions spend over a trillion dollars a year on this activity, which is approximately $4,000 for every man, woman, and child in the United States today.[4] In *reality*, corporate America has been focused on the enterprise of manufacturing consumers through the application of concepts and methods of the social sciences for the last forty years with remarkable success.

The terrible irony in all this is that many Americans view their increasingly commodified lives as evidence of their *participation* in the American dream rather than in its opposite. But as Michael Dawson points out in his book *The Consumer Trap*, "over time, our increasingly marketing-saturated life spaces make us dumber, lazier, fatter, more selfish, less skillful, more adolescent, less politically potent, more wasteful, and less happy than we could and should be." This degenerative process is also multileveled. On one level, corporate marketers coax us into purchasing habits that "clutter our homes, poison our bodies, undermine our independence, pollute our ecosphere, and waste our precious time and energy." This, in turn, changes the dynamics of personal living with fast food, shopping, and television taking the place of more meaningful interpersonal relationships. And as corporate marketers invent new marketing approaches "sensationalism and titillation—the two great cultivators of receptive advertising audiences—corrupt our mental, emotional, and practical capabilities."[5]

This is hardly a description of the American dream, and yet many people wander through their corporatized lives accepting this state of affairs and wondering why they feel as if something is not right with the world. To a significant degree, we are all victims of marketing efforts to keep our gaze focused on the back of Plato's cave, and the corporate control of the media plays a significant role in promoting this victimization.

In the remainder of this chapter, we will consider the role of America's largest corporations as image makers and distorters of the American dream. In the next two chapters we will discuss the intersection of this source of propaganda with the other great source of mind control in American society, the US government. At certain levels these two sources are indistinguishable, but there are points at which governmental and corporate interests diverge, and these points reveal a great deal about the limits of our freedom as citizens of the United States of America.

EXTREME MAKEOVER OF THE AMERICAN MIND

Here's some conventional wisdom. The most pervasive view of the role of corporations in American life is that corporations serve a need, namely, the need of the citizen to procure and use goods and services that make life possible. Corporations provide us with cars because we, the consumers, have a need for transportation; they provide us with news because we need and want to be informed; and they provide us with Viagra because we . . . well, you know. And so it is with all our other needs: corporations are there to serve us, and their livelihood depends on our willingness to satisfy those needs through our consumer choices. Moreover—so goes this conventional wisdom—corporations are therefore beholden to the customers that pay for their wares. Without us, the consumer, they are nothing. We could force them to close up shop by exercising different choices or foregoing certain things altogether.

The conventional wisdom is *conventional* for a good reason. There has been a concerted effort by individuals and groups variously associated with corporate interests to *make* this the conventional way of thinking about corporations. For example, W. W. Rostow claims in his influential book

The Stages of Economic Growth that the mechanisms of big business are beholden to "consumer sovereignty," that it is consumer freedom that drives corporate activity.[6] This analysis came at a time when the principles of modern marketing were already clear, when it was understood by corporate management that *manufacturing consumers* was going to be necessary for the survival of large corporations. It was recognized that, rather than merely responding to consumer needs, corporations would have to *create* needs on the consumer side if they were to keep demand for goods high.[7] More recently, Francis Fukuyama, author of *The End of History and the Last Man*, has argued that the pinnacle of history is the American economic system, a system in which the demands of the consumer govern supremely and genuine freedom is maximized. This is an idea so contrary to fact that it betrays itself as a marketing ploy to anyone with even a minimal grasp of reality. Such literature abounds, originating from far-flung advocates of the corporate establishment. (Fukuyama himself was a charter member of the Project for the New American Century [PNAC]. As will be discussed in later chapters, PNAC seeks corporate privatization as a key mechanism for achieving world domination.)

True, there was a time when America's corporations were beholden to those with the power to purchase their products, a time when genuine price wars worked in the interest of the citizen on the street, but those times are gone. After World War II, American business realized that in order to protect the bottom line against saturated markets and diminishing consumer resources, it would have to create the conditions that kept people buying. Rather than creating products to meet the needs of a sovereign consumer, corporations would have to create the consumer, establish a need, and design products accordingly (Americans' increasing debt is in part a function of this effort, as providing lines of credit opens up yet further opportunities for corporations to dig into the earnings, or potential earnings, of the citizenry). In a competitive market where businesses are vying for the same resources, this created a race to the bottom—an attempt to be more manipulative, more psychologically intrusive, and more effective than one's competitors. In short, America's corporate managers came to two important realizations: "(a) demand is not an uncontrollable, incorrigible force, and (b) demand can be governed to a large degree by the marketer."[8]

And so began the extreme makeover of the American mind. Armed with the resources of modern psychology, sociology, cultural anthropology, and the analytical power of modern mathematics, the marketing industry has systematically deconstructed the American psyche, exposing subconscious and preconscious motives and exploiting this information to create a sense of need that might otherwise not exist. Rather than trying to fit products into a pre-existing lifestyle, marketers have sought to *sell us a lifestyle and then populate that lifestyle with commodities*. Early historical examples of this kind of manipulation include the marketing program by Philip Morris to change the image of Marlboro cigarettes from a product for sissies and women (its filtered tip was the problem) to one for the rugged individualist braving the wild frontier—a very successful program, to be sure. Closer to our own time, corporate marketers sell us on the idea of retirement golf communities, hair color for men, designer pharmaceuticals, and a virtually endless litany of other commodities associated with emotionally charged images of the Good Life. It goes without saying that that life is one in which new needs and desires emerge and are then satisfied by the products created with the marketing images in mind. In the business, this is called *Demand Management*.

Thus, according to Dawson, rather than giving engineers, designers, and scientists free rein in using science and technology to give customers what they really want, marketers keep designers and scientists focused on producing products made to fit the make-believe needs that marketers drum up by selling us images and illusions. And, instead of letting users define product quality, marketers define quality in terms of what is most profitable, which "depends on threatening, enticing, and cajoling people to accept more commodified ways of living."[9]

The reality is that big business uses behavioral manipulation to make us *think* it is applying objective standards of engineering.[10] The whole idea that corporations are providing Americans with real choices, that the customer is guiding the direction of big business, and that corporations are fulfilling a socially important function is bunk. It's nonsense on stilts; pure propaganda.

Tying all this in with the reflections about the media in previous chapters depends on recognizing a simple truth, namely, that the media serve *primarily* as a delivery device for corporate marketing. That's right. Turn on your favorite sitcom or soap opera and you are settling into corporate America's behavioral modification program. As Leonard Hill, an independent television producer expresses the point: "With flagrant disregard for even the most dilute concept of public trusteeship responsibility, the networks are currently engaged in creating branded entertainment. . . . No longer content to simply plug products through calculated set dressing, networks now are attempting to engineer commercial messages into the very narrative of the series that are being broadcast. And this is not some dirty little secret. . . . *Corporate propaganda is no longer contained in clearly understood commercial blocks but has metastasized, silently invading every organ of mass communication*" (emphasis added).[11] This should hardly be surprising, given the connection between broadcasting and other big businesses. As you've seen, the media are owned by much larger businesses, businesses whose primary responsibility is to maximize their value for shareholders. Embedded as they are in the corporate framework, television and radio (and to an increasing degree, the Internet) serve as an extension of the marketing division, as a conduit both for advertisements and for the images and ideals that shape the way we view the world. At best, our favorite shows are attention grabbers that keep us tuned in to a freeway for commercials. At worst, our favorite shows themselves are extended advertisements, attempts to subtly influence our views on lifestyle, relationships, and the commodities that support them.

But how much does our constant exposure to marketing affect the way we look at the world? *Does* marketing affect us at all, or is this just a tempest in a teapot? If it weren't for the mythology about "sovereign consumers" and radical freedom propagated by advocates of corporate power—that is, if it weren't for careful marketing on the part of corporations to make themselves look good to the public—the answers to these questions would be too obvious to state. *Of course* marketing is effective. If it weren't, corporate America wouldn't spend a trillion dollars a year doing it.

The average American watches in excess of four hours of television a day, has seen over two hundred and fifty thousand commercials by the time he or she graduates from high school, uses cell phones and computers that serve as conduits for marketing, and is exposed to commercial messages through the radio, billboards, and a variety of other media. Is it likely that such saturation of advertisements and marketing techniques leaves our worldviews unchanged?

As a barometer of the impact of the media on our psyches, consider the influence of television violence on people's behavior. Health professionals have known for years that exposure to violence desensitizes viewers to acts of violence. Moreover, this influence is not restricted to children, who tend to be more impressionable than adults.

David Phillips, a researcher at the University of California in San Diego, discovered an alarming connection between the incidents of murder and televised boxing matches, a connection that suggests a tendency to model the violent behavior of an aggressor.[12] After careful analysis of the homicide rates following prize fights and correcting for factors such as differences in the time of year and day of the week, Phillips determined that between the third and fourth day following a fight the national murder rate increased significantly and that the victims in these murders were more likely to have physical features of the losing fighter—for example, black if the loser was black, white if the loser was white. The connection between media violence and the behavior of viewers is empirically well established.[13]

Of course influence is not the same thing as control, violence may not be typical of the impact of the media on our psyche, and it is unlikely that there is a simple, causal connection between what we view and who we are. No one can point to a commercial and say, "Ah ha. That's the one that pushed Americans over the edge." But it's a big mistake to assume that you would have to find a direct and obvious connection like this in order to show the negative effects of advertising on our choices and ideas. The influence is subtler than that, and the changes in our views may be incremental—just enough to push someone over the tipping point. As Max Sutherland, psychologist and director of MarketMind Technologies, points out, "Why is it so difficult to introspect on advertising and how it influences us? Because we look for major effects, that's why! . . . We look for a major effect rather than more subtle minor effects. . . . These minor effects are not obvious but they are more characteristic of the way advertising works."[14]

It is because the impact of advertising and marketing are subtle and cumulative that people don't question their radical freedom. We don't see the incremental changes in our worldview, the result of the seemingly endless bombardment of messages that communicate the same basic ethos: "Consume, consume, consume. You are a consumer. Hedonism is good! Indulge yourselves! Don't think, act." The erosion of our psyches, the gradual reshaping of our judgment is like the erosion of mountains at the hands of the elements, a gradual, glacial change that seduces us into believing in the unshakable stability of the world.

The *true* American dream is a dream of personal dignity and freedom. It's a dream of financial opportunity and of reaching your potential. It is a *human* dream, which is why America has been a beacon of hope to countless people across the globe.

But it is also a dream that is being morphed into a plastic, unreflective vision of the world by the powers that shape our thinking in the interests of profit. It is a perspective that sees alternative cultures as alien and dangerous; that sees familial relationships as exploitative rather than respectful; that desensitizes, dehumanizes, and propagates war and violence. It is a vision clouded by fear, preemptive strikes ("get 'em before they get you"), and blind trust in government to save us from our mortal enemy who hates us because we're "free."

This is a vision sustained by a false sense of freedom— of being politically free and of being autonomous consumers of ideas, services, and products. It is a vision sustained by a false sense that *we*—not the corporate monoliths—are the movers and shakers of production. It is a myth subtly propagated and programmed into us by a politico-corporate establishment, not for what conduces to the good of America or to the happiness of its individual citizens but all for the narrowest of self-aggrandizing purposes: money and power.

This is the empty, callous shell that's left of the noble American dream. But how exactly has the politico-corporate establishment managed to pull this off? How exactly has it managed to steal our freedom, leaving only a counterfeit façade? What mechanisms has it used to morph our concepts of culture (our own as well as foreign ones), family, and war? Here, knowing your *real* enemy is a useful principle in defeating it.

NOTES

1. "Leveraging Xenophobia and Other Bush Administration Policies," http://www.dailykos.com/storyonly/2006/4/10/141932/724 (accessed February 15, 2007).

2. Walter Lippmann, *Public Opinion* (New York: Free Press Paperbacks, 1997), p. 16.

3. Ibid., p. 28.

4. Michael Dawson, *The Consumer Trap: Big Business Marketing in American Life* (Chicago: University of Illinois Press, 2003), p. 1.

5. Ibid., p. 2.

6. W. W. Rostow, *The Stages of Economic Growth: A Non-Communist Manifesto*, 3rd ed. (Cambridge: Cambridge University Press, 1990), pp. 10–11.

7. Dawson, *The Consumer Trap*, chap. 1.

8. Richard Ott, *Creating Demand: Powerful Tips and Tactics for Marketing Your Product or Service* (Burr Ridge, IL: Irwin, 1992), p. viii.

9. Dawson, *The Consumer Trap*, pp. 94–95.

10. Ibid.

11. Elliot Cohen, ed., *News Incorporated: Corporate Media Ownership and Its Threat to Democracy* (Amherst, NY: Prometheus Books, 2005), pp. 225–26.

12. D. P. Phillips, "Natural Experiments on the Effects of Mass Media Violence on Fatal Aggression: Strengths and Weaknesses of a New Approach," in *Advances in Experimental Social Psychology*, ed. L. Berkowitz, vol. 19 (New York: Academic Press, 1986), pp. 207–50.

13. Anthony Pratkanis and Elliot Aronson, *Age of Propaganda: The Everyday Use and Abuse of Persuasion* (New York: Owl Books, 2001), pp. 147–48.

14. Quoted in Dawson, *The Consumer Trap*, p. 99.

Chapter 5

WASTING AWAY
IN MEDIAVILLE

The real damage done by the commercialization of entertainment is that it represents a squandered opportunity to reflect meaningfully on our own experience and to understand the successes and setbacks of our fellow men and women in the proper context. The American dream is about valuing the individual if it is about anything, and valuing others requires empathy and understanding. Unfortunately, the corporate media have systematically undermined human dignity in a relentless attempt to amass profit. This profit is paid for by sucking the life blood—respect for human dignity—out of democracy.

MANUFACTURING PREJUDICE

For years, social psychologists have known that the way to combat prejudice, the way to increase respect for people who are different from us is to promote responsible interaction. Caricatures and oversimplifications, depictions of women as sex objects, of Muslims as religious zealots bent on jihad, or of homosexual men as effeminate fashion mongers serve to reinforce rather than reduce prejudice. Consequently, entertainment that promotes such stereotypes contributes to a climate of declining empathy and dehumanization that tarnishes our own dignity as well as that of others. Such a climate makes it easier to float ideas to the American public that run counter to respect for the individual, ideas about who is worthy to marry, who is worthy to succeed, and, ultimately, who is worthy of life, liberty, and the pursuit of happiness.

Perhaps this point is no more salient than in the depiction of the Islamic world in popular entertainment. The portrayal on shows like Fox's *24* of Muslims as sinister, violence-prone anti-Christian zealots has become a source of concern for Islamic communities in the United States. The protagonist in *24*, played by Kiefer Sutherland, is a tough, no-nonsense counterterrorist agent bent on destroying sleeper cells in Los Angeles, and his adversaries are consistently depicted as dark-skinned, one-dimensional thugs whose irrational hatred of the West drives them to unspeakable crimes. This show is far from atypical. Hollywood films like *Diehard 3* and *True Lies* depict terrorists as Islamic fundamentalists of a particularly virulent type, an image that reinforces the idea that the Islamic world represents an irrational but serious threat to the ideals and livelihoods of the West. Such images are reinforced by news coverage that is either biased toward the West or too shallow to expose the fallacy in generalizing from a few extremists to over one billion Muslims worldwide. As Dr. Parvez Ahmed, a member of the board of directors for the Council on American-Islamic Relations, notes: "A search of past newspaper articles shows that terrorism, militancy or extremism by a Muslim is frequently linked to his faith. The association is 1000 to 1 times more likely for Muslims than any other faith group. This lopsided association is troubling given the fact that all religions, not just Islam, have in the recent past fallen prey to misinterpretation by a radical fringe. Certainly the ills of a misguided minority do not justify the victimization of the peaceful majority. The consequences of such imprudent associations are often overlooked."[1]

The consequences of such distortions can be measured in a very human cost. By seeing Muslims portrayed as irrational and dehumanized, viewers are desensitized to the killing of terrorists and Muslims alike. When one also considers the propensity of violence in television programming and video games to desensitize viewers to the horrific nature of violence, one has a recipe for propaganda that effectively contributes to the acceptance of war and its associated human costs. War has become a technological affair for the American viewer not only because news coverage focuses an inordinate amount of time on the virtues of smart munitions and stealth drones, but also because we are fighting an enemy that is perceived as less than human. War is a sterile, clinical affair, one that need not trouble the conscience except when our own boys lose their precious lives to "barbarian hordes" of the Middle East.

When we dehumanize others and treat them as inferior, we tarnish our own dignity. When we justify torture by saying someone deserves it, we become deserters of the American dream and enemies of our Constitution. The media's promotion of stereotypes and prejudice—either intentionally, to meet a political objective, or unintentionally, as a consequence of other marketing strategies—shapes our sense of the world and erodes our moral perspective.

EXPLOITING FAMILY RELATIONS

The impact of marketing is not restricted to our views of foreigners and official enemies; the interest of the corporate establishment in shaping the minds of the American people is eroding our respect for individuality and human dignity here at home. The source of our declining respect for the individual lies in the pervasiveness of corporate marketing and high-powered, exploitative techniques used to sell products. In particular, we are talking about the phenomena of viral and peer-to-peer marketing and overt marketing techniques that exploit human vulnerabilities and intrude upon the interpersonal relationships that serve as the backbone of a functional society.

Consider the marketing strategy developed by Lucy Hughes at Initiative Media Worldwide, one of the world's largest communications management companies, called the "Nag Factor." The Nag Factor exploits young children's capacity for incessant nagging, matching nagging strategies to parenting techniques in the interest of selling products. In an interview with Joel Bakan for the film *The Corporation*, Hughes states:

> We found . . . that the way a child nags isn't always the same. That there's one of two ways. That they nag either

with persistence or they nag with importance. When we talk about nagging with persistence, it's really whiny: "Mommy, I really, really want the Barbie Dream House, wah, wah, wah, wah." . . . Nagging with importance is that the child has associated some sort of importance to this product: "Mommy, I need the Barbie Dream House so Barbie and Ken can live together and have children and have their own family." . . . The way the child nags to the parent will have an impact on whether or not the parent will buy that product.[2]

Working closely with child psychologists, the strategists at Initiative Media discovered that different types of whining will be more effective on different kinds of parents. Those parents who are minimalists, who tend to resist the simple repetitious nagging of a child are more likely to succumb to the importance nagging that is built around a rationale for the product, whereas single mothers suffering from a sense of guilt about not spending time with their children are more inclined to respond to persistent nagging. Whatever the particular family dynamic, the marketing industry is intent on exploiting aspects of the parent-child relationship in the interest of selling products and it does so through manipulation. The basic principle marketers must adopt in justifying such strategies is that, when it comes to selling products, it is *okay* to ignore the social good and exploit the family. In other words, it is okay to treat people as a means to a corporate end and ignore the dignity of the individual.

A potential consequence of interjecting the corporation into the family is that it threatens to undermine healthy, respectful relationships between children and their parents. By encouraging a child to nag until she gets what she wants, advertisers are reinforcing an inherently antisocial form of behavior: rather than learning to respect the authority of her parents, the child is being encouraged to act on impulse and defy the will of the parent. To the extent that nagging is an effective way of getting what one wants, it becomes part of a child's behavioral repertoire and will likely carry over into her relationships as an adult. The Nag Factor is a marketing strategy that discourages self-control and the balancing of personal needs against the needs and interests of others and, hence, it feeds the image of one's self as a consumer. *And a consumer is not the same thing as a citizen*; if a person is bent on getting his own way, he's less likely to consider the needs and interests of others. Respect for others depends on setting limits to one's own interests, and this is precisely the thing that marketers want to avoid.

Unfortunately the Nag Factor is not the only, or the most *sinister*, method for mining social relationships in the interest of profit. Peer-to-peer marketing has emerged in recent years as a method for encouraging a "buzz" about a product by exploiting the social relationships of children and young adults. Now, there is nothing wrong with word of mouth, but traditionally word of mouth about a product was a function of its quality. In modern peer-to-peer marketing, what sounds like good advice from a person on the street is actually a sales pitch in disguise. Whether it is an unassuming young man playing with the latest video game technology over coffee at Starbucks, or the charming young couple on the street corner who, claiming to be tourists, ask you to take their picture with their new cell phone, marketers have figured out that exploiting natural human interactions pays big bucks. The unsuspecting person who is introduced to the latest video game technology by conversing with the young man at Starbucks believes that his interaction with a fellow citizen is authentic, when in fact it's a ruse. Malcolm Gladwell, author of *The Tipping Point*, characterizes this kind of marketing in the following way: "Well, there's an element, obviously, of deception involved that I don't think is the case in conventional advertising. Conventional advertising is about trying to charm us or trying to persuade us. But it's not usually about trying to trick us. And it's the trickery part, I think, that makes it different."[3]

What makes this form of marketing particularly dangerous is that marketing companies are recruiting young adults and children to employ these tactics with their friends, thereby introducing a profitability factor into the child's interpersonal relationship. Consider, for example, the buzz around the "tween" demographic among marketers. Tweens are young girls between the ages of eight and thirteen and they represent the most promising source of revenue since the baby boomers came of age. Marketers like Laura Groppe of Girls' Intelligence Agency (GIA) are mining this age group by exploiting the social behaviors that occur naturally among preteen girls, for example, slumber parties. Groppe recruits trendsetters, or "alpha girls," who are given merchandise to distribute at slumber parties in the interest of providing feedback about products and disseminating the good word about a product that is set to hit the market. As Groppe notes, "Each girl can personally evangelize to anywhere from 10 to 20 girls. . . . So that a slumber party can reach hundreds and hundreds of girls . . . through one [alpha] girl."[4] The tween market is worth $335 billion according to Groppe. "That's a powerful consumer, so that includes not only her spending, but the influence on the family spending."5

But if corporate America is excited about exploiting this virgin territory, America's parents should be less sanguine. Between the ages of eight and thirteen, girls are struggling with issues of body image and personal identity, and the desire for social approval makes them especially susceptible to predatory marketing practices that implicitly promise popularity. True, alpha girls are chosen because they have that *je ne sais qua*, that popularity factor that suggests their value to a marketing agency, but that popularity is not based on their willingness to distribute products to their peers. Once an alpha girl is operating as an agent of a marketing firm, she is encouraged to view her popularity in terms of profitability—at least implicitly, and the nature of her inter-personal relationships is glossed with the interest in main-taining her social position through the exploitation of others. Simply put, tween girls are being encouraged to view their peers as a means to continued popularity, not as individuals worthy of respect; they are being encouraged to adopt an ethos of deceit, to manipulate others, and to value material goods over the ethical principles at the heart of authentic relationships. Corporate America's logic of exploitation, its predation for profit is being injected into the psychology of those most vulnerable to the message.

In addition to potentially damaging an emerging sense of personal responsibility and the ethics of friendship, marketing to teens and preteens threatens an emerging sense of individ-uality and need for independence. In the interest of building an association between a brand and a lifestyle, marketers in recent years have actively investigated teen counterculture and used this information to market products. The classic example of this type of marketing is Coca-Cola's campaign to identify one of its products, Sprite, with the hip-hop movement during the 1990s. Hip-hop began as a countercultural movement, a critical and often caustic evaluation of the American establishment and an outlet for minority youth to express their anger and anxiety through music. Through the use of aggressive marketing and event sponsorships, Sprite became an icon of the movement, a fact that is as tragic as it is ironic, given that Coca-Cola is so much a part of the economic and political establishment hip-hop is reacting against. Once a counterculture is absorbed by the broader cultural forces it opposes, it can no longer serve as an outlet for the disenfranchised; the images and ideas of a counterculture have then been highjacked, and the creative impulses of its members aspire to even more radical or revolutionary expression.[6]

Even public broadcasting, a traditional bulwark of quality programming, has fallen victim in recent years to the hostile takeover of the American dream. Established in 1967 as a means for providing the public with high-quality, commercial-free programming, the Corporation for Public Broadcasting (CPB) has had its budget slashed by Congress over the years and has had to resort to corporate sponsorship as a way of subsidizing its operating budget. Among executives at PBS, the Public Broadcasting Service is referred to as "the new PBS," and potential corporate investors are wooed by selling PBS as a "brand" rather than as providing a public service.[7] This new attitude, largely a response to the 1995 congressional budget cuts, has led to a new partnership with America, but it is one that has the feel of a sellout to corporate interests. Families look to PBS to provide stimulating and socially responsible programming free of corporate interference, and this is precisely what is being lost through the corporate takeover of public television.

DUMBING DOWN AMERICA

Despite the diversity of approaches to selling products, there is a common theme (or at least a family resemblance) that unites them. Pitching products within the entertainment venue, constructing story lines and characters that promote consumption of our favorite TV shows, and exploiting interpersonal relationships for profit all encourage an impulsive, unreflective state of mind that seeks immediate gratification over enduring satisfaction. People are not being encouraged to *think* but to pursue their desires; it is *emotion* rather than *judgment* that will inspire us to purchase beyond our means and to indulge in the unhealthy conveniences of a fast-food economy. As David Walsh, a psychologist and president of the National Center on Media and the Family, states: "Emotion focuses attention, determines what we remember, shapes attitudes, motivates, and moves us to act. It should not come as a surprise, therefore, that the emotional centers of the brain become the primary target for marketers and advertisers. This list of the roles that emotions play could easily be mistaken for an advertiser's wish list. What advertiser would not want to capture a customer's attention, implant the message in his memory, shape his attitudes, motivate him and change his behavior?"[8]

Susan Linn reinforces this idea, noting the desirability of an unthinking public for the purpose of selling products:

"Advertising works best if it can evoke from its target audience a strong and positive emotional response. Advertisers have the best chance of evoking an emotional response strong enough to influence viewers when people don't know they're being influenced, or if they have a limited capacity for critical judgment."9

And here is where the marketing divisions of America's largest corporations overlap with their newsrooms. If your aim in life is to sell products—and selling products depends on dumbing down the population's capacity to think—and if, in addition, you *own* the news, then the newsroom inevitably becomes an extension of the marketing division. It is here that the conflict of interest inherent in corporate ownership of a public resource comes into plain view: in a functioning democracy, the media are there to promote the public good, where the public good is determined by the *public* rather than a corporate or governmental institution. As we have stressed throughout this book, when the news is part of an institution that is designed to maximize profit, it becomes the handmaiden of that overriding interest. Basic free-market assumptions suggest that the message about the world we would receive through the corporate media would be one that undermines serious, analytical thinking in favor of controlled emotional responses. We would anticipate a picture of the world that oversimplifies issues, puts a positive spin on events that might incite a re-evaluation of the consumptive lifestyle, or creates a sense of helplessness and confusion (a sense assuaged by yet more consumption).

In fact, this is precisely what we get from the news. The emphasis on sound bites rather than serious analysis in contemporary news coverage creates a vision of the world as somehow disconnected, a world in which things just happen, which results in the perception that human beings are somehow ineffectual at changing that world. As political scientist Michael Parenti rightly notes:

> Many things are reported in the news but few are explained. Little is said about how the social order is organized and for what purposes. Instead we are left to see the world as do mainstream pundits, as a scatter of events and personalities propelled by happenstance, circumstance, confused intentions, bungled operations, and individual ambitions—rarely by powerful class interests. Passive voice and impersonal subjects are essential rhetorical constructs for this mode of evasion. So we read or hear that "fighting broke out in the region," or "many people were killed in the disturbances," or "famine is on the increase." Recessions apparently just happen like some natural phenomenon ("our economy is in a slump"), having little to do with the constant war of capital against labor and the contradictions between productive power and earning power.[10]

By constructing an image of the world that is fragmented and chaotic, a series of disconnected happenings, corporate media eliminate the incentive to think critically, globally, and analytically about the policies and events that impact our lives. After all, if the message is that there is no connection between events, then it is irrational to seek a connection. The corporate news creates just this image, and as this image is offered up by public personae that appear credible and authoritative, the implicit suggestion is that one need not look further. In short, the idea that there are no deep problems and no deep issues encourages the misperception that deep thinking is incompatible with the world. Like the characters in Orwell's *1984*, the American people are losing the vocabulary necessary to articulate the growing threat of tyranny in this country and the decay of the American dream. "Don't think. Just get back to your bag of Doritos. Hey, did you hear about Anna Nicole Smith?"

The decline in critical thinking as a result of the intrusiveness of marketing in our lives thus serves a political function: it allows those in power to reshape our way of looking at the world without the fear that we will catch on. The Bush administration can talk about the value of domestic spying without fear that we will raise questions about the constitutionality of such a thing or that we will point out that the mechanisms were already in place to get the information with judicial oversight. The Bush administration can argue that Saddam Hussein was forging alliances with Osama bin Laden without the worry that we will have the wherewithal to grasp the practical impossibility of this connection. In other words, the Bush administration and its allies can mold our thinking to a point where fascism seems natural and where respect for the individual looks like a threat to our way of life. By dumbing down our thinking, corporate America is paving the way to the end of the American experiment in democracy.

MARKETING WAR

One of the most dangerous influences of the media on our decisions, and one of the most tragic, is their tendency to desensitize the public to the horrific nature of war and violence. In the hands of the MSM, war has become a "political necessity" devoid of the human tragedies that in more sensible times make war a last, desperate resort. Details of America's wars are primarily provided by the Pentagon rather than reporters on the ground. Vague, tactical information wrapped in patriotic rhetoric is systematically disseminated by an assortment of generals, and on the rare occasion that a serious question is posed by a journalist, the answers are almost always qualified by the assertion that details cannot be revealed because of national security issues.

The poor quality of the information provided by official sources is illustrated by the interest in the Jessica Lynch story in the early stages of the invasion of Iraq. During one Pentagon briefing, the dramatic details of Private Lynch's rescue dominated the discussion, despite the fact that US troops were still in combat operations and over the objections of some foreign journalists. As it turned out, the rescue of Jessica Lynch was largely staged, but it provided a dramatic element to the war effort that distracted the American public from the real issues and events.[11]

This thinning out of news coverage has a profound effect on the way we see and debate America's latest war. Just prior to the war, nearly 60 percent of Americans believed that Saddam Hussein was behind the 9/11 terrorist attacks, either directly or by providing material support to al Qaeda, despite a compelling body of evidence to the contrary.[12] Why? News coverage of the president's speeches prior to the invasion of Iraq highlighted this connection by televising segments that suggested the connection either implicitly or explicitly. And no one was asking the tough questions. No one was asking whether a secular state run by a dictator would be a likely partner of an ideologically driven group of religious fanatics. No one was emphasizing the fact that sixteen of the nineteen highjackers were Saudis, that none were Iraqis, or that Iraq had no meaningful weapons or technology to sell in the first place. The issues surrounding the buildup to the Iraq war were treated in seductive sound bites, catchphrases, and cheap rhetoric, just enough to give viewers the impression of being informed while providing no context, analysis, or depth necessary for real understanding. The result was a public that offered minimal objections to the Bush administration's push to invade a sovereign nation that represented no real threat to America or its allies. The result was a public that never knew that US General Tommy Franks was being sued for war crimes in Belgium before such efforts were manipulated away by US officials, or that the United States was using cluster bombs in civilian areas in clear violation of the Geneva Conventions.[13]

The coverage of the war by embedded reporters also narrowed the scope of discussion about the war and hence affected people's decision to support the war. As mentioned in chapter 3, while the idea of embedding reporters with the troops sounds like a way of guaranteeing up-to-the-minute coverage, in actual fact it is a way of controlling the content of the news. Not only were the journalists who accompanied the troops carefully screened by the military, but the perspective of the war offered by these reporters was inevitably conditioned by the restrictions imposed on coverage by the commanding officers of the embedding units. In effect, the coverage of the war was restricted by a de facto military censor, and such censorship is incompatible with the ethics of journalism, the principles of democracy, and the interests of the American people. The result was an extremely one-sided and sterilized account of the war from the US point of view.

In addition to the mechanisms used to distort the coverage of the war, viewers at home were subjected to countless stories about the accuracy of the weaponry in the US arsenal and were bombarded with images of smart bombs hitting their targets while missing a mosque, a hospital, or school. The coverage of such weapons gives the impression that the utmost care was being taken to avoid collateral damage (i.e., the killing of innocent people), thus suggesting, at least implicitly, that there was no need to worry about coverage of civilian casualties. After all, if our weapons are that good, there shouldn't be any such casualties; only the Bad Guys are getting killed, buildings are being destroyed, and that is a Good Thing.

Discussions of the US military strategy to subdue any opposition through a massive bombing campaign (euphemistically called "Shock and Awe" instead of the more accurate denomination "Let's Slaughter Tens of Thousands of People Using Our Own Weapons of Mass Destruction"), were also devoid of the human side of the war. Various spokespeople offered up asinine reflections suggesting that the enemy would drop their weapons where they stood, completely overwhelmed by American firepower. There was no mention of the fact that policymakers were hoping that by bombing Iraqis into the Stone Age, they could impose a free-market system on the country without anybody caring or perhaps even noticing.[14] Instead of getting the facts, we were given a picture of a war being fought for principled reasons, for the good of all humankind, a war that was as clean and humane as war could ever be, a war that would allow its advocates to sleep well at night.

To support a war is to exercise a choice. To support a president who would take us to war without the scrutiny of Congress is to exercise a choice. To sign up for a war that one believes is just, or to accept the deaths of thousands upon thousands of people, American and Iraqi, is to exercise choice. These choices are *conditioned* by the quality of the coverage of the events leading up to a war, of its initial execution, and of the aftermath. These choices are *constrained* by the impression that the majority of Americans supported unilateral military action against Iraq, even though this was not true.[15] Our choices are *influenced* by the constant exposure to violence on television and in the movies, by the tendency to cast violence as an inevitable consequence of competition, and by the associated view that competition is an inevitable part of life. We have war in our entertainment and entertainment in our war coverage, and by conditioning consumers of mass media to view the world through a lens of corporate profiteering, we are less inclined to step back and question the sanity of what we do. We are less inclined to remember that war is always terrible, and that the weight of an Iraqi corpse on our conscience should equal that of an American one. We are less inclined to remember that Iraqis, like Americans, love their children, and that the death of a child is a calamity so horrible that it must be avoided at all costs. Our view of the world and of ourselves determines the range of choices we envision, and the corporate media are bent on constraining and restricting that view in the interest of maximizing profit.

The influence of the corporate media on the quality of

news coverage, entertainment, and advertising gives Americans a picture of the world that is fragmented, illogical, and, hence, deeply irrational. In this fabricated universe of artificially created consumer needs and values, the surreal has merged with the real and the superficial and insignificant has switched seats with the profound and important. Stuck inside this matrix of deception, America is in grave danger of becoming hopelessly credulous. Like the prisoners in Plato's underground cavern who know only the shadows cast on the wall before them, the American public is a gullible audience for those who pull the corporate strings.

We are not claiming that corporations intentionally try to dumb down America for their own sake, however. In actual fact, there are competing interests *among* America's corporations, and hence there are competing forces that push and pull the public in different directions. Yet the common interest in making a profit brings with it the intense institutional pressure to manipulate the interests and behaviors of the public—to create a consumer state of mind where it did not previously exist. It is this common interest that moves corporate America in the same general direction, not a conspiracy of corporate executives to deceive the public for deception's sake.

In chapter 9, we will see how corporate America's marketing strategies work to the political advantage of those who *are* conspiring to use the power of corporations to subvert our democracy. Our interest in this chapter has been to expose some of the mechanisms that are working against the need to inform and educate the public in a way that is necessary for the preservation of democracy. It is these forces that have contributed to the steady pace at which this nation has morphed closer and closer to a fascist state in just six years: the declaring of "preemptive" war by the president (not Congress) on fraudulent grounds without informed consent of Congress and the American people; the abridgment of the Fourth Amendment protection against warrantless search and seizure of personal records and communications (e-mail messages, phone calls, and financial transactions); the attempt to usurp judicial checks on legislative and executive authority by intimidating "activist judges"; the unlawful suspension of the right of habeas corpus for anyone the president deems an "enemy combatant"; the torture and humiliation of prisoners of war; the threat to prosecute journalists for treason; the surveillance of antiwar groups; the attack on freedom in cyberspace; and (as you will see) the assault on the right to vote.

But how can this be happening to a nation that has, until now, managed to survive assaults on its democratic principles? After all, our democracy has managed to withstand Watergate and the attempt by the Nixon administration to place the president above the law. What's different now? As will become clear in the chapters ahead, the plan is much more organized, systematic, and evolved and is backed by several decades of planning and marketing experience.

NOTES

1. Parvez Ahmed, "Attitudes of Ignorance—A Consequence of Media Portrayal of Islam and Muslims," http://www.common dreams.org/views04/0810-02.htm (accessed February 16, 2007).

2. Quoted in Joel Bakan, *The Corporation: The Pathological Pursuit of Profit and Power* (New York: Free Press, 2004), pp. 119–20.

3. "Undercover Marketing Uncovered," CBSNews.com, July 25, 2004.

4. "Tweens: A Billon-Dollar Market," CBS News, December 15, 2004.

5. Ibid.

6. *Frontline*, "Merchants of Cool," http://www.pbs.org/wgbh/pages/frontline/shows/cool/ (accessed February 16, 2007).

7. Susan Linn, *Consuming Kids: The Hostile Takeover of Childhood* (New York: New Press, 2004), p. 45.

8. David Walsh, "Slipping under the Radar: Advertising and the Mind," presented at the World Health Organization Conference, "Health: Marketing and Youth," Fabrica, Treviso, Italy, April 18, 2002, http://www.who.int/healthmktg/walshpaper.pdf (accessed February 16, 2007).

9. Linn, *Consuming Kids*, p. 51.

10. Quoted in Elliot D. Cohen, ed., *News Incorporated: Corporate Media Ownership and Its Threat to Democracy* (Amherst, NY: Prometheus Books, 2005), p. 107.

11. The staging of Jessica Lynch's rescue is recounted in the BBC documentary titled *War Spin*, aired on Sunday, May 18, 2003. A transcript of the documentary is available online at http://news.bbc.co.uk/nol/shared/spl/hi/programmes/correspondent/transcripts/18.5.031.txt (accessed February 16, 2007).

12. See the Program on International Policy Attitudes (PIPA) survey, "Misperceptions, the Media, and the Iraq War," October 2, 2003, http://65.109.167.118/pipa/pdf/oct03/IraqMedia_Oct03_rpt.pdf (accessed February 16, 2007).

13. "Belgium: Government Seeks to Block War Crimes Case against US General Tommy Franks," Richard Tyler, World Socialist Web site, May 20, 2003, http://www.wsws.org/articles/2003/may2003/belg-m20.shtml (accessed February 17, 2007);

Amnesty International press release, "Iraq: Use of Cluster Bombs —Civilians Pay the Price," April 2, 2003, http://web.amnesty.org/ library/index/engmde140652003 (accessed February 12, 2007).

14. Naomi Klein, "Baghdad Year Zero: Pillaging Iraq in Pursuit of a Neocon Utopia," *Harpers*, September 2004.

15. Gallup International Iraq Poll, 2003; response to the question "Are you in favor of military action in Iraq?" http://www .gallup-international.com/download/GIA%20press%20release %20Iraq%20Survey%202003.pdf (accessed February 4, 2007).

Chapter 6

BLAMING
THE LIBERALS

In 1973, Jules Archer published *The Plot to Seize the White House* in which he purported to expose a conspiracy by members of the business community to reshape American government into a military state advantageous to the interests of big business.[1] The inspiration for this coup was Franklin Delano Roosevelt's New Deal, a policy shift designed to control and offset corporate power in response to the harsh economic conditions during the Great Depression and the inherently inequitable system of favor trading and corporate exploitation. While many in the business community agreed with Roosevelt that the New Deal was necessary, others viewed FDR's policies as a threat to capitalism itself and took action to thwart this populist move. Archer claimed that a cabal of businessmen tried to recruit a former marine general named Smedley Darlington Butler to be the public face of a military coup that would overthrow Roosevelt and place Butler at the helm of a fascist state.[2] The coup failed as a result of Butler's commitment to preserving the political order, but the incident—whether real or fictitious—speaks volumes about the conflict that exists between the public and private interests.

Archer's tale of the plot to overthrow FDR's presidency is captivating because of our sense of the power differential between big business and the average citizen, as well as the widely held idea that money is the real force behind politics. The plausibility of the tale is also increased by more recent events in American history like the assassination of John F. Kennedy and his brother Robert in the 1960s, events that suggest the possibility of hidden powers behind the public face of American government. The conflict between the interests of the little guy and the business mogul, between labor and capital, is a constant theme in political history and on more than one occasion this conflict has inspired the overthrow of governments (sometimes with American complicity). The story of FDR's New Deal and the thwarted coup attempt appeals to our love of underdogs and advocates for what is right and just; it capitalizes on our suspicions about monopolies and robber barons and gives us a picture of hope fulfilled.

However one evaluates Archer's account, the tale of Smedley Darlington Butler raises important questions for us: What is it about America that prevents such an event from happening? What is it that keeps a lid on the inherent tension between the public welfare and private interests that has inspired revolution? Let us not forget that America was borne of the revolutionary spirit; the Founding Fathers predicated American independence on idea that the economic and political policies of the English were unjust. What is it about the America of recent history that dampens the revolutionary ethos?

THE QUIET PLOT TO STEAL AMERICA

Part of the answer lies in the pervasiveness of the mass media and its power to shape the attitudes and interests of the public. The conflict between privilege and peasantry has not abated in recent years; America is not free of the forces that inspire political treachery. Far from it. The difference is that the propaganda machinery is now available to those with controlling interests in American society. Coups are passé. People object to taking things by force, as the tenacious insurgency in Iraq demonstrates. Moreover, overthrowing the government by force strips the usurping regime of its moral credibility. The beauty of utilizing the media to promote market-friendly totalitarianism is that one avoids the messiness of imposing one's will with a stick. Get the people to *choose* their servitude, to *give away* their rights, and you secure your objectives with much less effort and much greater control over the results. From a business perspective, dismantling the welfare state through stealth and deceit is the clear winner in a cost-benefit analysis.

During the decades following FDR's New Deal, business advocates were thinking along these lines and making their views public. In 1971, the wealthy corporate lawyer and soon-to-be Supreme Court justice Lewis Powell circulated a memorandum that echoed the very sentiments that motivated Archer's coup but without the call for a military overthrow of the US government. Powell argued that the system of free enterprise in America was being undermined by four institutions, namely, the courts, the political establishment, colleges and universities, and the media. In response, Powell asserted, the business community should put its resources and expertise to work in an effort to dominate these institutions. As David Brock, founder of Media Matters for America, points out,

> Powell . . . laid out the strategy that the Right would follow in the coming decades, whereby conservative business interests would create and underwrite a "movement" to front its agenda in the media. Under Powell's plan, heavily subsidized "scholars, writers, and thinkers" speaking "for the movement" would press for "balance" and "equal time" to penetrate the media, thereby shaping news coverage, reframing issues, influencing the views of political elites, and changing mass public opinion. These would be the manufactured "intellectuals" . . . marketed in the media to "expand the spectrum." They would be housed in new "national organizations" in an effort "undertaken long term" with "generous financial support."[3]

Powell's concerns were both echoed and ramified by other, more politically minded supporters of corporate power in America. For example, William E. Simon, the corporate oligarch and far-right activist, published *A Time for Truth* in 1978, a book that identified modern environmentalism, consumer advocacy, and the workers' rights movement as direct threats to business interests. Clearly, if business interests are taken to mean the unrestricted pursuit of profit, then Simon and Powell are correct. Protecting the environment from the predatory practices of the corporation is to say, in effect, "These resources are off limits to corporate raiders. These resources are not to be exploited." The workers' rights movement, from the corporate standpoint, represents an attack on the bottom line, as greater compensation to workers means less compensation for shareholders. And consumer advocacy—the idea that citizens have certain protections against corporations interested in picking their pockets—runs directly counter to the central principles of modern marketing (see chapter 8). The response to these threats was massive, systematic, and enduring, as business elites like Joseph Coors, Richard Mellon Scaife, and a handful of others became financiers of Powell's social engineering project.

Powell's proposal resonated not only with business leaders but with social conservatives who viewed the cultural revolution of the 1960s as a direct attack on traditional American values. Rather than recognizing the distinct characters of the different social movements of the period—the environmental and feminist movements, for example—and addressing each on its own terms, social conservatives moved in unison against progressive values and policies. In the spirit of the old adage "The enemy of my enemy is my friend," social conservatives realized that the conflict between corporate interests and advocacy for the little guy could be exploited to hoist a conservative political agenda on the American people. Similarly, leaders in the corporate world realized that the language of consumerism and corporate profiteering would not be persuasive and that the corporate agenda would have to be anointed and legitimized by the Holy Warriors of Right. The result was the convergence of business interests and right-wing politics in a politico-corporate movement to reshape the social landscape of the country, a movement that by its very nature was *anti-environment, anticonsumer-rights*, and *antilabor*.[4]

The mechanisms by which this new movement would come to power and change America's view of itself are complex, but the financing of conservative think tanks would prove an essential part of the tour de force of the Right. The Heritage Foundation, the Institute for Contemporary Studies, the Rocky Mountain Legal Foundation, the Hudson Institute, the Lynde and Harry Bradley Foundation, and a host of other organizations committed to reshaping academia and the judiciary and to dismantling the federal government churned out pseudo-policy papers, created their own publications, and propped up wannabe intellectuals ready to fight for the cause. With the institutional resources of corporate America behind it, this new movement has become the prime mover of American society in recent decades, as a former Heritage Foundation operator notes: "[the network of conservative think tanks serve as] . . . the shock troops of the conservative revolution."[5] And, as professor and author Robert Bothwell notes, "When it comes to 'winning' political battles, ultimate success results less from who's doing the right thing, and more from whose view of reality dominates the battlefield. . . . It doesn't take a rocket scientist to figure out that the millions spent by conservative think tanks have enabled them virtually to dictate the issues and terms of national debate."[6]

If the resources and coordination of this new movement are impressive, the tactics are even more so. Apparently truth is not important when money is at stake or, ironically, when salvation is at stake. The modus operandi of the

Right's corporate movement grew right out of cold war propaganda tactics and took aim at the institutions essential to a functional democracy as well as the people who espoused truly democratic ideals. Indeed, the cold war provided cover for the attempt to reshape the American landscape: communism's emphasis on distributing wealth based on need rather than opportunity as well as its thoroughly secular view of the world made it an easy target for capitalists and religious zealots alike. Domestically, any social program or public service (for example, Social Security and progressive taxation) that helps to level the playing field for working-class Americans and provide a fighting chance at the American dream was demonized, and the specter of communism provided the rationale for doing so. Interestingly, many of the tactics that emerged in the Right's war to win the hearts and minds of the American people grew right out of communism itself, for example, the Leninist strategies for manipulating the public mind and shaping the public debate. Along with the guerrilla tactics on the ground, the funded think tanks, and phony scholarship there emerged

> a neolexicon—a language invented by conservative practitioners trained in the use of manipulative, often Orwellian, rhetoric. Agenda items like gutting Social Security, rolling back civil rights protections, and slashing taxes inequitably would be smoothed out with deceptive Madison Avenue-type branding slogans of the kind used to sell commercial products: "privatization," "the new federalism," the "flat tax," and so on. Americans would be told that poverty is a "behavioral" condition, that any advance gained by members of a minority group amounted to "reverse discrimination," and that providing

government subsidies for private and parochial schools while draining resources from public education was to be thought of as "school choice."[7]

Truth be told, over the last forty years Americans have been subjected to a propaganda campaign that combines the marketing resources of corporate America with the rhetoric of family values. We have been conditioned to believe that the public sector is inherently bad, that corporate capitalism is inherently good, and that it is our own fault if we don't get a shot at the American dream. Conveniently, liberalism has also fallen by the wayside, a consequence of the Right's skill in connecting the word *liberal* with hot-button terms such as *communist*, *traitor*, and *unbeliever*. Liberalism has become synonymous with *un-American* and serves as the whipping boy for corporate America and the Right while they sell off the American dream to the highest bidder. The idea that corporate America would promote a hostile takeover of the US government is utterly absurd in this kind of environment, since a much more effective and sinister plan for stealing America has been playing itself out over the last forty years to great effect.

Welcome to Orwell's *1984*.

THE MYTH OF LIBERAL BIAS

In chapter 2 we said that the claim that the MSM is liberal is not so much false as it is unintelligible. And throughout this book we have given numerous examples of how the MSM has sold out journalistic integrity in proffering the right-wing agenda. But what we haven't done yet is expose the roots of this myth in the politico-corporate movement. It is one thing to recognize that the press is not doing its job and that the failure of the news media is a function of consolidation, but it is something else entirely to understand the *ideology* driving powerful people who actively seek to compromise the media for political reasons. The idea of liberal bias in the media serves to hide the misdeeds of those who will stop at nothing to reshape America to fit the conservative agenda. Understanding the myth of liberal bias is important for understanding the way this idea has served to shut down public debate and diminish public awareness.

To begin with, we should be clear about what is meant by "liberal bias." As emphasized earlier (chapter 3), when uttered by conservatives, the term "liberal" is obviously negative. As Tom DeLay noted in his parting shot at Congress on June 8, 2006, liberalism means big government, higher taxes, and less control over our own lives. What DeLay did not say is that this view of liberalism is the one constructed for public consumption by members of his own party and their corporate collaborators (which means that his characterization was pure propaganda). What he did not say is that liberalism is not about big government or squeezing the little guy, but about making sure that the public sector is protected from private interests that would happily plunder our treasury, steal our educational and financial opportunities, and pollute the air, water, and food supply with corporate sludge. Liberalism is itself a casualty of the war for the hearts and minds of Americans—a war fought by and for conservatives—and it has come to be associated with falsehoods of the most outrageous kinds: according to the propaganda, liberals are without morals, hate religion, and hate America. So the term *liberal bias* is apparently meant to describe a particular slant in the media that favors the views of those who—according to DeLay and others—do not love our country and who would support the enemies of America by protesting its wars, its use of torture, and its curtailing of civil liberties. *Liberal bias* is meant to indicate a prejudicial and dangerous misuse of the public airwaves—according to those who support DeLay's mythology—and prevents good, well-intentioned leaders like President Bush from implementing policies the American people want and deserve.

But this view of liberal bias is a pure, unadulterated fabrication, a *useful* fabrication for the Right, to be sure, but a lie by any rational measure. If liberal bias *were* a reality, one would expect certain observable consequences—one would expect, for example, that reporters would be badgering members of the Bush administration, skewing the facts in favor of "liberal" interests, and so on. You would expect a disproportionate number of "liberals" to occupy positions of leadership at news organizations, positions such as editor in chief, for example, and that liberal think tanks and organizations would be cited more frequently than their conservative counterparts. You would expect the liberal press to be lenient with "liberal" politicians and relentless with conservatives like George Bush. In short, you could *test* the idea that liberal bias exists in responsible, verifiable ways by looking at the consequences of that bias on media coverage.

Even a casual glance at news coverage in America today reveals the falsity of the claim about liberal bias in the press. As we've seen in earlier chapters, the press is far more lenient with conservatives and advocates of big business than it is with those who would champion the little guy. President Bush's less-than-honorable stint in the armed services, his questionable business practices while in the private sector, his prior problems with alcohol, his former use of cocaine, and his staggering lack of political wisdom and common sense have never been exploited by the press in a way remotely comparable to the slash-and-burn treatment of the Clinton administration. Surely, if the press was liberal, there would be plenty of ammunition it could use to undermine the Bush administration. It could exploit the fact that President Bush is guilty of crimes at least as egregious as those of the Nazis tried in Nuremberg, that his NSA surveillance program violates the Constitution, that his business and personal connections with the bin Laden family and his family's connection with the defense industry make him unfit to lead the country in a time of war (even a fabricated, disingenuous war on terrorism, a war that provides cover for those who want to turn America into a fascist, theocratic breeding ground for the corporate pillaging of the American people)—all this and more could be exploited by the "liberal" press to bring down the country's most overtly religious conservative leader in its history.[8]

As mentioned in chapter 3, right-wing conservatives (among them what John Dean calls "conservatives without consciences") have set their sights on a common inside enemy to rally support against. In fact, the right-wing attack on the liberal press has its roots in an old political strategy Kevin Baker terms the "Stab in the Back":

> Every state must have its enemies. Great powers must have especially monstrous foes. Above all, these foes must

arise from within, for national pride does not admit that a great nation can be defeated by any outside force. That is why, though its origins are elsewhere, the stab in the back has become the sustaining myth of modern American nationalism. Since the end of World War II it has been the device by which the American right wing has both revitalized itself and repeatedly avoided responsibility for its own worst blunders. Indeed, the right has distilled its tale of betrayal into a formula: Advocate some momentarily popular but reckless policy. Deny culpability when that policy is exposed as disastrous. Blame the disaster on internal enemies who hate America. Repeat, always making sure to increase the number of internal enemies.[9]

In recent history, the Nixon administration used this tactic to leverage support for the Vietnam War, blaming failed policies on hordes of internal enemies who had nothing better to do than subvert the US government for subversion's sake. According to David Brock, it was a young Pat Buchanan who promoted the idea of curtailing the media's effectiveness in exposing the failings of Nixon's Vietnam policies by charging the media with a bias toward antiwar activists.[10] It is therefore no coincidence that during the Nixon years one of the first books devoted to the "liberal bias" issue—Edith Efron's *The News Twisters*—hit the best-seller list. This highly partisan distortion of the media coverage was bought up by political mechanics of the Nixon White House for the express purpose of getting it on the best-seller list. The book itself was underwritten by the conservative Historical Research Foundation and promoted by members of Right's politico-corporate movement such as Irving Kristol and William F. Buckley Jr.

An intentional consequence of the attempt to manufacture internal enemies is that Americans today are pitted one against another on values that are highly *personal*. Rather than debating the conditions of freedom, we are receiving challenges to our faith, to our patriotism, to our attitudes toward marriage and child-rearing. Dividing the public and stirring up hostility toward others in this way serves a *political* function: it allows the power brokers to blame internal enemies for failed policies and turn the political will of the people inward, against themselves. Dividing the country on personal matters and creating the sense of an internal enemy also gets people to set aside moral scruples about how to attain political ends, since the appearance of an imminent threat at the door instills a sense of urgency and fervor. As pointed out in chapter 1, the Nazis used this tactic on the German people to neutralize their political will and forward the genocidal policies of Hitler's government.

Accusing the MSM of being liberal created a common internal enemy, a ruse designed to advance the right-wing agenda. The basic plan: First, define a common enemy—"the liberal"—who seeks to undermine America (through lack of patriotism in supporting the "war on terror," a "cut-and-run" military stance, weakness on crime, reverse discrimination, and whatever else would imperil America). Second, poison the well against the MSM by accusing it of being "liberal." The anticipated result: intimidation of the corporate media into catering to right-wing interests (explicitly or implicitly). And this plan has worked like a charm. Since it's more cost-effective to concede than to lose credibility among consumers, the MSM has rolled over and, while feigning loyalty, has sold out.

Caught up in and promoted by the propaganda machine of the Right, the claim about liberal bias became a battle cry of conservative shock troops on the ground. The strategy for compromising the coverage of important issues was to fight for what conservatives called "balanced reporting": every perspective that runs counter to the preferred point of view, that is, the *conservative* point of view, would be offset by a point of view favorable to conservative interests. Of course, there was never a shortage of "experts" to stand in for the Right, since the emerging and well-funded think tanks had been producing legions of scholars-for-hire for this very purpose. All that was needed was access, and access could be handled if the right people own the media. Hence the value of consolidation: corporate coconspirators could be counted on to push for "fair and balanced" reporting in America's newsrooms.

To most people on the receiving end of this "fair and balanced" approach to the news, the idea of offering different points of view seems pretty reasonable. This is typical of effective propaganda: corrosive and outright caustic policies and ideas are offered up to the public in language that would make any challenge to the idea seem unreasonable. Who, after all, would object to something as progressive as Bush's Clear Skies Initiative, the "environmental" policy that actually allows corporate polluters more leeway to poison the American people? "Fair and balanced" makes it seem like there will be a legitimate democratic forum for the expression of diverse perspectives and that the news media are finally doing their jobs. But this inclusive, democratic language in the hands of the right-wing conservatives has been used as a ruse for smuggling in half-baked facts, lies, prejudice, and hate mongering under a label that makes it sound morally compelling.

So, is it any wonder why the push for "balance" in the newsrooms has been a central objective of the Right's politico-corporate movement? Imagine if the Right had simply come out and said, "Hey, we believe in abolishing the division between church and state. We believe that we are living in the End Times and that it is our job here on Earth to help bring about the prophecies of Revelations." Or, imagine corporate America coming right out and saying, "Our objective is to make as much money as possible for our wealthy shareholders and unfortunately for you, the American public, that means fleecing you of your hard-earned cash. We are going to promote wars, eliminate your health care, pollute your backyards, and poison your children—but hey, on the bright side, we are also going to brainwash you into thinking this is a *good* thing." Instead of the media reporting on corporate malfeasance and the slash-and-burn guerilla tactics of the Right—remember Tom DeLay's hired shock troops who bullied election officials in Florida into stopping the recount in 2000?—they report instead on peripheral or fabricated issues by staging discussions between handpicked "experts" who make the conservative perspective sound superior. "Fair and balanced" "We report, you decide." Please!

Or consider the coverage of the war in Iraq (or, perhaps more appropriately, the lack of coverage). Yes, there were stories about possible terrorist links between al Qaeda and Saddam Hussein (the terrorist link idea came straight out of the vice president's office); there were benign stories by embedded reporters (as mentioned earlier, the reports of embeds were by contract subject to military censor); and there was even the occasional piece on the role of private contractors in Iraq. Typically, each piece was utterly non-committal, made no meaningful inroads, and, consequently, whitewashed and played down the plundering of our national treasury and the destruction of a sovereign country.

✓ What was not said was that the war in Iraq was planned well before 9/11 and that it had nothing to do with WMD or terrorism. The war in Iraq was largely about profit, not just from the proceeds of Iraq's assets that were to be given away to favored corporations but from the American taxpayer as well. By hiring private corporations, some of which had direct links to the Bush administration (such as Halliburton, which received no bid contracts from the government to manage the war effort), dollars from the US Treasury were simply handed over to corporate interests behind the military effort under the aegis of a bogus war.[11] But this is a point of view substantiated by facts—facts that would have made the Bush administration look like plunderers and thieves. One would think that the "liberal" news media would have hit the Bush administration hard on this, but there was barely a trace of real reporting on this from the MSM.

In what seemed like a real boost for the Right's political machine, there emerged some apparent validation of the claim of liberal bias in the media in the form of a 1995 survey of Washington-based political journalists (the publication preceded a similar 1997 study of the same topic and postdated the highly partisan 1986 book *The Media Elite*, which tarnished the reputation of the media as liberal). The Roper Center and Freedom Foundation Survey discovered that 89 percent of Washington journalists had voted for Bill Clinton in the 1992 presidential election, a number that far exceeded the percentage of the citizenry who voted democratic that year (44 percent). Clearly, this is evidence of liberal bias—or so the Right would have us believe.

In actual fact, the 1995 study shows *no* connection between the personal views of reporters and the quality of the news coverage, *no* connection between the voting patterns of reporters and "liberal bias." What the study does is obscure the political and corporate influences on the news by focusing on the personal character of journalists. By directing the focus on the journalist, the report distracts us from the influence of the editorial process, the bottom line, and the threat of political retribution. To say that the news is liberal on the basis of a survey of journalists' private political views is like saying that healthcare policies are liberal because a majority of healthcare workers voted for Clinton in the 1992 presidential election. In any event, it is false that "democrat" can be equated with "liberal." For example, the views of Sen. Joseph Lieberman (I-CT) are as right wing as those of many staunchly conservative Republicans.[12] In addition, as media critic Eric Alterman correctly pointed out, Clinton himself was hardly liberal in his foreign policy, a fact that won him the support of such conservative columnists as William Safire as well as other hard-core neocons.[13]

Those who would tout this survey as evidence of liberal bias do so out of ignorance or political interests. A serious inquiry into the issue of liberal bias would consider not only the methods for collecting and distributing news, but also such factors as who owns the news, how ownership affects the focus of the coverage, what conflicts of interest might arise from corporate ownership, and so on. The business executives at the top of the media food chain don't have formal training in journalism, aren't driven by the interest in uncovering recalcitrant facts, and hence often lack the appreciation for the editorial integrity of America's newsrooms. As a result, the political leanings of corporate executives have a greater likelihood of finding their way into the newsrooms than do those of individual journalists who are generally at the bottom of the corporate food chain. Lack of training and interest in journalism as well as the power to wield real influence create the mechanisms by which personal interest can become part of the media message, and this message is largely a *paid* political announcement—paid for by trading away the public interest (the good of the American people) for an increase in the corporate bottom line. You should hardly be surprised to find, as David Croteau, a researcher at Virginia Commonwealth University has, that "content analysis of the news media have, at a minimum, shown the absence of any . . . systematic liberal/left tilt; some studies have found a remarkably predictable press usually reflecting the narrow range of views of those in positions of power, as well as a spectrum of opinion that tilts toward the right."[14] There's a slant all right, but not in the direction that the politicos currently in Washington and their corporate bedfellows want us to know about.

The truth is that the claim about liberal bias in the news seems plausible only if we succumb to the politico-corporate propaganda that is fed to us on a moment-by-moment basis. That propaganda is designed to make us impulsive, to view thinking, reasoning, and rational inquiry as undesirable or impossible, in the interest of molding us into consumers. When we embrace this consumer mentality while evaluating the news, it is natural to apply the same irrational standards that underlie our buying behavior: all things are subjective;

every point of view is as good as every other, so news must be about reporters' views on the world. And unfortunately, much of what people see on television these days is subjective and impulsive, a consequence of connecting media with the profit-making drive of big business. But journalism, properly understood, is not about my point of view or yours. It's about facts, ideas supported through evidence, and about responsible, rational inquiry. Just as science is not "political" in the conventional sense of that term, journalism is not "political" unless you make it so. And making the news political—forcing a particular political point of view on the public—is precisely what corporate America and the political right have done. That's what makes real propaganda attractive to those who lack conscience: it allows them to get away with the very crimes they accuse their opponents of committing.

In short, the claim that the MSM is biased toward the liberal point of view is a propaganda ploy to dupe the American people into thinking that anything that approximates the free exchange of ideas is an imminent threat to civilization as we know it. Believe the attack dogs and intellectual hacks on the right, and you wind up thinking that black is white, up is down, and that a corporate-controlled press in the pocket of the Bush administration is actually an instrument of Fidel Castro's communist Cuba. But unlike the propaganda of past totalitarian regimes, the mechanisms of deception employed in America today have several decades of corporate marketing experience behind them. The scale, sophistication, and pervasiveness of politico-corporate propaganda emanating from the White House and its far-flung minions would make Joseph Stalin blush for its manipulative power. Want an illegal war in Iraq? We can do that.

Want to cover up a botched job in managing the war? We can do that. Want to frighten the American people into throwing their Constitution on the dung heap, supporting torture, embracing domestic spying by their government, and giving over their money to corporate raiders? No problem. We can even get the people to think George Bush is the Second Coming and that Karl Rove is a national hero (though on the Karl Rove thing we have to work with a bit of a handicap).

Not surprisingly, the same bogus balancing strategy waged against the "liberal media" is now being waged against the "liberal professors" who are alleged to be tilting higher education to the left. The call is now out for what has been called "the Foxification of higher education."[15] For example, in 2005, Rep. Dennis Baxley (R- FL) sponsored House Bill 837, a "Student and Faculty Academic Freedom in Postsecondary Education" act that was marketed to the public as a way of controlling "leftist" professors who corrupt America's youth by promulgating outrageous political ideas. In actual fact, this bill would have placed the power to determine the content of Florida's classrooms in the hands of legislators and stripped professors of their right (and responsibility) to use their knowledge in the service of the public good. Baxley's bill would have mandated a "fair and balanced" approach to teaching, requiring that different perspectives on the issues get equal playing time (for example, intelligent design theory might have to be taught alongside evolution). It would also have paved the way for students to sue their professors when they feel their beliefs are being unfairly challenged or misrepresented—a recipe for disaster, as every educator knows. In other words, the bill would give the government the right to determine what views are "appropriate" and "inappropriate" for the classroom and would use intimidation and threats of lawsuits to muzzle left-leaning professors. Put bluntly, it would shut down academic freedom in the classroom.

While Baxley's bill did not become law in Florida (at least not yet), there have been similar bills floated in other states. And it is no wonder. Ideally, universities represent bastions of critical thinking, and as such they present a threat to a fascist regime bent on blind obedience to state authority. People who think for themselves make poor subjects of a totalitarian state. So, under the guise of making higher education in America more "balanced" by ridding it of its purported liberal bias—thereby striking another blow to the "enemy"—the conservatives have added "the liberal professors" to their enemies list.

The collective cost of this propaganda effort—the myth of liberal bias in the press as well as equally damaging lies about activist judges, subversive professors in the academe, and so on—should be alarming. Democracy requires a balance of power and a free market of ideas in which democratic debate can flourish. The attack on progressive policies effectively undermines both. The success of probusiness, conservative candidates in both the presidential and congressional races in the last decade have resulted, in part, from the success of the corporate propaganda machine's sympathetic stance toward those whose ideas embrace corporate America's economic objectives (although, as we shall see in chapter 11, corporate America has been providing more than just face time to its favored candidates in recent elections). The consolidation of power in a single party is the result: not only does the Republican Party have undue influence in all three branches of government, but Republicans are attempting to undermine the two-party system that serves to moderate extremism and keep the country on the right track. And all of this is going on under the noses of the American people as a result of the distorted view of the world promoted by the politico-corporate propaganda machine.

Once upon a time liberalism was understood to promote open political debate and diversity of views out of respect for the individual. Once upon a time liberal democracy was understood as a system built on the sanctity of individual rights and the protection of the citizenry from the tyranny of despots. Liberalism is a product of the Enlightenment and the offspring of a tired Europe that suffered too long under the weight of internal strife and persecution. Liberalism was an optimistic vision, holding as it did to the idea that we, as individuals, have the capacity to make the world a better place through government by and for the people. But this dignified idea has been twisted and distorted into something utterly grotesque. The democratic process is now characterized, at the hands of the corporate media, as an attack on truth, as the promotion of amoral political institutions, and, hence, as a system that undermines what is good, right, and just. Debate itself has been demonized, and those who promote tolerance are viewed as advocates of an "anything goes" mentality. A consequence of this myth about the logic of tolerance and diversity is that it provides a further rationale for embracing dogmatism over critical—and *moral*—reflection.

One result of the maligning of liberalism is that those who would defend the public interest have been pitted against conservatives on issues that, other things being equal, they might agree on (we're talking about *real* conservatives here, not the *faux* conservativism that hides the zealotry of the Right). The principles of individual liberty are, after all, part of the fabric of our Constitution, a Constitution that people from virtually every aspect of the political spectrum accept (the Bush administration excepted—see below). What has been obscured by corporate demagoguery is that popular ideas of justice and fairness are at the center of the American vision of government—both liberal and conservative. If conservativism can be fairly associated with the attempt to satisfy the conditions that establish a free republic, conditions such as property ownership, self-sufficiency, and an education that "enable[s] every man to judge for himself what will secure or endanger his freedom," then certainly the attributes of liberalism help foster this ideal.[16] Local governance by the people would be a far cry from the vision embraced by the founding fathers if intolerance for opposing points of view became the rule rather than the exception. True democracy would be impossible if the ruling majority imposed its way of life, its mores, or its religion on the minority. The principles of liberalism—rational adjudication of disputes, fairness, and the recognition that private interest must, in a free republic, be moderated by respect for the rights of the individual—are part of the conditions that make up the political ideal of self-rule. They are not merely values in themselves, independent of the political objectives they are meant to secure but *preconditions* for nurturing values—family or otherwise—in the fertile soil of self-government.

Ultimately, then, the war on liberalism at the hands of the Right coupled with corporate America's efforts to minimize the conditions that interfere with the pursuit of profit have combined to create the illusion that standing up for working-class interests is un-American. The financiers of this project to shape the American mind have deliberately injected political ideas—most notably misinformation about liberal ideology—into the corporate conduit, using a variety of techniques and strategies. The push for a counterfeit form of "fair and balanced reporting," the funding of conservative think tanks, the promotion of pseudo-scholarship that supports the cause, and so on, have had a profound and lasting effect on the American mind-set minimizing the opposition to one-sided policies. These are the true myth makers of American society—the right wing of the Republican Party and corporate America—and we the people are the unwitting recipients of a propaganda effort of historic proportions.

This propaganda machine runs deep and has many layers. As you will see in the next chapter, fear mongering goes even further than evoking (pseudo) fear of liberals and liberalism. It also includes using terrorist tactics (in a quite literal sense) to strike fear into the hearts and minds of millions of innocent Americans.

NOTES

1. Jules Archer, *The Plot to Seize the White House* (New York: Hawthorne Books, 1973).

2. For a good synopsis of Archer's thesis, see Joel Bakan, *The Corporation: The Pathological Pursuit of Profit and Power* (New York: Free Press, 2004).

3. David Brock, *The Republican Noise Machine: Right-Wing Media and How It Corrupts Democracy* (New York: Crown, 2004), p. 40.

4. See ibid., chap. 3.

5. Quoted in ibid., p. 48.

6. Ibid., p. 49.

7. Ibid., pp. 41–42.

8. See "The Constitution in Crisis: The Downing Street Minutes and Deception, Manipulation, Torture, Retribution, and Cover-Ups in the Iraq War," prepared by Representative Conyers's staff and available on the Conyers Web site.

9. Kevin Baker, "Stabbed in the Back," *Harpers*, June 2006.

10. Brock, *The Republican Noise Machine*, p. 21.

11. Vice President Cheney was former CEO of this company and still had financial ties to it when these contracts were awarded.

12. Lieberman was a democrat until he was unseated by Ned Lamont in the Connecticut primary, at which time he became an independent so he could run against Lamont in the general election. With the help of Republicans, Lieberman won reelection. One wonders if Lieberman realized that selling his soul was part of the deal.

13. Eric Alterman, "The Myth of the Liberal Media," in *News Incorporated: Corporate Media Ownership and Its Threat to Democracy*, ed. Elliot D. Cohen (Amherst, NY: Prometheus Books, 2005), p. 111.

14. David Croteau, "Examining the 'Liberal Media' Claim," http://www.fair.org/reports/journalist-survey.html (accessed April 17, 2006).

15. Robert L. Rexroad, "The Foxification of Higher Education," TVNewsLies.org, April 16, 2005, http://www.tvnewslies .org/phpbb/viewtopic.php?t=1248&sid=db15781951c420e272 620c5dbc8b3593 (accessed July 22, 2006).

16. Quoted from http://www.pbs.org/kcet/publicschool/pdf/ pr.pdf (accessed February 12, 2007).

Chapter 7

SHOCK AND AWE

AMERICAN TERRORISM
(THE MSM COVERS UP THE BLOOD)

When the United States launched its "preemptive" strikes on Iraq, the mainstream news headlines were rife with "Shock and Awe." As innocent Iraqis—many of them children—lost their lives, their limbs, and their homes, the media sounded its deferent trumpet to the beat of government. How much more draconian a message could imaginably be put forth by a society that had formerly prided itself as a moral leader? Just picture it. Death and destruction at every corner; people petrified with fear as bombs fell from the sky; buildings around them exploded in flames; skies lit up in a blaze; bodies laid limp in the street; women and children cried, screamed, and clamored for their lives. This is what shock and awe means in human terms. It is also the gut meaning of terrorism, the kind of dreadful horror that those trapped in the World Trade Center towers during 9/11 experienced. It is also the meaning attached to the hollow feeling that the families of the victims experienced. But this was the headline Americans saw on March 23, 2003, on CNN: "Shock and awe campaign underway in Iraq" with comments by secretary of defense Donald Rumsfeld, proclaiming how "the strike had taken place 'on a scale that indicates to Iraqis' that Saddam and his leadership were finished." And Rumsfeld declared that the American objective of ridding Iraq of its "illegal" weapons of mass destruction, thereby "liberating the Iraqi people," was under way. Of course, the mission was never accomplished. There were no such weapons!

Nor were there any Iraqis to be found among the lot of hijackers directly responsible for the 9/11 attacks. So the claim of retaliation—"giving 'em a taste of their own medicine"—cannot vindicate the terror struck in the hearts of innocent Iraqis during the US invasion of their homeland.

What the corporate media *never* covered were the photographs of bodies heaped upon one another. Roland Huguenin-Benjamin, a spokesperson for the International Committee of the Red Cross in Iraq, described the onslaught in Hilla, south of Baghdad, as "a horror, dozens of severed bodies and scattered limbs." As Pepe Escobar recounts in the April 4, 2003, issue of the *Asia Times*, there were "babies cut in half, amputated limbs, kids with their faces a web of deep cuts caused by American shellfire and cluster bombs." While corporate media possessed such photos, uncensored versions were never publicized in the West. Yet when Saddam's brothers were "hunted down" and killed, newspapers obediently plastered their lifeless corpses on their front pages.

This was an American victory. The bodies of civilian Iraqis were merely "collateral damage" to be buried and hidden from sight. At the time of this writing, there have been as many as 65,000 civilian deaths attributable to US-led military intervention in Iraq.

Nor have the dead bodies of American troops been shown to us, as though we, who have already been desensitized by persistent, graphic violence in the MSM and who were expected to *delight* in "shock and awe," were also somehow too fragile to handle the death and destruction of war. This is hypocrisy on stilts, but not merely such. No, this double standard was a carefully contrived plan to manipulate us into supporting a war that was waged on false pretenses—on lies propagated with the help of the corporate media.

On April 30, 2004, when Ted Koppel, host of *Nightline*, was to read the names of US servicemen and servicewomen killed in action in Iraq, Sinclair Broadcast Group—the nation's largest independent owner of stations—ordered its ABC affiliates not to broadcast the show. Sinclair defended its action by accusing Koppel of being "motivated by a political agenda designed to undermine the efforts of the United States in Iraq."[1] But Koppel had consistently responded that his interest was not political, rather, he wished to pay tribute to those who had died in the line of duty. It is worth noting that, since 1997, Sinclair had donated more than $200,000 to Republican candidates and had inserted its own ultraconservative "news" into its programming.

Now, keep in mind, Koppel's plan was to merely read off names, not show bodies of the deceased soldiers. What was commonplace during the Vietnam War (the display of bodies on TV) had now become utterly too chilling for our "shock and awe" constitutions. During the Vietnam War, the media did not retreat from its obligation to report on the destruction of war. But then again there was also considerable coverage of antiwar protests. When, in 1974, Nixon ended the war, there had been a buildup of antiwar sentiment among the American people that made it politically risky to keep it going. Today, the media has relinquished its role as watchdog of government and consequently has changed an important variable in the way in which wars can be challenged. Now wars can be sanitized and stripped of their reality by media in cooperation with government. Today, real war is no more real in its appearance than the images that move to and fro on a video game screen. We have been deceived into forgetting the distinction between real and virtual blood. But, to be sure, Americans are really dying, every day, on foreign soil. We cannot see their faces, yet we have gotten used to the daily death tally of American troops, "insurgents," and "sectarians" reported as a matter of fact on the evening news alongside sports scores.

BUSH'S WAR ON TERROR: KEEP US AFRAID, WE'LL SUBMIT

Iraqis are not the only people who appear to have been "shocked and awed" by the US government. On October 6, 2005, at 10:00 AM, EST, president Bush addressed the Endowment for Democracy, emphasizing the war on terror and claiming that since 9/11 his administration had foiled at least ten terrorist plots. At 3:00 PM, EST, five hours later, the Associated Press reported that Bush's senior adviser Karl

Rove would testify before the grand jury that was created to investigate the outing of CIA agent Valerie Plame, and that special prosecutor Patrick Fitzgerald had told Rove that he could not guarantee that he would not be indicted. Then at 5:17 PM, EST, that same day, New York officials warned of a bomb threat to the city's subway system based on information provided by the federal government. However, it turned out that New York television station WNBC had received the story about the bomb threat several days earlier, but was asked by "high-ranking federal officials" to hold off airing the story. What is more, the New York police had known about the threat for at least three days before it was publicized and had already increased police surveillance of the New York subways. Finally, a Homeland Security spokesperson had admitted that the threat was based on intelligence of "doubtful credibility." Other sources quoted by media organizations including the *New York Post*, and NBC News said that the informant simply made up the threat.

According to Keith Olbermann there have been at least twelve other occasions in which the terrorism alerts and a change in alert status (color coding) had been preceded by a political downturn for the Bush administration.[2] While Olbermann warns that one can't simply suppose that A causes B because A is followed by B, he also cites the words of former Homeland Security director Tom Ridge, who said, "More often than not we were the least inclined to raise it. Sometimes we disagreed with the intelligence assessment. Sometimes we thought even if the intelligence was good, you don't necessarily put the country on (alert) . . . there were times when some people were really aggressive about raising it, and we said 'for that?'"

Was this "shock and awe" to keep America frightened and deferent to the Bush administration? When a government lies to its citizens in order to wage a war; when it engages in clandestine violation of civil liberties and violates the rule of law, it is no stretch to suppose that this is "shock and awe" once again, calculated to strike terror into our hearts, keeping us dependent and afraid.

The case for the "shock and awe" factor continues to mount as fear-inducing MSM headlines consistently dwarf setbacks for the Bush administration. For example, on June 23, 2006, the day after Senate Democrats spearheaded a vote to withdraw from Iraq, the FBI nabbed seven Miami "homegrown terrorists" who were allegedly plotting to blow up the Sears Tower in Chicago. These "aspirational" terrorists, who had no known means of carrying out such a terrorist attack, were infiltrated by an FBI informant who acted as ringleader, attempting to entrap the other members. In any event, the story stole the front-page headlines, and the Senate movement to end the Iraq war disappeared off the MSM radar, never to return.

On August 10, 2006, the day after Connecticut "Democrat" Joseph Lieberman lost the Democratic primary to antiwar candidate Ned Lamont, MSM coverage of this grand defeat for the Bush administration ended abruptly the next day when a UK plot by at least twenty-four British Muslims to blow up nine or ten planes bound from Heathrow for a few major US cities was foiled. Allegedly, the plot was to be carried out by smuggling liquid explosives onboard the aircrafts, although, according to the BBC, at the time of the arrest of the suspects, British Intelligence was unable to locate the explosives. The alleged terrorists had been watched by British intelligence for months, but it was only after US intelligence admonished that the group was just days away from a dry run that the Brits closed in. In fact, according to the BBC, British intelligence had urged the Bush administration to give it another week until it had gathered more evidence, but the Bush administration refused. The timing was perfect: just as MSM coverage of Ned Lamont's decisive victory over Bush's favorite son, Joseph Lieberman, came to a screeching halt.

Although at the time of this writing the MSM could provide no convincing evidence that the alleged terrorist plot was linked to al Qaeda, it consistently suggested that the plot had all the "earmarks" of al Qaeda. Here was yet another post-9/11 attempt to shock and awe the minds of Americans, and it appears to have worked. According to one survey taken after the story broke, 55 percent of Americans—up about 15 percent—believed that the Bush administration was doing a good job in protecting them against another terrorist attack. Like Pavlov's dogs conditioned to associate feeding time with the ringing of a bell, Americans succumbed to the MSM's attempt to link "Bush" to "Savior." This form of state terrorism—terrorizing citizens in order to achieve a political purpose—is not just filthy, rotten politics. It is inhumane and degrading. It is indeed the stuff of movies such as *V for Vendetta*, in which a government (in this case, Britain's) establishes absolute rule over its citizens by clandestinely launching a bioterrorism attack on its own people. Martial law declared, the government seizes control of the corporate media, which it uses to propagate its self-serving lies. Dissidents are murdered or imprisoned, and the people, fearful for their lives, come to believe that their only hope for survival is to relinquish their freedom to absolute government authority.

Sound at least vaguely familiar?

In October of 2005, President Bush called for martial law, including forced quarantines, in the event of an avian flu pandemic.[3] In the aftermath of Hurricane Katrina, he called for the use of the military to enforce the law in case of a natural disaster. Some government officials, such as Texas Republican congressman Ron Paul, have seen such strategizing as pretext for fear mongering to create a police state. Said Paul, "To me it's so strange that the president can make these proposals and it's even plausible. When he talks about martial law dealing with some epidemic that might come later on and having forced quarantines, doing away with Posse Comitatus [legal prohibition against use of the military for law enforcement] in order to deal with natural disasters, and hardly anybody says anything. People must be scared to death."[4]

Taking this plot a step further, former CIA analyst Ray McGovern warned that if another major terrorist attack took place, we shouldn't believe what the government tells us because the government itself might actually be the perpetrator![5] The issue is not whether the Bush administration or any subsequent administration is sinister and arrogant enough to try to pull this off. Indeed, history is rife with examples of democratically elected regimes, even that of Hitler, which sought absolute power. It's plainly naive to assume that this could never happen in America. But, whether such an ominous scheme can succeed in the end depends largely on whether or not the media is doing its job. Unfortunately, the MSM has fallen asleep at the watch.

While the mainstream media can claim to have "covered" Bush's ideas about declaring martial law, it nevertheless played down the illegal and dangerous nature of permitting government to use the military to enforce law. Also not covered were admonitions from congressmen like Ron Paul or twenty-seven-year veteran CIA analysts like McGovern.

It is a serious blow to democracy when government straight-facedly tells Americans that it may have to declare martial law in the not-so-distant future. Well, perhaps you are thinking that Congress would first have to authorize the use of such power. True enough, but one might also have thought that *Congress* would have to declare war. After all, that is what Article 1, Section 8 of the US Constitution states. However, Congress didn't declare war when the United States invaded Iraq. Instead, it relinquished its authority to the president!

The president didn't accept Congress's legal condemnation of cruel and unusual forms of torture when he issued a "signing statement" granting himself the authority to bypass it. Nor did he worry about going to the FISA court to get warrants before unlawfully wiretapping American citizens. Nor did he give much credence to national security (let alone law) when he authorized Vice President Cheney's former chief adviser Scooter Libby to discuss classified, sensitive information with reporters for self-serving political purposes (we will address this below). Realistically, in an environment where the rule of law is itself disregarded, it is sheer folly to assume its protections.

When the rule of law dangles on a thread, fear mongering, intimidation, witch-hunting, and jingoism are often its cheap substitutes. Insidiously linking Saddam to the 9/11 attacks, the Bush administration "shocked and awed" us into waving the flag and supporting a war in Iraq. Said Bush in his 2003 State of the Union, "Before September the 11th, many in the world believed that Saddam Hussein could be contained. But chemical agents, lethal viruses and shadowy terrorist networks are not easily contained. Imagine those nineteen hijackers with other weapons and other plans—this time armed by Saddam Hussein. It would take one vial, one canister, one crate slipped into this country to bring a day of horror like none we have ever known. We will do everything in our power to make sure that that day never comes." (Applause.)

If we didn't attack the Iraqi leader on his soil, he would attack us on ours. Here again was the use of fear mongering—terrifying an already traumatized people with trumped-up prognostications of even greater horrors to come—unless, of course, we repose our trust in the president and rally behind him.

Far from blowing the whistle on such vacuous psychological manipulation, the MSM actually helped to propagate the myth that Saddam harbored dangerous and deadly weapons of mass destruction. By ghoulishly reporting the words of officialdom instead of vigorously questioning it, this defrocked Fourth Estate helped mislead most Americans (around 70 percent of us!) into thinking that there truly was a connection between the attacks of 9/11 and Saddam Hussein.

One reporter who may have done the most in helping to propagate this myth worked for the *New York Times*—Judith Miller. In a first-person account of her testimony in a federal grand jury inquiry into whether she received classified information from Scooter Libby, she uttered these words: "During the Iraq war, the Pentagon had given me clearance to see secret information as part of my assignment 'embedded' with a special military unit hunting for unconventional weapons. . . . I was not permitted to discuss with editors some of the more sensitive information about Iraq." As journalist Normal Solomon points out, had Miller worked for the government as an intelligence officer, her refusal to speak with her editors might have been understandable.[6] But as a reporter for the *New York Times*, this was an abomination of her role as journalist.

Furthermore, in printing Miller's government lines, the *New York Times* was itself complicit. As mentioned in chapter 1, while the *Times* editors later denounced its shoddy prewar reporting of WMD in Iraq (attributing it to having fallen into "groupthink"), this self-serving admission of a reputable paper caught with its pants down was published only as a couple of editor's notes, not as front-page news in its own paper.

When I (EC) was interviewed by the *New York Times*, I had a special fact-checker assigned to my story. Where was the fact-checker *in this case*, in which thousands of American and Iraqi lives hung in the balance? Where was the Fourth Estate when we needed it? Instead of doing its job of exposing government abuse of power, it was complicit in it!

WHO TERRORIZED WHOM ON 9/11?

And how diligent was the press in investigating what happened on September 11, 2001, when the twin towers of the

World Trade Center in Manhattan and the Pentagon in Washington, DC, were attacked? While the Internet and progressive radio still continue to buzz with questions, the mainstream has glossed over many facts that raise serious questions.[7]

Here are some of the facts—and some of the questions raised by examining the facts. According to eyewitness accounts, there appeared to be violent explosions from bombs going off in the basement level of the twin tower buildings similar to what had transpired in the attacks of 1993. Just before 9/11, workers allegedly replaced cables in the sealed inner shafts of the towers, which is where explosives would have had to have been placed in order to destroy the support columns. Suspicions about the nature of these events might have been laid to rest had the iron from the buildings been available for inspection, to check for residue from explosives. However, prior to any inspection, the iron from the toppled towers was sold and shipped off to China to be used for scrap metal!

As for the attack on the Pentagon, how could a rookie pilot known to have been incompetent based on flight school reports have managed to maneuver a giant commercial Boeing 757 (American Airlines Flight 77), flying at about 500 MPH, making a dramatically sharp 270-degree turn, descending 7,000 feet in two and a half minutes, and flying a few feet above ground several hundred meters before striking its target? The Pentagon now offers this as a satisfactory explanation of what happened on that dreadful day. Yet in April 2001, just about five months before the attack, the Pentagon had explicitly rejected the same scenario of a hijacked airliner flying into the Pentagon as too "unrealistic" to prepare against.[8]

Why didn't NORAD (North American Air Defense),

which is charged with defending our skies, intercept the hijacked airliners? Why weren't the two F-16 fighter jets at Andrews Air Force Base, about ten miles away from the Pentagon and supposed to defend the skies over Washington, DC, scrambled in time to intercept rogue Flight 77? NORAD had one hour and twenty-three minutes after loss of ground control communication with the flight to scramble these fighters. Federal agency regulations require air traffic control to immediately request military interception in such cases.

And why did the F-15s launched out of Otis Air National Guard Base in Cape Cod fly toward Manhattan at less than one-third of their top speed of 1,875 MPH, only to arrive too late?

Why did then acting head of the Joint Chiefs of Staff, General Richard Myers, choose to remain in a meeting even after hearing a TV report that a plane had struck the North Tower of the World Trade Center? Instead of being taken to task for his failure to act responsibly to defend his nation, President Bush commended him for his "calm manner, sound judgment, and his clear strategic thinking," and on October 1, 2001, less than one month after the September 11 attacks, Myers took command of the entire US military as the fifteenth chairman of the Joint Chiefs of Staff. Was this payback for turning a blind eye?

Why was the damage to the Pentagon incommensurate with the size of the Boeing 757 that allegedly crashed into it? This jumbo jet, with a wingspan of almost 125 feet and a tail end spanning 44.5 feet high, left no identifiable imprint of wings and tail on the Pentagon, nor was the area of damage nearly as wide or high as the dimensions of this plane. In fact, the area of damage to the Pentagon was no more than 90 feet wide on the first floor, 13 feet on the second, and no more than 26 feet high. Further, what happened to the large pieces of American Airlines Flight 77, such as its huge wing sections, which seemed to have disappeared into the Pentagon?

On May 16, 2006, in response to a Freedom of Information Act request file by Judicial Watch (a conservative non-profit, public-interest law firm), the Pentagon released an obscure series of still shots captured by Pentagon security cameras. These shots, which included a shot previously released in 2002, showed lots of smoke but no identifiable signs of the massive American Airlines Boeing 757. The government also failed to release the footage from the nearby Sheraton, which was confiscated by the FBI immediately after the attack.

Why did Bush continue to read *The Pet Goat* to the children at the Booker Elementary School in Florida after chief of staff Andy Card informed him of the attack? Wouldn't the Secret Service have immediately escorted him off, especially since it was known prior to 9/11 that the president would be at this location?

Was it merely a coincidence that the Bush administration had finalized war plans to invade Afghanistan two days before 9/11 with strategic placement of 44,000 US troops and 18,000 British troops in Tajikistan and Uzbekistan?

In December 2001, about three months after the September 11 attacks, CIA field commander Gary Berntsen and his US and Northern Alliance fighters, who were in pursuit of Osama bin Laden in the White Mountains of Afghanistan, were told to "stand down" rather than to hunt him down. Why did the government thwart the attempt to capture the suspected mastermind of the September 11 attacks?

Why was the bin Laden family whisked out of the

United States after the attacks rather than being detained for interrogation? In any other criminal investigation, wouldn't the family of the suspect have been questioned?

Just as chilling as these questions are the prophetic words of the Project for the New American Century (PNAC), a Washington-based, neoconservative think tank founded by William Kristol and Robert Kagan in 1997 and financed by the oil and weapons industries. As mentioned by Peter Phillips in the introduction to this book, the main mission of PNAC is to usher in a "New American Century" in which the United States uses its military might to dominate and force corporate privatization throughout the world. According to its document "Rebuilding America's Defenses" (RAD), published in 2000, "the process of transformation, even if it brings revolutionary change, is likely to be a long one, absent some catastrophic and catalyzing event—like a new Pearl Harbor . . ."

"Like a new Pearl Harbor"? Wasn't that precisely what the 9/11 attacks "turned out" to be? And was this "turning out" mere coincidence?

PNAC's strategy as prescribed in RAD also included forced regime change in Iraq and buildup of permanent US military presence in Iraq. It proclaimed that "while the unresolved conflict with Iraq provides the immediate justification, the need for a substantial American force presence in the Gulf transcends the issue of the regime of Saddam Hussein." In other words, going to war to depose Saddam was just a crock. The whole damn thing was, from the very start, about achieving US dominance in the Middle East. So, in the immortal words of the Downing Street memo, the facts needed to be "made to fit the policy."

This policy was carved in stone by September 11, 2001. In 1998, PNAC drafted and got congressional approval of the Iraq Liberation Act. This act's main purpose was "to support efforts to remove the regime headed by Saddam Hussein from power in Iraq and to promote the emergence of a democratic government to replace that regime."

Chillingly, if you had used PNAC as your crystal ball, you would have been able to predict 9/11 as well as the war in Iraq at least as far back as 2000. In fact, RAD flatly states, "We hope that the Project's report will be useful as a road map for the nation's immediate and future defense plans." It has also targeted Iran, stating that "even should U.S.-Iranian relations improve, retaining forward-based forces in the region would still be an essential element in U.S. security strategy given the longstanding American interests in the region." In other words, whether or not Iran poses an imminent threat to our national security, we still have good enough reason to send in the troops.

And sending in the troops is not unlikely in the foreseeable future. Presently, the scenario playing out with regard to Iran is one strikingly similar to that which played out in the leadup to the Iraq war. According to a recent 2007 Pentagon investigation of pre–Iraq War intelligence, then secretary of defense Donald Rumsfeld and his deputy, Paul Wolfowitz (both PNAC members), conducted their own, alternative intelligence analysis for the express purpose of finding a link between Saddam Hussein and al Qaeda after the intelligence community found no such link. This alternative assessment drew the groundless conclusions that there was a "mature symbiotic relationship" between Iraq and al Qaeda involving "shared interest and pursuit of" unconventional weapons, and that there were "some indications" of cooperation between Iraq and al Qaeda on the September 11, 2001, terrorist attacks. These disingenuous claims, which were susequently discredited by the September 11 Commission, were nevertheless parroted by the MSM and used to manipulate the public into supporting a bloody, groundless war.

History now appears to be repeating itself. Despite the fact that a recent National Intelligence Estimate Report has stated that Iranian involvement is probably not a major cause of the bloodshed in Iraq, Bush has maintained that Tehran has been arming "Shiite extremists" to kill Americans. And, in a manner reminescent of Rumsfeld and Wolfowitz, Secretary of Defense Robert Gates has begun the process of finding evidence to fit the policy. According to Gates,"*I think* there's some serial numbers, there *may* be some markings on some of the projectile fragments that we found," that point to Iran" (my italics). If the future resembles the past, these doubtfully expressed claims will morph into certainties and a "convincing" case for war with Iran will be made—albeit based on shoddy intelligence.

Bush has also maintained that Iran has an agressive program to develop nuclear weapons. However, the Iranians maintain that their uranium refineries are geared toward peaceful uses of nuclear energy. Much as Bush raised the alarm about a WMD program in Iraq prior to his "preemptive attack," he has sounded the alarm about a nuclear weapons program in Iran. As in the case of Iraq, the evidentiary basis for drawing his conclusion that Iran has a nuclear weapons program is the negative one that Iran has not proven that it does *not* have one. In other words, his inference rests on ignorance, not evidence.

In the face of doubt about the true intentions of the Iranians, a rational approach to a resolution of these doubts might be arranging inspections of its nuclear facilities under the auspices of the United Nations. Iran has already given some indication that it might be receptive to such a possibility. Recently, it has opened up its nuclear plants to Arab officials and journalists from neighboring nations allegedly to ease their uncertainty about Iranian intentions. Further, Iran has maintained that it is against development of nuclear weapons and that if it truly intended to build such a weapon it would have withdrawn from the Non-Proliferation Treaty.

While Bush has claimed warfare is "the last option," he has already dispatched two US naval aircraft carrier strike forces to the region. The CIA and the air force have been flying missions over Iran to scope out military and nuclear targets, and have engaged Turkey to allow US strike aircraft to use its airspace to attack northern Iran. They have also deployed Patriot antimissile missiles to the area. It thus appear at this juncture that Bush's war plan is already in place.

Strategic targets in the quest for world domination is what "axis of evil" really means. Accordingly, the chain of events presently unfolding is predictable. Yet, as in the weeks prior to Bush's invasion of Iraq, the MSM, still not having learned its bloody lesson, drones out the latest breaking "news" from the White House.

And what else would PNAC be willing to approve in the name of world domination? In words that might well have been uttered by Adolf Hitler himself, PNAC looks forward to a time when "advanced forms of biological warfare that can 'target' specific genotypes may transform biological warfare from the realm of terror to a politically useful tool."

This exuberant desire to speak of genocidal terrorism of the most macabre strain using the euphemism "a politically useful tool" shows the pathological extremes to which this group would go to attain world domination. There is here an uncomfortable legitimizing of the most grotesque forms of terrorism imaginable under the rubric of political expedience. Would a group willing to go this far, and that has already admitted the need for a "new Pearl Harbor," have reluctance in staging the attacks of 9/11 in the name of political expedience?

Now, if PNAC were an organization of fringe radicals who had little influence on Capitol Hill, we all might rest comfortably in the belief that our national leaders would not swallow any of this. But the most chilling fact of all is that the members of PNAC have emerged as key players in the Bush administration. Some of the more prominent members include vice president Dick Cheney; former chief adviser to the vice president I. Lewis "Scooter" Libby Jr.; former secretary of defense Donald Rumsfeld; former deputy secretary of defense and current president of the World Bank Paul Wolfowitz; former US ambassador to the United Nations John Bolton; former chairman of the Defense Policy Board Richard Pearle; and even the president's brother, Jeb Bush.

According to the PNAC Statement of Principles, "We need to strengthen our ties to democratic allies and to challenge regimes hostile to our interests and values." In other words, anyone who stands in the way of American economic growth and expansion; any nation or group that refuses to adopt American values; to acquiesce in its corporate culture and to feed its bottom line, are to be counted among "regimes hostile to our interests and values." To the extent that terrorists and other extremists fall into this category, they make suitable military targets. Thus it was never really about stopping terrorism as such. And, indeed, any nation that happens to be "swimming in oil" like Iraq provides a prime target for engaging military action to stem the "hostility."

Bush's doctrine of preemption—of getting "the enemy" before it gets us—is therefore a gross oversimplification of its true doctrine. It's really about power and domination, of strategically advancing US power and influence throughout the world. It is this ideology—its own subjective vision of what the ideal world order would be like—that has allowed the Bush administration to rationalize away and to demand the "sacrifice" of hundreds of thousands of lives, Iraqi and American alike. As a matter of historical record, it has been one ideology or another—from religious extremism to Nazism—that has enabled human beings to brutally kill or oppress without being deterred by a guilty conscience. In the case of the Bush administration, it was its ideology of world domination that inspired invading Iraq in the first place, and it is now the likely basis for Bush's refusal to leave.

To see this, just listen to the PNAC manifesto of war as stated in RAD:

> We cannot allow North Korea, Iran, Iraq or similar states to undermine American leadership, intimidate American allies or threaten the American homeland itself. . . . Keeping the American peace requires the U.S. military to undertake a broad array of missions today and rise to very different challenges tomorrow, *but there can be no retreat from these missions without compromising American leadership and the benevolent order it secures.* This is the choice we face. It is not a choice between preeminence

today and preeminence tomorrow. Global leadership is
not something exercised at our leisure, when the mood
strikes us or when our core national security interests are
directly threatened; then it is already too late. Rather, it is
a choice whether or not to maintain American military
preeminence, to secure American geopolitical leadership,
and to preserve the American peace. (my italics)

From which, Bush's "logic" for remaining in Iraq can easily
be gleaned:

1. Do not retreat from any military mission essential to
   establishing American world domination.
2. The mission in Iraq is such an essential mission.
   Therefore, do not retreat from the mission in Iraq.

Sadly, the first premise is morally repugnant. It is the same
old megalomaniac, dictatorial ideology that has led to world
war and holocaust. And the second premise, which treats
Iraq as a pawn in attaining global preeminence, is specula-
tive and without empirical grounding.

Nevertheless, in the face of a bloody civil war, an Iraqi
government on the brink of collapse, mounting casualties on
all sides, and against the sober advice of a bipartisan Iraq
Study Group, Bush has predictably dug in his heels even
deeper by pledging to "surge" more American troops with an
increase of about ninety-two thousand (which does not
include support troops that may more than double this
amount) in the next five years; so solidifying his resolve
never to back down. After all, the PNAC manifesto is to do
whatever it takes to secure military victory. Human life is for
him the cost of such "victory." And how does one ultimately

define "victory"? In terms of the larger PNAC mission: world domination. Here then is his positive "logic" for escalating the war:

1. Do whatever it takes to secure military victory essential for establishing American world domination.
2. Sending more troops into harms way in Iraq is necessary to secure such a military victory.
   Therefore, we should send more troops into Iraq.

Regarding premise 2, most military experts have come to the opposite conclusion. This logic is clear and simple but it is clearly and simply wrong, and fraught with peril. Unfortunately, most Americans know little or nothing about the ideological basis on which the blood of American troops is being spent. Instead, they are fed lies and propaganda and only sound bites of the truth.

A media that truly perceived itself as an adversary of government would not have kept these facts and chilling connections out of the mainstream. It would not have simply parroted the official government accounts of 9/11, the Iraq war, and its emerging policy regarding Iran. If all this was and is part of a prearranged government plot, then it is one of the most heinous abuses of government power wielded against its own citizens in the history of this planet. Even if, in the end, the media were unable to connect all the dots, it should have at least given the American people the opportunity to hear and judge for themselves. That's what a *democratic* media would have done!

BIG BROTHER IS WATCHING US

From domestic wiretapping to the waging of war abroad, the government has relied on manipulation and lies to get what it wants. Its modus operandi has been to strike fear into our hearts and minds by using the threat of terrorism as a pretense. The government is playing us like a fiddle. Just tell us that it will stop terrorists from launching another attack, and we willfully surrender our civil liberties. And it really works! Consider that in a May 2006 *Washington Post* poll, when asked if, *for purposes of detecting terrorist activities*, they would permit the National Security Agency to keep track of every phone call (both domestic and foreign) they made and received, about two-thirds of Americans polled said that it would be all right. Never mind that this agency doesn't have legal authority to track Americans. After all, who cares about the rule of law when you are afraid of terrorists? Never mind that this poll played on fear of terrorism and completely avoided mention that this information might also be used for illicit purposes.

This is not to say that every ploy to scare us into submission has been successful. Undoubtedly some techniques have worked better than others. A few years ago, the media reported that the Bush administration was building a giant database called Total Information Awareness. The program was to be directed by John Poindexter, a convicted felon. The logo for the program was a big eye. The blatant in-your-face association with Big Brother watching our every move didn't go over very well, even with the usual scare tactics. So the government scrapped the big eye, but not the program.

Now the government is creating files on every American. Not only do these files include your phone log; they also include your medical records, bills, credit card purchases, and even your voter status. And, there is currently under way a plan to add your DNA to your file.

Some of this information is being collected by Choice-Points, Inc., a company with well-established, close ties to the Bush administration. This company collects data on Americans for allegedly commercial purposes and sells it to the federal government. According to journalist Greg Palast, this is the same company that compiled the infamous felons list in 2000 prior to the presidential election, which prevented hundreds of rightful voters, mostly black and Democrats, from being allowed to vote.

So what is the MSM saying about all of this? After the May 11, 2006, *USA Today* story about the government's tracking of our phone calls broke, the mainstream media did indeed "carry" this story. Its coverage abundantly emphasized how this program was somehow supposed to protect us from terrorists. It was ritualistically repeated that this program was only mining telephone numbers (admittedly easily linked to our names and addresses by using the Net), merely looking for patterns, and that it was not tapping the content of these calls. It also stressed that the program was "legal." There was even a shot of the president on the CNN Web site standing in front of honest George Washington, declaring that he was not "data mining or trolling" American citizens' phone calls.

What was left out was that it is illegal for the NSA to engage in such domestic spying unless it is investigating a crime. Nor was it mentioned that the NSA's program of warrantless surveillance (not to mention its secret AT&T program for wholesale scanning of domestic and foreign e-mail messages) could also provide the content of at least some of these calls.[9] And since they were, after all, warrant-less, there were no legal constraints in place to prevent the Bush administration from eavesdropping on domestic calls placed to parties *within* the nation as well as international calls. Nor was it made clear that the files being assembled are also linked to Americans' health, credit card, and billing records. Nor was it made clear that this is just Total Information Awareness—"Big Brother"—back again, only this time incognito. Nor was it pointed out that this information is not merely being used to track terrorists but also, among other things, to keep track of those who oppose them. Instead, the MSM paid lip service to reporting the story while helping government successfully "shock and awe" about two-thirds of Americans into relinquishing their right to privacy on the pretext of being protected against future terrorist attacks.

DISSIDENTS BEWARE:
THE OUTING OF CIA OPERATIVE VALERIE PLAME

The government's modus operandi of "shock and awe" also includes quelling any opposition from *individuals* courageous or patriotic enough to stand up against it. Those who get in its way are branded "enemies of state," where the latter simply means anyone who disagrees with its policies and objectives. Joe Wilson is a good example of how the government handles American "dissidence."

In February 2002, Joseph Wilson, a former US ambassador to Gabon went to Niger (Africa), at the behest of the

CIA to investigate the possible purchase of uranium yellow-cake (a processed form of ore) by Iraq for purposes of creating nuclear weapons. On July 6, 2003, Wilson published a brief account of his findings in the *New York Times* in an article titled "What I Didn't Find in Africa." The article began with these words: "Did the Bush administration manipulate intelligence about Saddam Hussein's weapons programs to justify an invasion of Iraq? Based on my experience with the administration in the months leading up to the war, I have little choice but to conclude that some of the intelligence related to Iraq's nuclear weapons program was twisted to exaggerate the Iraqi threat." After having spoken with Niger government officials, including the current US ambassador and those involved directly in uranium mining, he came away with a clear sense that Bush's intelligence, a report of dubious origin obtained from the British that attested to a uranium sale to Iraq in the late 1990s, was bogus.

Yet, Wilson's conclusion, which was presented in several reports including one filed by the ambassador to Niger and one by the CIA itself, was still not acknowledged by the Bush administration. On January 29, 2003, according to Bush's State of the Union address: "The British government has learned that Saddam Hussein recently sought significant quantities of uranium from Africa. Our intelligence sources tell us that he has attempted to purchase high strength aluminum tubes suitable for nuclear weapons production."

On July 14, 2003, about one week after Wilson's *New York Times* article debunking Bush's uranium claim was published, Robert Novak, a right-wing reporter for the *Chicago Sun Times*, published an article titled "Mission to Niger," which included these treacherous words: "Wilson never worked for the CIA, but his wife, Valerie Plame, is an Agency operative on weapons of mass destruction." With these words, the identity of a CIA operative working under-cover on something as vital to national security as WMD was divulged, and therewith, she and her agency affiliates were put in harms' way and their operations blown. In fact, as it later became known, Plame and company had been investigating the claim that Iran was attempting to acquire nuclear weapons.

According to Wilson, the outing of his wife was the Bush administration's attempt to "punish" him for casting doubt on the legitimacy of its case for going to war in Iraq, a case that was groundless from its very inception. So, under the guise of national security, the Bush administration actu-ally jeopardized national security by outing one of its covert CIA agents and, by implication, the others who were working uncover with her.

On October 7, 2003, President Bush said, regarding determining the identity of the leaker, "I want to know the truth. I want to see to it that the truth prevails."

In December 2003 Patrick J. Fitzgerald was appointed special counsel to investigate the leak. In fact, as it turned out, there were at least six journalists to whom classified information was leaked, among them the then *New York Times* reporter Judith Miller, mentioned above. After spending eighty-five days in jail for refusing to reveal her source, Miller cooperated with Fitzgerald and disclosed her source: Scooter Libby. According to Miller, she had met three times with Libby, first on June 23, 2003, second on July 8, 2003, and third on July 12, 2003. Miller claimed that, according to her notes, Libby told her that Joseph Wilson's wife "may have worked on unconventional weapons at the C.I.A.," but she also claimed that this was "well before Mr. Wilson published his critique"—a statement, which if true, would disconfirm Mr. Wilson's timely complaint that the outing of his wife was done to punish him for publishing his July 6, 2003, *New York Times* article. On the other hand, Libby himself testified that he did *not* discuss Ms. Wilson with Miller because "he had forgotten by that time that he learned about Ms. Wilson's C.I.A. employment a month earlier from the vice president." Both witnesses could not have spoken the truth as their testimonies were logically inconsistent—although both could conceivably have been speaking falsely.

On January 29, 2007, former White House press secretary Ari Fleisher testified that Libby told him at a lunch meeting on July 7, 2003, that Plame worked for the CIA. Yet, Libby told a grand jury that he first learned of Plames CIA identity from MSNBC reporter Tim Russert at a July 10, 2003, meeting. However, Russert never discussed Plame's identity with Libby at that meeting. In the end, Libby was found guilty of perjury. But the important question was "Why did he lie?" Who was he trying to protect?

On April 6, 2006, Libby testified that the president gave him instructions to speak with a reporter about selected prewar intelligence, which included the refuted charge that Iraq had attempted to purchase yellowcake from Niger. However, Libby stopped short of saying that he was also instructed to leak Valerie Plame's covert identity to the press. So Libby took a leak for the president, who himself condemned leaking. Said Bush on September 30, 2003, in response to an investigation into the leaking of the classified information: "Let me just say something about leaks in Washington. There are too many leaks of classified information in Washington. There's leaks at the executive branch; there's leaks in the legislative branch. There's just too many leaks. And if there is a leak out of my administration, I want to know who it is. And if the person has violated law, the person will be taken care of."

So what, perchance, was the president's rationale for leaking classified information *himself*? Bush retorted, "I wanted people to see the truth and thought it made sense for people to see the truth. And that's why I declassified the document."

The truth? But the president was fully aware that this intelligence was severely flawed—there was no attempt by Iraq to purchase uranium from Niger. He publicly admitted as much on July 7, 2003, when the White House issued a statement saying it had been a mistake to include the words about the sale of uranium in the president's 2003 State of the Union speech. This was falsehood, not truth, and Bush had already admitted it!

But the plot thickens still. How, in fact, did Novak acquire classified information about Plame's identity? At first Novak claimed two "senior administration officials" gave him the information. These sources were later (July 2006) revealed to be senior White House adviser Karl Rove and then spokesperson for the Central Intelligence Agency Bill Harlow. However, according to Novak, neither of these two were his primary source, which he refused to divulge. So there were really three sources. Would any of these high-level officers of the Bush administration incur the risk of intentionally blowing the cover of a covert CIA operative without at least a wink and a nod from the president, or at least from the vice president? You do the math!

What about the other journalists who received the info? Well, on October 12, 2003, the *Washington Post* quoted an "administration official" as saying that "two top White House officials disclosed Plame's identity to at least six Washington journalists." According to the *Post*, the source said that "officials brought up Plame as part of their broader case against Wilson. . . . It was unsolicited. . . . They were pushing back. They used everything they had."

Obviously, the Bush administration perceived Wilson's finding as a threat to its contrived rationale for going to war with Iraq. It therefore had ample reason to try to discredit Wilson. There is, however, a further question, the answer to which one can only speculate. Was the outing of secret agent Valerie Plame calculated merely to punish Wilson (a rather lame way to discredit him) or was it also intended to serve some even more nefarious (albeit useful) purpose? Plame was, after all, herself investigating the claim that Iran had a nuclear weapons program, and in order to continue to do so, she needed to retain her covert status.

PROSECUTING JOURNALISTS AS TRAITORS FOR DOING THEIR JOB

On Mary 21, 2006, Attorney General Alberto Gonzales said journalists can be prosecuted for publishing classified leaks, and he had in mind the *New York Times* reporting of the Bush administration's program of warrantless (and illegal!) eavesdropping on American phone calls and e-mail messages. He admonished that, if the government's probe into the NSA leak determines that there has been criminal activity, prosecutors have an "obligation to enforce the law."

This new attempt to "shock and awe" journalists into lockstep with the government marks the beginning of a further severe and devastating blow to what remains of the Fourth Estate. While journalists have often ended up sitting in prison for refusing to reveal their source, they have not typically had to fear being found guilty of violating espionage laws for doing their job.

Stated Gonzales, "There are some statutes on the book which, if you read the language carefully, would seem to indicate that that is a possibility. . . . We have an obligation to enforce those laws. We have an obligation to ensure that our national security is protected."

Once again, here is the fear tactic in motion, encroaching once again on our civil liberties, severing the lifeline that protects us from the abuses of government power: a free and independent press.

"Freedom of the press," said Gonzales, "should not be absolute when it comes to national security." But Gonzales needs to be reminded that there are limits to what can legitimately be claimed in the name of "national security." Is it a matter of national security that the Bush administration should be permitted to engage in *warrantless* eavesdropping of American citizens? The issue here is not whether there are grounds to engage in eavesdropping. Rather, the issue is whether the executive branch should have the power to circumvent the lawful judicial process of getting a warrant.

National security requires that a system of checks and balances on executive authority be in place. It requires that the judicial branch of government be left to do its job. It requires that the media be permitted to disclose the unlawful activities of government. National security is not protected by surrendering these constitutional protections to the absolute authority of a dictator.

In 1971, when President Richard Nixon attempted to halt the New York Times's publication of the Pentagon Papers, the Supreme Court ruled 6 to 3 to overturn a federal court injunction prohibiting continued publication. These papers painted a picture of how the United States government had lied and deceived the American people in order to escalate an illegal war in Vietnam. While the justices wrote separate opinions, the majority concurred that the government failed to meet the heavy burden of proof that must be met in attempting to restrain freedom of the press in the name of national security. Indeed, for some, such as Justice Black, this freedom is in fact inviolable. Said Black, "To find that the president has 'inherent power' to halt the publication of news by resort to the courts would wipe out the First Amendment and destroy the fundamental liberty and security of the very people the Government hopes to make 'secure.'"[10]

Quite obviously, an attempt by government to constrain journalists from exposing its own *illegal* activities would not pass constitutional muster on any legitimate interpretation of presidential powers. However, the Bush administration does not think it needs to meet *any* burden of proof whatsoever. For Bush, reality is whatever he says it is when it comes to fighting "the war on terror." Here, the president's power to interpret what is required to keep us safe and secure is entirely up to his judgment. "The United States is a battlefield in the war on terror," affirmed solicitor general Paul D. Clements in defending Bush's right to capture a US citizen on American soil and hold him indefinitely as an enemy combatant.[11] If the entire nation is such a "battlefield," Bush doesn't need a warrant to invade your privacy! Forget, too, about the Fourth Amendment. Even your bedroom is a battlefield!

Attorney General Alberto Gonzales proposed using 18 USC, 793 of the Espionage Act of 1917 to prosecute journalists for disclosing classified leaks. This eighty-nine-year-old statute, which was never used nor intended to prosecute journalists, makes it a crime for an unauthorized person to receive national defense information and to transmit it to others. In keeping with its MO of "shock and awe," the Bush administration wants to send a consistent message to journalists: "Say only what we condone or you can expect to suffer our wrath."

So what can be expected if the Bush administration, including its cronies in the Justice Department, gets its way? Predictably, the prosecution of journalists will be inconsistent and selective. Journalists like those at the *New York Times* who disclosed Bush's illegal domestic eavesdropping program will be indicted and prosecuted as spies. On the other hand, "freedom-loving" patriots like Robert Novak, who are compliant with the Bush administration in doing its dirty work, will escape prosecution altogether. In the end, whatever is now left of our noble Fourth Estate will be chilled under threat of imprisonment.

As you have seen, since giant, profit-seeking corporate media are beholden to government for their financial prosperity, they already have a strong incentive to walk lockstep with the Bush administration. But that doesn't mean that these companies won't occasionally step out of line. As discussed in chapter 2, this is especially true of smaller, more news-centered companies like the *New York Times*. So, another tier of political control (threatening to charge non-compliant journalists with treason) is still necessary to attain media dominance. Even so, the attempt to silence individual journalists who step out of line is but one more fail-safe level of an even broader government plot to bring the media under its full control.

Now that the Internet has become a major independent news and information source, controlling the MSM is simply not enough. Government's attempt to put a dictatorial lid on the purveyors of truth has therefore escalated into an all-out attack on the free and open architecture of the Internet. True to form, the Bush administration is now plotting to take control of cyberspace.

NOTES

1. Sinclair Broadcast Group, "ABC Nightline Pre-emption," http://www.sbgi.net/ (accessed February 12, 2007).

2. Keith Olbermann, "Bloggermann," MSNBC, December 13, 2005, http://www.msnbc.msn.com/id/9665308/ (accessed February 12, 2007).

3. CNN, "Bush Military Bird Flew Role Slammed," October 6, 2005, http://edition.cnn.com/2005/POLITICS/10/05/bush.reax/ (accessed February 12, 2007).

4. Paul Joseph Watson and Alex Jones, "Republican Congressman Slams Bush on Militarized Police State Preparation," PrisonPlanet.com, October 12, 2005, http://www.prisonplanet.com/articles/october2005/121005slamsbush.htm (accessed February 12, 2007).

5. "Former CIA Analyst: Government May Be Manufac-

turing Fake Terrorism: A Government Openly Promoting Torture, a President Acting Like a King Cannot Be Trusted, Must Be Impeached," PrisonPlanet.com, October 19, 2005, http://www .prisonplanet.com/articles/october2005/191005McGovern.htm (accessed February 12, 2007).

6. Norman Solomon, "Judith Miller, the Fourth Estate and the Warfare State," *Free Press*, October 17, 2005, http://www .freepress.org/columns/display/5/2005/1234 (accessed February 12, 2007).

7. Alex Jones and Paul Joseph Watson, "Actor Charlie Sheen Questions Official 9/11 Story: Calls for Truly Independent Investigation, Joins Growing Ranks of Prominent Credible Whistleblowers," PrisonPlanet.com, March 20, 2006, http://www .prisonplanet.com/articles/march2006/200306charliesheen.htm (accessed February 12, 2007).

8. Eric Schmitt, "Pentagon Rejected Pre-9/11 Hijacking Exercise," *New York Times*, April 14, 2004, http://www.nytimes .com/2004/04/14/politics/14PENT.html?ex=1397361600&en= 0592fe7d878e9a7f&ei=5007&partner=USERLAND (accessed February 12, 2007).

9. See chapter 1.

10. Justice Black, Concurring Opinion, *New York Times Co. v. United States*, 403 US 713 (1971), http://supct.law.cornell.edu/ supct/html/historics/USSC_CR_0403_0713_ZC.html (accessed February 12, 2007).

11. Tom Jackman, "U.S. a Battlefield, Solicitor General Tells Judges," *Washington Post*, July 20, 2005, http://www.washington post.com/wp-dyn/content/article/2005/07/19/AR2005071901023 .html (accessed February 12, 2007).

Chapter 8

PROJECT FOR THE
NEW AMERICAN NET

The days are numbered for surfing an uncensored, open-access Internet, using your favorite search engine to search a bottomless cyber-sea of information in the grandest democratic forum ever conceived by humankind. Instead you can look forward to Googling about on a walled-off, carefully selected corpus of government propaganda and sanitized information "safe" for public consumption. Indoctrinated and sealed off from the outer world, you will inhabit a matrix where every ounce of creative, independent thinking that challenges government policies and values will be squelched. Not just some wild conspiracy theory, this Project for the New American Net (PNAN) is documented in the annals of the Project for the New American Century (PNAC).[1]

THE PNAN PLAN

As mentioned earlier in this book, the main mission of PNAC has been to attain world domination through corporate globalization and the increase in US military dominance throughout the world. In its blueprint of what would be required for the transition, it stresses the necessity of government control of the Internet.[2] In one of its documents, "Rebuilding America's Defenses" (2000), the PNAC states, "as with space, access to and use of cyberspace and the Internet are emerging elements in global commerce, politics and power. Any nation wishing to assert itself globally must take account of this other new "'global commons.'" Speaking of "cyber-war" it states: "Although . . . the role of the Defense Department in establishing 'control,' or even what 'security' on the Internet means, requires a consideration of a host of legal, moral and political issues, there nonetheless will remain an imperative to be able to deny America and its allies' enemies the ability to disrupt or paralyze either the military's or the commercial sector's computer networks. Conversely, an offensive capability could offer America's military and political leaders an invaluable tool in disabling an adversary in a decisive manner." It is mind-boggling to think what the terms *control* and *security* might mean for a militaristic government bent on defeating its "enemy." If this seems a stretch from the current political climate, then it is worth reminding you that many of the prominent members of PNAC occupy or have occupied high positions in the Bush administration, including the vice president himself (see chapter 7).

At this time, it's not hard to outline the broad stages of

the PNAN plan for transforming the Net into a vehicle of world domination:

- **Corporatize:** bring Net under corporate control
- **Sanitize:** censor whatever conflicts with government interests
- **Propagandize:** insert false and misleading government "information"
- **Militarize:** police Net for subversive content and communication, and use it to rally support for government interests and to defeat "enemies"
- **Globalize:** enclose the world inside one *Great American Firewall*

As long as the Internet remains an open forum for independent content providers, it can flourish as a democratic forum. In contrast, corporatization of mass media means homogenization and sanitization. Media broadcast corporations like CBS, ABC, and NBC control the spectrum that carries their broadcasts; they are therefore able to determine the content of their programming. Cable TV news networks like News Corp's Fox News and Time-Warner's CNN own the cables that carry their news shows and therefore can control what passes as "news." Gigantic radio empires like Clear Channel and Infinity have crowded out the smaller broadcasters and now determine the content of mainstream radio. The Corporation for Public Broadcasting, now on a campaign to restrict "liberal" programming, controls National Public Radio (NPR) and the Public Broadcasting System (PBS). Colossal media corporations like Time Warner, which also own mainstream movie distribution companies, control the content of the movies most Americans watch. Publishers of books are also part of this intricate corporate media web. For example, News Corp owns Harper-Collins and Viacom owns Simon & Schuster.

As noted earlier, all of these companies have well-entrenched business relationships with the government, for example, dependence on government officialdom for the content of their news reports; enormous financial incentives to receive government contracts (for example, General Electric's NBC has interests in military contracts to produce jet engines); interests in government deregulation of media ownership caps and cross-market ownership, and lucrative tax incentives. As a result of this intricate web of quid pro quo, the MSM is to America what *Pravda* used to be to the now defunct Soviet Union: disseminators of an array of government-friendly, self-censored, whitewashed propaganda.

The principle of control governing this Pravda-ization of mass media is quite clear: *Whoever controls the conduit (the physical medium of conductivity such as airwaves, cables, and phone lines) will also control the content.* In the case of the Internet, the dominant physical media are presently cable and phone lines, while radio frequencies are now also being used in the emerging technology of wireless Internet. To the extent that telecom companies exercise control over these physical media, they will have the power to determine what Web sites we can surf.

THE SUPREME BETRAYAL
OF INTERNET FREEDOM

The corporate commandeering of the Internet is already well under way and it is progressing rapidly with the support of the federal government. The beginning of the end came on June 27, 2005, when in a 6 to 3 decision in *National Cable & Telecommunications Association vs. Brand X Internet Services*, the United States Supreme Court ruled that giant cable companies like Comcast and Verizon are not required to share their cables with other Internet service providers (ISPs). The Court opinion, written by Justice Clarence Thomas, was contrived to serve corporate interests. Instead of taking up the question of whether corporate monopolies would destroy the open-access architecture of the Internet, it used sophistry and legally suspect arguments to obscure its constitutional duty to protect media diversity, free speech, and the public interest.

The Court accepted the FCC's conclusion reached in 2002 that cable companies don't "offer" telecommunication services as defined by the 1996 Telecommunication Act, which defines telecommunication purely in terms of transmission of information among or between users. According to the FCC, cable modem service (which is what carries broadband Internet) is not a telecommunications offering. This is because consumers use high-speed wire transmission as a necessary part of other services like browsing the Web and sending and receiving e-mail messages. These latter services, claimed the FCC, are information services because they manipulate and transform data instead of merely transmitting them. Since the act requires companies offering telecommunication services only to share their lines with other ISPs (the so-called common carriage requirement), the FCC concluded that cable companies are exempt from this requirement.

Keep in mind the significance of this. This technical drivel means the difference between a free Internet and one that is dominated and controlled by the mega-telecom corporations. It is roughly the difference between a private road on which trespassers can be arrested (or shot!) and a public highway. The FCC is saying that the cables that carry high-speed Internet are private property, and that therefore it can control who operates on them—and, accordingly, what information is transmitted back and forth along these lines.

This decision by the FCC was aimed to satisfy corporate avarice at the expense of the public interest. Defying all logic, its basis for classifying cable modem services as informational was groundless. Not even the FCC could deny that people use their cable modems to transmit information from one point to another, regardless of whatever else they use them for. The FCC's classification could not possibly have provided a reasonable interpretation of the 1996 Telecommunication Act, since it was inconsistent with it.

Section 706 (C) (1) of this act defines "advanced telecommunications capability" as being "without regard to any transmission media or technology, as high-speed, switched, broadband telecommunications capability that enables users to originate and receive high-quality voice, data, graphics, and video telecommunications using any technology." If high-speed, cable Internet doesn't fit this definition, then what else does? It's baffling how the Court could have concluded otherwise! To classify broadband Internet service instead as an information service is to treat it like a cable TV station such as Fox News or CNN. These networks send information down a *one-way* pipe, unlike Internet transmissions, which, in contrast, are interactive two-way exchanges resembling telephone conversations.

In 1999, before the FCC rendered its construction in 2002, the US 9th Circuit Court of Appeals in *AT&T v. Portland* made this point quite clear. It stated: "Accessing Web pages, navigating the Web's hypertext links, corresponding via e-mail, and participating in live chat groups involve two-way communication and information exchange unmatched by the act of electing to receive a one-way transmission of cable or pay-per-view television programming. . . . Surfing cable channels is one thing; surfing the Internet over a cable broadband connection is quite another."

In *AT&T v. Portland*, the US 9th Circuit Court of Appeals also had this to say:

> Under the Communications Act, this principle of telecommunications common carriage governs cable broadband as it does other means of Internet transmission such as telephone service and DSL, "regardless of the facilities used." 47 U.S.C. S 153(46). The Internet's protocols themselves manifest a related principle called "end-to-end": control lies at the ends of the network where the users are, leaving a simple network that is neutral with respect to the data it transmits, like any common carrier. On this rule of the Internet, the codes of the legislator and the programmer agree.

Here the 9th Circuit Court was quite clear that there is no question about whether cable broadband must be regarded as a telecommunications service and hence subject to "common carriage." This means broadband Internet must be open to all, and that telecommunication companies cannot discriminate against users. These companies must respect "end to end" control by users whereby the network is "neutral with respect to the data it transmits." Just as a phone company cannot determine who converses and what is said over the lines, so, too, must the cable companies honor this principle of "common carriage." Here is the essence of Net neutrality, and it is the lifeline of democracy on the Internet.

Groping for a practical anchor to its specious decision, the United States Supreme Court cited the FCC's claim that "broadband services should exist in a minimal regulatory environment that promotes investment and innovation in a competitive market. This," the Court maintained, "is adequate rational justification for the Commission's conclusions."

What "rational justification" was the Court talking about? When one uses the term *rational justification* it implies that one has at least *a* reason, let alone a good reason. But the Court did not cite *any* reason for concluding that giving cable companies monopolies on broadband Internet cable service—thereby doing away with open access—would spawn more competition. In reality, such deregulation could mean less competition from independent service providers!

Further, even if creating monopolies on cable modem service *could* encourage more investment in relevant technologies, not all technologies are worthy of using and some may even be grotesquely antidemocratic, for example, using innovative filtering technologies to build a great American firewall around the Net and increasing the speed and efficiency by which government propaganda can reach consumers.

The Court's decision simply covered up the fact that there was *no* justified defense given by the FCC for its construction. The more *plausible* explanation (not at all a justification) is this: by giving big-cable business what it wants (namely, big money), big government will get what *it* wants in return: *control over what people are permitted to know.*

In the absence of any technical, practical, or moral argument for siding with the FCC, the Supreme Court, in the end, rested its decision on its own *Chevron* ruling. According to this purely procedural rule, courts should defer to government agencies, such as the FCC on matters of statutory interpretation so long as the statute in question is ambiguous and the agency's interpretation is reasonable. Despite the fact that there was *un*ambiguous, prior precedent for considering the Internet to be a telecommunication service rather than an information service (*AT&T Corporation vs. Portland* noted above); and despite the fact that treating an interactive service such as the Internet like a one-way cable TV station defied rationality, it still deferred to the FCC.

By deferring to the FCC instead of exercising its own judicial discretion in determining what really was reasonable, the Court mooted the point of having an independent, ultimate court of appeals in the first place. That point is to provide checks and balances on the activities of the other two branches of government and to settle controversial, politically significant cases with far-reaching social consequences. Instead, the Court abandoned its constitutional charge to protect the First Amendment right of all Americans to freedom of speech in cyberspace from encroachment by √ big business acting in concert with the federal government.

This decision has set the legal stage for a further

maneuver in the dismal saga of the declining free Internet. In 2006 there was extreme pressure on Congress by telecom lobbyists to pass the Communications Opportunity, Promotion, and Enhancement Act (COPE), which included a measure that would have granted the FCC exclusive authority to make all decisions regarding broadband policy and principles. Had telecom lobbyists gotten their way (while COPE passed the House, it died in the Senate), the FCC would no longer have had to rely on *Chevron* to attain deference. Instead, it would have been given a blank check to enforce its own mandates. This would have meant that, in the future, courts would have scant authority to challenge and overturn the Supreme Court's decisions. Unfortunately, the FCC holds a political bias that would make granting this authority dangerous. Under the direction of former FCC chair Michael Powell, and now under its current chair, Kevin Martin, the FCC has repeatedly moved toward increased deregulation of telecom and media companies, and there is now little reason to expect that this trend will reverse. The consequence is the thickening of the plot to increase corporate control of the Internet.

SILENCING THE LITTLE GUY: THE MEGA TELECOM "PAY FOR PLAY" PLAN

Thanks to the Supreme Court working together with the FCC and telecom monopolies, the Internet cables and phone lines are now sufficiently under the corporate control needed to take things to the next level of corporate domination. Presently, behemoth telecom corporations like Comcast,

Verizon, and AT&T are poised to set up tollbooths on the Internet. What they have proposed is a "pay for play" approach according to which content providers will get what they pay for.

Whether you're a small business or a giant corporation, if you want to provide visitors with a faster and more secure connection, then you will simply have to pay for it. Mega-telecom companies such as Comcast, Verizon, and AT&T argue that they can't simply rely on subscribers to their Internet services in order to make enough money to upgrade their networks and to invest in new technology. They maintain that, unless they also bill Web site operators (large and small, profit and nonprofit) for the quality of their connection and level of security, they will not be able to give their subscribers the technologically advanced and efficient product they demand. This would include improved video, faster online gaming, improved quality voice-over IP services, and so forth.

As you can see, this is, in the first place, a variation of the rationale the FCC used before to deregulate the mega-telecoms and to grant them broadband monopolies. It is the slippery slope of demanding more and more control and less and less constraints, all in the name of satisfying the consumer.

Of course, it's only fair that you should get what you pay for, right? That's exactly what the mega-telecoms want you to think. But the fly in the ointment is that not everybody can *equally* afford to pay. Wouldn't it be nice if everyone, rich and poor alike, could afford lifesaving organ transplant surgery? The reality, however, is that insurance companies would rather let people who can't afford the hefty premium die.

Similarly, according to the "pay for play" plan, only content providers with deep pockets would be given optimum Internet connectivity or "bandwidth." Giant corporations like News Corp and Time Warner would have the means to get their messages out there while the rest of the Internet community (which includes you and me) would be left spinning slowly in cyberspace or not at all. The "Net" result would be the demise of Internet neutrality. No longer would all of us have an equal voice within the freest and most comprehensive democratic forum ever devised by humankind. Instead, money would dictate what perspectives count as worthy of being heard. Since government ultimately controls the purse strings of large corporations, this would provide the leverage a dictatorial government bent on global domination would need to constrain what people see and hear.

THE GREAT AMERICAN FIREWALL

This trend is not without chilling precedent in other nations burdened with forms of dictatorship, notably China. There, a "Great Firewall" has been erected by the Chinese government around its Internet. Accordingly, sites considered "subversive"—anything the government disapproves of—are slowed down and/or phased out. There are thirty thousand Internet police whose job it is to comb the Internet looking for dissidents.

Recently, the search engine giant Google cooperated with the Chinese government in creating Google.cn, a government-censored version of itself. This is an instructive example of how corporate power can yield to the authority holding the purse strings. While this company's motto has always been "Don't be evil," feeding its bottom line by capturing the burgeoning Chinese Internet market appears to have meant more than remaining true to its motto. Now a corporate giant, it has partnerships with News Corp and profits that exceed Time Warner.

In fact, Google is prepared to sell its respect for customer privacy to the highest bidder. Many cities in the United States now have or are planning to have citywide wireless Internet zones that provide affordable Internet connectivity to the masses. For instance, Google, now also in the Wi-Fi business, has recently teamed up with EarthLink to offer a package deal that includes free Internet service as well as low-cost service. For example, it plans to provide the city of San Francisco slow Internet service for free while its partner provides low-cost ($20.00 per month) faster service. The hitch for the free service is that cookies would be planted in the user's computer that would collect personal data. This data would in turn be used to sell products that are matched to the user's personal profile. And it would collect this data without even informing the user that it is being collected!

As you have already seen, giant telecom companies such as AT&T, Verizon, and BellSouth have already begun to cooperate with the government in creating personal files on every American. Now, just as the government has a record of every phone call you ever made, it will have unprecedented ability to monitor your Internet activity by gaining access to these data mines.

Will Google cooperate in such blatant privacy violations? To its credit, Google has resisted the Justice Department's recent attempt to force the company to hand over some of its search records, allegedly to study how much pornography turns up in children's searches. In contrast MSN, Yahoo, and AOL fully cooperated with the government request.

Nevertheless, as is evident from its willingness to cooperate with an oppressive foreign government like China and to encroach on the personal privacy of Americans through a system of clandestine Wi-Fi data mining, Google, like other corporate monoliths, has its price. Its recent resistance to a government subpoena to hand over some of its search records does not disconfirm this claim. In cases where Google has stood to substantially increase its bottom line, its obligation to its shareholders has invariably taken priority over fighting government censorship and intrusions of privacy. Corporations of the magnitude of Google cannot be trusted to consult their moral consciences in resisting evil, because they have no such consciences. It was good for Google's image to resist a government subpoena. After all, it is into advertising, and this was cost-effective PR. On the other hand, if government took steps to deregulate Google out of existence if it failed to fork over its users' private records, I suspect Google would hand them over on a silver platter.

In any event, even if Google were to emerge as the oddball case of a colossal corporation that persistently bit the government hand that fed it, there would always be a corporate competitor more willing to play ball. Unfortunately, in the behemoth corporate universe of dog-eat-dog, there is little room for nice guys—unless being nice pays.

The German philosopher Immanuel Kant made a useful distinction between acting *out of a sense of duty* and acting *in accordance with duty*. When I said earlier that corporations don't have moral consciences, what I meant is that they don't ordinarily act out of a sense of duty. To act out of sense of duty is to do your duty *because* it's your duty. On the other hand, to act *in accordance with duty* is to do what duty requires, but not necessarily because it *is* your duty. Corporations sometimes act in accordance with duty—although not out of a sense of duty—because doing what's right maximizes their bottom line.

Google or Yahoo or MSN or AOL or any of their competitors are capable of doing nice things, including giving to charity, supporting social programs, and providing services that improve the quality of our lives. However, they do these things because they are calculated to advance their bottom lines, either directly (providing a tax write-off, for example), or indirectly (promoting a corporate image that sells). The logic of corporate decision making typically excludes doing nice things that can be calculated to adversely affect the bottom line—at least in the long run. Giant corporations do not typically act out of a sense of duty. They do what's morally incumbent on them only if it also pays.

What this means is that we shouldn't depend on these monolithic corporations to regulate themselves for the common good. If there is no disruption of current trends, the Internet will predictably fall in line with a rigid program of censorship that will fundamentally devour the free spirit with which the Internet was conceived. This is a Net born of a free, interactive, democratic mission, not a profit-maximizing vehicle of corporations. It's not surprising therefore that under the auspices of the latter, in concert with a government with an insatiable appetite for power, which has the ability to make or break these corporations, the Internet would undergo an identity crisis. It is a blatant fallacy to suppose that profit maximization equates to democracy no less than to morality. To the contrary, in the present corporate context it equates to the marginalizing of any perspectives that are not cost-effective.

As mentioned earlier, when the *London Times* leaked the "Downing Street memo," the Internet buzzed with how Americans were deceived and lied to about the Bush administration's reasons for going to war in Iraq. While at first the MSM gave scant attention to this memo, the shockwaves sent out from the Internet were simply too strong to be ignored indefinitely. Even so, the mainstream broadcast media, from NBC's Chris Matthews to Fox's Bill O'Reilly, still ignored the substance of the memo (namely, that "the facts" about the threat to US security posed by Saddam Hussein were being "fixed" to fit a policy of preemptive war). Instead, the MSM focused on peripheral issues (such as whether the Bush administration had an exit plan) and largely dismissed the memo as "nothing new."

So what if the Internet was but another extension of Fox News or CNN? Then no American would have even been aware of the memo's existence! And the Bush administration would have avoided being placed in the position of having to answer to the American people. Without a free Internet, Americans are vulnerable with no defense against media and government propaganda. The government is protected against the people instead of the converse. Walled off from a free Internet, America is walled off from the truth, and there is no longer freedom in America.

The MSM has systematically played down the ongoing corporate assault on the free Internet. There was in fact a virtual mainstream blackout of the Supreme Court's decision to

224 THE LAST DAYS OF DEMOCRACY

deregulate broadband cable Internet just as it ignored the Downing Street memo. The decision was not even mentioned by cable TV networks like Fox and CNN. The *New York Times* covered it only at the bottom of the business section while the details of the BTK killer got front-page press along with other decisions handed down by the Supreme Court on June 27 (including the Grokster file-sharing case). The *Palm Beach Post*, which is published by Cox—another MSM company in the cable business—didn't cover it at all. Censoring stories that have potential to subvert corporate and government interests has already become the rule in this brave new world of corporate media coverage. And with open-access Internet now under siege, things are likely to worsen.

In fact, I (EC) wound up with the coveted Project Censored Award for a story I wrote on this subject. The article, "Web of Deceit: How Internet Freedom Got the Federal Ax, and How Corporate Media Censored the Story," was selected as the number one "most censored" story of 2005–2006. This article attempted to raise awareness about the Brand X case, which was hushed up by the MSM. The story, originally published on the Internet (on Buzzflash), was eventually plastered all over progressive Web sites but didn't see the light of the MSM. And this is precisely the problem.

I had to rely on progressive radio talk shows such as ones on the Air America network to get the word out. Only recently has the MSM even begun to test the waters. For example, to his credit, John Reinan, an Internet reporter for the *Minneapolis Tribune*, wrote an excellent article titled "Access to the Internet: Is it a Right or a Privilege?" (*Minneapolis Tribune*, May 27, 2006).

While this article laid out what was at stake in abridging

Net neutrality, it did not cover some of the more chilling facts that I had presented in my interview. In particular, I had discussed the PNAC plan for weaponizing the Internet in connection with the ongoing corporate takeover. When I later queried the reporter about why this admittedly more provocative aspect was not broached in the story, he explained that he "had to keep the story to a certain length"; and that, "while provocative, the PNAC angle was too far a field . . . to follow on this one." But he also told me he would probably cover it in his blog, which he indeed did. So, once again, the dicey story got some Internet attention while still remaining off the beaten path of the mainstream.

Let me reiterate. What we have said here is not speculation! What has happened to cable and network TV is now well on its way to happening to the Internet. Further, due to its cosmopolitan nature, the Bush administration has a special interest in the Net. Currently in motion is a plan to turn the Internet into a *global* weapon of mass deception. Read the PNAC plan, it makes it clear that the Internet is a "commons" that must be "controlled" and "secured" by the Defense Department in order to attain world domination. And world domination, through military might, is precisely what the United States is now seeking.

If you are like us (the authors of this book) and love basking in Net freedom and neutrality, then the worst thing you can do is hide your head in the sand. This trend toward the demise of democracy online will not go away by denying its reality. To the contrary, it will proceed whether or not you believe it exists, and one day in the not-so-distant future you will no longer be able to deny the painful truth, by which time it will simply be too late.

I (EC) have frequently been challenged by those who argue that there will always be technological ways to outsmart any authority that tries to control Net content. The solution, according to these critics, lies in the use of proxy servers that can transmit data below the radar of the Internet gestapo. I have no fundamental disagreement with the ingenuity of a clever geek to get around whatever firewall might be constructed to wall off information the government considers subversive. But, as the China experience clearly shows, there are grave risks in trying to outsmart a tyrannical government. Since use of proxy servers is illegal, those who attempt to escape their cyber shackles will become outlaws risking imprisonment. Moreover, relative to the general population, there are few among us who have the knowledge and sophistication to pull it off. As a result, most of us will see little alternative to falling in line with the rest of the herd. No firewall will ever be completely impenetrable, but it is not perfection that the government is after. It is not likely to surrender to a small band of Internet pirates. It will simply make this enterprise very risky and difficult. In the end, the masses will be subtly brainwashed into swallowing the government line.

Presently in Senate committee is the "Internet Freedom Preservation Act" (S 215)." This act, if passed, could provide at least a temporary stopgap for the mega-telecoms in their attempt to undermine Net neutrality. This act would make it unlawful for a broadband provider to

> block, interfere with, discriminate against, impair, or degrade the ability of any person to use a broadband service to access, use, send, post, receive, or offer any lawful content, application, or service made available via the Internet . . .

These words are fighting words for the telecom giants as they are for the Bush administration. These powerful opponents of Internet freedom can be predicted to fight cooperatively to kill this act, and if they are unable, they will work through the FCC and/or the Supreme Court as they have done in the past to reconstruct it in a manner favorable to the giant telecom companies. This is not to say that S.215 is not important; it is. It's not to say that there is no hope of defeating the well-organized attack on the free Internet; there is. However, this is a battle that cannot be won if the citizens of this great nation are unaware of what's going on. The corporate-political establishment is only too happy to keep us in the dark. Enlightened citizens cannot so easily be fooled. Don't be fooled!

Formerly under the direction of Michael Powell and now Kevin Martin, the FCC has consistently justified deregulating the monolithic media and telecom companies on the grounds that there are other technological frontiers in the mix that will contribute to a robust, diverse, and democratic media. For example, Powell argued for relaxing the national media ownership rules for broadcast TV on the grounds that the days are gone "when three networks reigned, when the number of television, radio stations were substantially less—before cable television was even a service; today 84 percent of Americans get television from cable—before direct broadcast satellite offered an alternative, and before anybody even dreamed of something called the Internet or, for that matter, VCR's and Blockbuster and the kinds of entertainment explosion we've seen."[3]

However, what Powell conveniently left out of the equation is the fact that the giant media corporations have maintained a stranglehold over each emergent technology. Thus, Powell failed to mention that Blockbuster is owned by Viacom, which also owns the CBS network, MTV, Infinity (radio) Broadcasting, and Paramount Pictures, among others. And the major satellite television provider, DirecTV, is now owned by News Corp, which also owns Fox Broadcasting Network, Fox Cable News, and 20th Century Fox, among others. Thus, the media explosion of which Powell speaks has been bought out by just a handful of owners who are in the position to call the shots about what we Americans can see and hear.

NOW UNDER WAY: THE HOSTILE TAKEOVER OF WI-FI INTERNET

Now that other Internet technologies are emerging, such as wireless (Wi-Fi) Internet, the FCC has appealed to these technologies to try to justify granting broadband monopolies to telecom companies like Verizon and Comcast. So, what has happened to broadcast TV, cable TV, satellite TV, and broadcast radio is now also happening to broadband cable and DSL Internet. In *Brand X*, the Supreme Court succinctly summed up the FCC's position: ". . . changed market conditions warrant different treatment of cable modem service . . . substitute forms of Internet transmission exist today, including wireline, cable, terrestrial wireless, and satellite. The commission therefore concluded that broadband services should exist in a minimal regulatory environment that promotes investment and innovation in a competitive market."

"Don't worry," we are told. "There are still other technologies coming of age." But what we have not been told is that all of these newer technologies have been or are in the process of being swallowed up by the same gigantic telecom corporations.

Presently, the mega-telecoms have powerful state and federal lobbies to pass legislation preventing states from creating their own infrastructures for wireless community Internet. There have already been fourteen states that have outlawed their municipalities from setting up community hot spots for receipt of Wi-Fi. These companies have argued that local governments are not equipped to efficiently run such systems and that competition and technological development will be stymied if communities are allowed to build their own wireless networks.

But the reality is that community Internet has the potential to spawn new market competition, since municipalities would hire private contractors to consult, build, supervise, and/or operate their networks. Municipalities would save money on deployment and operational costs. These savings could then be invested locally instead of diverting money away from the community to fill the deep pockets of the mega-telecoms. Community Internet would provide coverage in rural, less populated, or poorer areas not considered cost-effective enough by the telecoms to service. It would provide protection against discriminatory practices (so-called redlining) by providing affordable Internet to *everyone* in the community. It would encourage local businesses to conduct more of their activities online, increasing their efficiency. The low cost of doing business online would stimulate creation of new businesses, and the availability of such an opportunity would provide an incentive for other businesses to relocate to the community.

Local governments have had many years of successful experience in handling public utilities, from power plants to intricate subway systems, and there is no reason to assume that operating a Wi-Fi system as a public utility would be any less successful. As Robert McChesney insightfully probes, "If these systems are destined to fail, why are the telephone and cable companies expending so much energy trying to stop them?"[4]

The giant telecoms seek to destroy any competition from local governments in providing Wi-Fi. But that isn't all they stand to lose. These companies fear that community Internet would greatly bite into their revenues from cellular services, which currently include not only cell phone service but also e-mail and Internet services. These services are very expensive for consumers and provide a substantial source of telecom revenue. But if communities build their own wireless systems, there will be a substantial decrease in the demand for such services. These companies are not concerned about the quality of the services the customers would receive from their local governments. They care only about their bottom lines

There have been some municipal Wi-Fi projects launched, such as in the city of Philadelphia, which has plans to turn Philly into a giant 135-square-mile hot spot, permitting receipt of wireless Internet throughout the city. Companies like Verizon have fought hard to quash this project and have already successfully lobbied to pass legislation outlawing the construction of other such systems in the state.

The city of St. Cloud, Florida, with about 28,000 residents, has recently built and deployed a system that provides free wireless Internet to all of its residents. The system, funded by tax dollars, cost each of the ten thousand households in St. Cloud a total of $200 to deploy and $3.33 per month to operate. Prior to the system's deployment, residents paid $600 per year ($50.00 per month) to receive the identical service, which is now also available throughout the city. Would Bush's tax cuts have saved the average American this much?!

The St. Cloud project can and should serve as an inspiration for the rest of us. While 98 percent of broadband Internet service is now under the control of the mega-telecoms, community Internet still remains a frontier that might be won. For this to happen, municipalities must stand firm against a seductive, disingenuous foe whose arguments are contrived exclusively for purposes of increasing its bottom line. Communities can do their part in saving the free Internet by following the lead of St. Cloud. Unless such opposition is well organized and has strong community backing, the likely consequence is that Wi-Fi will become yet another outpost of the MSM.

NOTES

1. "Project for the New American Net (PNAN)" is our term of reference. Giving this aspect of PNAC a distinct name should make tracking its future progress easier.

2. See also Elliot D. Cohen, "The Great American Firewall: Why the Net Is Poised to Become a Global Weapon of Mass Deception," *Buzzflash*, May 2006, http://www.buzzflash.com/contributors/06/05/con06169.html (accessed February 19, 2007).

3. Online News Hour, "FCC Chairman Powell" (transcript), August 9, 2001, http://www.pbs.org/newshour/bb/media/july-dec 01/powell_8-9.html (accessed February 11, 2007).

4. Robert McChesney, "Let There Be Wi-Fi: Broadband Is the Electricity of the 21st Century—And Much of America Is Being Left in the Dark," *Washington Monthly*, January/February 2006, http://www.findarticles.com/p/articles/mi_m1316/is_1-2 _38/ai_n16068246 (accessed February 11, 2007).

Chapter 9
PAX AMERICANA

The last chapter showed how giant telecom companies and the federal government—from the FCC to the Supreme Court—have been working symbiotically to shut down open access to cyberspace. Now the Internet is poised to become an extension of the MSM. Notice how this media metastasis follows a discernible pattern in which giant corporations are given the green light by government to gobble up more and more of the information market. This corporate expansion is not granted without a price, however. The only options are to play ball with the administration and support it—and this means *politically*—or to pay dearly.

The real bottom line is that corporations are *systematically* being forced (sometimes reluctantly) into submitting to the Bush administration; they are becoming extensions of the GOP, and the politicization of our private lives is the intentional consequence of this move. In making this claim, we are qualifying the commonly held view that corporations control the government and that politics must be understood in economic terms (an idea that harks back to the philosophy of Karl Marx). In our view, this common vision of American politics fails to explain our current political experience and overlooks a dangerous *ideological* agenda that is driving much of America's current domestic and foreign policy decisions. By exposing this agenda and tracing the influence of the policy wonks known as the neoconservatives, we— the American people—will be in a much better position to understand our nation's current trajectory toward fascism and the loss of personal and political freedoms that accompanies this degenerative process.

AMERICA THE TYRANNICAL: THE NEOCONSERVATIVE VISION FOR THE TWENTY-FIRST CENTURY

Recall Plato's metaphorical account of how members of society are deceived by those in power. We used his account to introduce the idea that the vision of the American dream so central to our political identity is being systematically eroded and distorted by corporate marketers (see chap. 4). What we didn't say at the time, and what now clearly must be said, is that Plato believed deceiving the public is a *good thing*. Plato was not a believer in democracy and in fact argued vehemently against the notion that the public at large should rule. For Plato—and, as we shall see, for many influential members of America's political establishment— democracy is the rule of the ignorant over the educated, of the immoral over the virtuous. Plato believed that a ruling elite was necessary for a republic to function properly and that the masses should be lied to, diverted, and controlled for their own good and the good of the state.

As it turns out, this antiquated view of politics is not so antiquated after all; the political elitism espoused by Plato has been consciously embraced by members of both political parties. Alexander Hamilton's idea of a ruling elite that preserves and consolidates power by bringing wealthy business leaders into the political fold is not some aberration in American politics, *it is the rule*. As Boston University historian Howard Zinn asserts: "Around 1776, certain important people in the English colonies made a discovery that would prove enormously useful for the next two hundred years. They found that by creating a nation, a symbol, a legal unity called the United States, they could take over land, profits and political power from favorites of the British Empire. In the process, they could hold back a number of potential rebellions and create a consensus of popular support for the rule of a new, privileged leadership."[1]

This idea of a privileged class in America has found expression in various ways throughout our history, but it wasn't until the twentieth century that elitism and the science of mass deception came together in a way that made this guiding political theme so difficult to detect. By the time of Woodrow Wilson and the onset of the First World War, it was clear that mass communication could be an instrument of mass deception, and that mass deception was necessary if America's political elite was to fight off a populist challenge to its authority. As Noam Chomsky points out, "By Wilson's day, it was widely recognized by elite sectors in the US and

Britain that within their societies, coercion was a tool of diminishing utility, and that it would be necessary to devise new means to tame the beast [i.e., the public at large], primarily through control of opinion and attitude. Huge industries have since developed devoted to these ends."[2]

Wilson's interest in getting the United States involved in the First World War spawned a propaganda program run through his Committee on Public Information (also known as the Creel Committee, after George Creel, the journalist who was the public face of the efforts to engineer public support for the war). This program was remarkably successful as a result of the orchestrated efforts to manipulate the public mind through a variety of media—radio, film, public meetings, popular art, and the like—and inspired thinkers like Walter Lippmann and Edward Bernays to explore in greater detail the purposes and techniques of thought control.[3] To a large extent, the Creel Committee is responsible for the birth of the modern public relations industry, spawning as it did the application of social science research to the task of controlling public opinion through the new media of mass communication.

The most disturbing aspect of the Creel Committee's legacy is the extent to which the effectiveness of Wilson's propaganda machine has made thought control the centerpiece of public policy. The opening remarks of Bernays's famous work *Propaganda* are particularly telling in this regard: "The conscious and intelligent manipulation of the organized habits and opinions of the masses is an important element in democratic society. Those who manipulate this unseen mechanism of society constitute an invisible government which is the true ruling power of our country."[4] As he notes later in the same text:

In theory, every citizen makes up his mind on the public questions and matters of private conduct. In practice, if all men had to study for themselves the abstruse economic, political, and ethical data involved in every question, they would find it impossible to come to a conclusion about anything. We have voluntarily agreed to let an invisible government sift the data and high-spot the outstanding issue so that our field of choice shall be narrowed to practical proportions. From our leaders and the media they use to reach the public, we accept the evidence and the demarcation of issues bearing upon public question. . . .[5]

The function of political parties, according to Bernays, is to serve as a selection committee, providing manageable choices to a public that is not up to the task of grasping the issues at hand. This idea is central to the view of democracy embraced by Walter Lippmann as well, who describes a "revolution" in "the practice of democracy" as "the manufacture of consent." According to Lippmann, the manufacture of consent is a consequence of the fact that "the common interests very largely elude public opinion entirely, and can be managed only by a specialized class whose personal interests reach beyond the locality."[6] In short, the public at large is a *herd* that must be kept within its proper confines and driven in whatever direction the ruling elite deem necessary.

If one is in a charitable mood, the ideas of Bernays and Lippmann seem almost palatable. We can't all be experts in domestic and foreign policy, after all, just as we can't all be experts in the goings-on of America's social and economic institutions. Turning the decision making over to those who have the requisite expertise becomes a practical necessity given that most people don't have the knowledge to make informed decisions on their own. The problem, though, is that if this system of government is going to work, if it is going to serve the interests of the public, *then those in power must act with the public interest in mind.* This is what separates the more "acceptable" view of a ruling class from tyranny—the use and abuse of power to serve the interests of the ruling class. In short, if the view of government embraced by Bernays and others is to be at all defensible, it depends on a *moral* ruling class, a *compassionate* ruling class, a ruling class that recognizes its prime responsibility as the upholding of the public trust.

This idea, too, is one that Plato accepted, the idea that the ruling class must be made up of virtuous men and women who can take on the arduous task of ruling the republic. But, as you might expect, Plato's view implies a profound difference between those who lead and those who don't. It is not just education that separates leaders from followers in Plato's scheme, but natural abilities. Some people are *better* than others, and only the best people should rule. One wonders how moral a ruling class is going to be, however, if the leadership believes that they are superior to those they lead. As Lord Acton quite rightly noted, "[P]ower corrupts and absolute power corrupts absolutely." Remaining virtuous and protecting the public good seems an unlikely eventuality given the human propensity for self-aggrandizement and opportunism.

In our own time, Plato's ideas about democracy and the ruling elite have a direct connection to the policies and attitudes of the Bush administration. The group of policy makers and politicos known as the neoconservatives has more than a casual link to Plato's political philosophy due to its connection to the teachings of Leo Strauss, the highly influential political philosopher. Indeed, Strauss was a staunch advocate of a ruling elite and a critic of liberal democracy:

> In Strauss's view, there can be no universal community of men because a community is by its nature exclusive. A society that includes all of mankind is not a society; for the latter is by its nature a bond that unites members of a group by what distinguishes them from others. And that is precisely the trouble with liberal democracy—it is supposedly so all-inclusive that it is a void. Liberalism allegedly binds men not by what makes them distinctive . . . but by what all mankind have in common—which is to say, the desire for survival, ease, and security. Strauss does not think that a sense of justice is a universal attribute of humanity; he implies that what we have in common is our animality, and that is the basis for liberal democracy.[7]

Strauss was an esoteric philosopher who collected around him intelligent men who had a taste for elitism and an interest in reviving the concept of *regime*. Believers in the idea that the public is not up to the task of being virtuous or understanding much, Strauss and his followers embraced the idea that public discourse should hide the real intent of the powerful, and that government should be a "behind-the-scenes" affair. As humanities educator Earl Shorris notes, "Because [Strauss] was an extreme conservative, many of the young men . . . who sat at his feet were already dabblers in conservative or reactionary thought. They idolized Strauss as an earlier generation had embraced Marx. They saw a chance to change the order of the world. In the excitement of this unlimited ambition, the Straussian cult was born."[8]

Among the followers of Strauss is Paul D. Wolfowitz, the Pentagon's former undersecretary for policy and architect of the controversial policy paper outlining the role of the United States as the dominant world power in the post–cold war environment. The paper, referred to at the Pentagon as "Defense Policy Guidance" (DPG), called for the United States to take measures that would prevent the rise of competitors on the international scene, even if those competitors are pursuing their own legitimate interests. "With its focus on this concept of benevolent domination by one power, the Pentagon document articulates the clearest rejection to date of collective internationalism, the strategy that emerged from World War II when the five victorious powers sought to form a United Nations that could mediate disputes and police outbreaks of violence."[9] In other words, under a defense policy articulated by Wolfowitz, America should transcend the framework of international law and diplomacy established in the twentieth century and strive for a position of world dominance. "The document is conspicuously devoid of references to collective action through the United Nations, which provided the mandate for the allied assault on Iraqi forces in Kuwait. . . ."[10] The central thesis of the Wolfowitz piece is an attack on democratic principles and the rule of law and, therewith, an expression of the elitism referenced above.

Wolfowitz's attitude is hardly an anomaly among the neoconservatives. Other influential followers of Leo Strauss are committed to the idea that an American regime that dominates the globe is the next great phase of political history on our planet. As mentioned in chapter 7, Dick Cheney, I. Lewis "Scooter" Libby Jr., Donald Rumsfeld, John Bolton, Richard Pearle, and Jeb Bush, among other high-level officials, are all committed to the concept of a new world order based on American economic, military, and cultural power (*power*, not the rule of law). And remember Francis Fukuyama, the former State Department official and author of the book *The End of History and the Last Man*. He, too, has deep connections to the cabal of neocons bent on re-engineering world politics.

Fukuyama's membership in this now notorious group of policy elites is worth highlighting for a moment, as it suggests the convergence of two lines of thought we've been exploring in this book. Leo Strauss was committed to the idea that the old world order of independent nation-states should be replaced by a universal politics to which independent nations are subordinate (not to be confused with universal democracy, mind you); Fukuyama's idea that corporate capitalism is part of the system for the expression of human freedom suggests that Strauss's view has been recast as a call for a global free market system where the transnational corporation reigns supreme. What we see, then, in the connection between corporate capitalism and the political elitism of the neoconservatives, is the harnessing of corporate power in the service of a political ideal: corporations are viewed as the mechanism by which a new world order will be established and maintained, and the idea that this dominance ultimately promotes human freedom is the pretext for undermining democratic principles in the process. It should come as no surprise, then, that the neoconservatives are also ardent supporters of globalization—the opening and managing of global markets to the world's largest corporations. It is also worth noting that among the conditions of membership in the World Trade Organization (WTO), a country must be willing to sign over its power to make and enforce certain laws that bear on the way corporations conduct business (for example, environmental protections)—yet another example of how citizens of free nations are having their power usurped by corporations.[11]

The commitment to a global system dominated by American economic interests would be incomplete—and the global system unworkable—without the military force necessary to protect corporate interests. World domination can be a messy business after all. Not everybody likes the idea of having virtually every aspect of their lives controlled by the mandates of the transnational corporation, and not everybody is willing to hand over public resources to private interests in foreign lands. So an adaptable, quickly deployable military is an important asset for ensuring access to lucrative markets and for stomping out the political backlash that is guaranteed to arise in the face of corporate tyranny. Just like the American Express slogan "Don't leave home without it," corporations need the assurances that come with the threat of US military might or the hired guns of client states and petty dictators. Corporate products and the threat of "Shock and Awe" are the proverbial carrot and stick that keep the world on track to complete subordination to US interests.

As mentioned earlier, this relationship between private interest and state muscle is the very essence of the vision of the world embraced by the Project for the New American Century (PNAC), the "nonprofit organization" discussed earlier in this book. Founded with seed money from the conservative Bradley Foundation, PNAC is committed to the principles of national defense articulated by Wolfowitz in 1992 (as is evident from the remarks of one of its defining policy papers). With reference to its review of US defense policy and subsequent recommendations, authors writing for PNAC note: "In broad terms, we saw the project as building upon the defense strategy outlined by the Cheney Defense Department in the waning days of the Bush Administration. The Defense Policy Guidance (DPG) drafted in the early months of 1992 provided a blueprint for maintaining U.S. preeminence, precluding the rise of a great power rival, and shaping the international security order in line with American principles and interests."

Here is the "Pax Americana," the present-day equivalent of the Roman Empire (Pax Romana), where America establishes its preeminent global reign through its unparalleled military strength. The PNAC authors note that this defense strategy was sidelined by the Clinton administration, but, writing in 2000, they go on to state: "Although the experience of the past eight years has modified our understanding of particular military requirements for carrying out such a strategy, the basic tenets of the DPG, in our judgment, remain sound."[12]

In other words, the neoconservative vision for the world expressed in Paul Wolfowitz's 1992 paper on US defense policy after the cold war is the *right* one. At its core, this vision is elitist, undemocratic, and—to the extent that military might is used in the service of this vision—thoroughly despotic. The Bush doctrine of preemptive war, though marketed to the public as part of a "war on terror," is actually part of a strategy spelled out long before 9/11, which represents a tectonic shift in US policy toward reshaping the "international security order." So, too, is the president's sneering disdain for the United Nations and international law: such antiquated ideas as diplomacy, international cooperation, and the rule of law are part of "Old Europe" and an Old World. The New World—a *Brave New World*—is to be shaped by the American übermensch, the man of character who, by nature, is above the law and guides the children of lesser gods with a sure and sometimes brutal hand. With complete faith in the character and intentions of the leadership, what is most important, and what is required of every citizen, is *loyalty*—loyalty not to principle but to the person who leads, to the embodiment of American Regime. "*W. The President*" reads the bumper sticker. Perhaps that says it all.

Taken in the context of the neoconservative worldview, the Bush administration's systematic (and, we should add, *highly successful*) attack on the checks and balances in American government is hardly surprising. Unitary Executive Theory, the idea that the executive branch of government should have unbridled power (a euphemism for dictatorship), is embraced by the Bush administration wholeheartedly. It is—and we should be really alarmed by this—embraced by at least one of the two Supreme Court justices appointed by President Bush, namely, Justice Samuel Alito, and perhaps by Justice John Roberts as well. (The June 2006 ruling by the Supreme Court, which overturns a ruling of the Court made just over a decade ago, on the right of police to enter a home without the "knock and announce" rule, is indicative of the impact of this faith in authority. Police officers are now no longer required to announce their presence at your door and, with warrant in hand, can simply barge in and search your home.)

Recall that the Project for the New American Century has articulated the need for a major event, "another Pearl Harbor," to unite America behind its fight for global dominance. The commitment to this idea is no accident given the lineage between PNAC and Leo Strauss. Strauss believed that "a political order can be stable only if it is united by an external threat; and following Machiavelli, he maintains that if no external threat exists, then one has to be manufactured."[13] The attacks of 9/11 were the event that united America in a war on terror, an amorphous war against a shady, elusive enemy that poses a constant threat to American security. The 9/11 attacks were this century's Pearl Harbor, and it was the inspiration for the PATRIOT Act, military tribunals, and the invasion of the neoconservative rallying point in the Middle East, Iraq. Is it so far-fetched to believe that, with considerable intelligence information about an impending attack on US soil available to the highest members of the US government, 9/11 was *allowed* to happen? If Dick Cheney, one of the founding members of PNAC, were privy to that information, would he take steps to prevent an attack? What about Karl Rove or Donald Rumsfeld? What about W. *the president*? People forget that elitism fosters disdain for those not among the privileged class. What are a few dead civilians in New York when compared to the prospects of world domination?

What is absolutely crucial to realize here, and what is really the point of this entire chapter, is that in a certain sense corporations are in the same boat as private citizens when it comes to standing up to the Bush administration. Again, people tend to think that corporations have seized government when in fact corporations are at the mercy of the same vindictive and arbitrary will of the Bush administration as the rest of us. There is a difference of degree here, to be sure, and that difference matters. But governmental power is one that threatens the welfare of individuals *and* institutions that don't fall in line behind Karl Rove and his cronies. As evidence of this claim, we turn to the Republican Party's extreme makeover of Washington's lobbying firms known as the K Street Project (K Street is the center of Washington's lobbying industry). The K Street Project is the result of the strong-arm tactics of Tom DeLay, former Speaker of the House of Representatives, Rick Santorum, the junior senator from Pennsylvania, Grover Norquist, the influential ideologue, and a cadre of Republican lawmakers who have forced corporations into the ranks of the Republican Party. The transformation of K Street in the last decade is a clear indication of the power of government over the private sector.

THE GODFATHERS OF K STREET

Once upon a time, Washington's lobbying firms were pragmatic about the ways they influenced politics, that is, lobbying was less about ideology and more about getting a client some face time with a member of Congress who could make his business life a little easier. And it made good business sense to be pragmatic: as the future can not be foretold, K Street companies hedged their bets and contributed roughly equal amounts to Democrats and Republicans; no matter who was in power, someone on the payroll could be counted on to go to bat for you. K Street's corporate posse also tended to hire as many Democrats as Republicans—pragmatists all—in the interest of using political connections for business advantage. This nonpartisan approach to buying access to lawmakers had the effect of diluting the power of both political parties and tied legislation more directly to the interests of lobbyists and their corporate clients.[14] Those were the good ol' days, the days when corporate money had real power and gave corporations some measure of control over government (though, of course, that control was never absolute, as lawmakers had the power to legislate corporations out of existence). But those days are gone.

After Republicans took control of Congress in 1994, the new leadership set in motion an effort to remake K Street and bring corporate America in line with a Republican agenda. Newt Gingrich, Tom DeLay, Dick Armey, and a handful of other lawmakers—supported by advisers like Grover Norquist and Ed Gillespie—sought to undermine the pragmatism of K Street by forcing lobbying firms to give generously to Republicans and cut off the flow of funding to Democrats. The strategy involved two basic thrusts. First, House Republicans and their allies sought to eliminate Democrats from the lobbying firms on K Street and replace them with Republican activists. Second, the Republican-led Congress would resort to a form of extortion to get corporations to follow a Republican agenda—a "pay to play" system that would require big donations in order to get access to Republican lawmakers. This effort met with some resistance while Democrats still dominated various committees in Congress and could block legislation if donations weren't made to the right people (the right Dems), but the decline of Democratic power between 1994 and 2006 (thanks in part to DeLay's illegal redistricting of Texas) and the stealing of the White House by Republicans in 2000 (and 2004—see the next chapter) accelerated the K Street Project considerably.

The result of this effort was that the balance of power between Republicans and Democrats, measured in terms of dollars and cents, was shifted to the right and corporations were made the handmaidens of the Republican leadership. And it's easy to see why. With Republican lawmakers using their political might as leverage to find their understudies key jobs on K Street, pragmatism gave way to dogmatism. "The corporate lobbyists who once ran the show, loyal only to the parochial interest of their employer, are being replaced by party activists who are loyal first and foremost to the GOP. Through them, Republican leaders can now marshal armies of lobbyists, lawyers, and public relations experts—not to mention enormous amounts of money—to meet the party's goals."[15] Ironically, the incentive to hire Republican activists was itself a pragmatic move on the part of K Street firms: if you don't hire the right people, you and your clients will be cut out of the loop, or worse. For example,

> [In 2004] retribution was taken against the Motion Picture Association of America, which—after first approaching without success a Republican congressman about to retire—hired as its new head Dan Glickman, a former Democratic representative from Kansas and secretary of agriculture in the Clinton administration. After Glickman was hired, House Republicans removed from a pending bill some $1.5 billion in tax relief for the motion picture industry. [Grover] Norquist told me [Elizabeth Drew], "No other industry is interested in taking a $1.5 billion hit

to hire a Clinton friend." After Glickman was selected, the Capitol Hill newspaper *Roll Call* reported last year, "Santorum has begun discussing what the consequences are for the movie industry." Norquist said publicly that . . . the motion picture industry's "ability to work with the House and Senate is greatly reduced."[16]

Another example of the strong-arm tactics of the Republican leadership comes from a *Washington Post* article on February 15, 2003, where it is revealed that Michael Oxley, Ohio Republican and former chairman of the House Financial Services Committee, pressured a consortium of mutual fund companies, the Investment Company Institute (ICI), to fire its chief lobbyist, Julie Domenick, who happened to be a Democrat. According to the *Post* story—which cited six sources, some of them Republican—members of Oxley's staff made it clear that a pending congressional investigation of the mutual fund industry "might ease up if the mutual fund trade group complies with their wishes." The reason for pushing Domenick out was the fact that Oxley and other law makers were interested in getting Social Security privatized, and the ICI had been somewhat resistant to the idea. Republicans believed Domenick was part of the problem.

The impact of this forced reorganization of lobbying firms went beyond K Street itself; it ramified through the corporate world as well:

> Such is the GOP's influence that it has been able to marshal on behalf of party objectives not just corporate lobbyists, but the corporations themselves. During the Iraq war, for instance, the media conglomerate Clear Channel Communications Inc. had its stations sponser [*sic*] pro-

war rallies nationwide and even banned the Dixie Chicks, who had criticized White House policy, from its national play list. Likewise, last spring Norquist and the White House convinced a number of corporations and financial service firms to lobby customers to support Bush's dividends tax cut. Firms like General Motors and Verizon included flyers touting the plan with dividends checks mailed to stockholders; Morgan Stanley included a letter from its CEO with the annual report it mailed to millions of customers.[17]

The leverage over corporations as a result of the K-street project came not only from the legislative power of Congress, but also from the new "spoils system" that was set up by members of the Republican leadership. This is the real advantage of privatization—privatization of the military, of Social Security, of Medicare, and so on. By privatizing the hallmarks of "liberal" government, one not only achieves the political objective of downsizing government but one creates windfall profits for the private-sector participants who subsequently manage the programs. But not everybody is going to make it to the feeding trough. Those who get in line and promote the Republican agenda are welcome and those who don't are free to starve. According to Paul Krugman of the *New York Times*, this was the real motivation behind President Bush's push to privatize eight hundred and fifty thousand federal jobs during his first term: those jobs become political spoils that ultimately find their way into the hands of obedient corporations.[18]

The message from the White House to the corporate world has consistently been either play ball or pay dearly:

When Bush's recently passed dividends tax cut proposal was first announced, the life insurance industry complained that the bill would sharply reduce the tax advantage of annuities sold by insurance companies, potentially costing them hundreds of millions of dollars. The industry's lobbyists were told to get behind the president's proposal anyway—or lose any chance to plead their case. So they did. In mid-March, Frank Keating, the head of the industry's trade group and a close friend of Bush's, hand-delivered a letter to the White House co-signed by nearly 50 CEOs, endorsing the president's proposal while meekly raising the hope that taxes on dividends from annuities would also be included in the final repeal (which they weren't). Those firms that didn't play ball on Bush's plan paid the price. The Electronics Industries Alliance was one of the few big business lobbies that declined to back the tax cut, in large part because the high-tech companies that make up a good portion of its membership don't even issue dividends. As a result, the trade group was frozen out of all tax discussions at the White House.[19]

So what we have, in effect, is a system of extortion for squeezing large corporations for political donations and coercing them into doing the Bush administration's bidding. By privatizing the public sector, purging K Street of Democrats and pragmatic Republicans, and controlling the way contracts are doled out to businesses (no-bid contracts offered through the Department of Defense, for example), Republicans were increasingly bringing American business capital into the fold of the Republican Party. The conventional idea that corporations own the government and lock out the American people in the interest of profit is therefore only partly true. The bigger picture is the way American government forces corporations into line by threatening to starve those businesses that diverge from the political interests of the leadership. President Bush's brother, Jeb, who just finished his second term as governor of Florida, used this very system to build the state party in Florida with impressive results. Corporations awarded contracts by the state were those that gave generously to the Republican Party. Brother Bush in the White House is looking to make this system national, something that effectively destroys the two-party system and takes us one step closer to tyranny.

Let's take a moment to reflect on the behavior of America's corporations in light of this discussion. It is commonly believed that, somehow, corporations have driven America to war with Iraq, and that the war is all about money. True, there is a lot of money to be made in war: having privatized a significant portion of the US military (from laundry and dining services to the maintenance of computers and infrastructure), tax-payer dollars are finding their way into the pockets of companies like Halliburton and Bechtel. (In effect, war has become a mechanism for redistributing wealth upward, away from the working class and toward the corporate elite). In reality, however, these corporations are serving political ends as well as financial ones. The neoconservative push for an invasion of Iraq expressed in the early 1990s and reiterated in the doctrines of the Project for the New American Century has found expression through the pay-to-play program set up by the Republican leadership. In the 2004 election cycle, Halliburton contributed more than $200k to Republicans, not to *buy* influence but to prevent itself from being locked out of a very

lucrative spoils system. Similarly, America's media corporations would have effectively hanged themselves were they to
question the motivation to go to war with Iraq (the Bush
administration would have cut off access to government officials as "sources" of news, for example). Across the board,
America's corporations increasingly depend on the good
graces of the White House to pursue their essential mission
of maximizing profit for shareholders. America's corporations are still pragmatic, it would seem, in that they are
willing to support a one-party system for the sake of profit.

It remains to be seen what kind of effect the recent political shift in Congress will have on the K Street project and
the subordination of corporate America to the GOP. On the
one hand, the Democratic majority in Congress after the
2006 midterm elections might provide the foundation for
stealing back some of the political leverage the GOP has
used to bring businesses in line with the White House's
agenda (recall that the Democratic control over congressional committees in the midnineties was used to assure significant amounts of lobbying money go to democratic
incumbents). On the other hand, the damage done by the K
Street project may prove to be so great that a power play
from the Left cannot get any real traction. It strikes us that
the latter possibility is more likely than the former, given the
very real possibility that the tables will turn in the GOP's
favor in the 2008 elections (see chapter 10) and that the
political machinery set in motion by Norquest and others
may take decades to derail. Moreover, the Democrats may
have been so emasculated at this point that the power of the
new Congress is greatly diminished. But whatever the case,
one thing is certain: the forces that have been moving

America toward fascism over the last half a century are not going away, and the degree to which those forces are entrenched in America's political institutions virtually assures a resurgence.

DECONSTRUCTING POLITICO-CORPORATE POWER

If one accepts the idea that the American people are at the mercy of the modern transnational corporation, while the corporate establishment is, in turn, at the mercy of the political leadership, one is embracing a picture of American politics in which the government utilizes the economic power of the transnational corporation as a way of influencing the attitudes and behaviors of the public. More bluntly, one is embracing a picture of American politics that looks a lot like tyranny, where the tyrants pull the strings of corporate institutions and place the American people at the center of some politico-economic drama. This is the picture of America set out by Walter Karp, and it is one that not only explains the relationship between government and special interest in terms of political rather than *economic* power, but it goes some distance in explaining how political content ends up in the mouths of corporate advertisers. As Karp notes,

> The reason for both [political favors to special interests and the rise of monopolies] is rooted in a political truth first boldly applied in America by Alexander Hamilton himself—that a political oligarchy could survive in this Republic only if it could bring into its camp a substantial portion of the wealth and social influence existing in society at large. Through the private influence of such

influential allies, the oligarchs would have at their disposal a prime requisite of their rule—a safe means to impinge directly on the minds of the citizenry and to shape them to oligarchic requirements. Men of wealth and influence would, as Hamilton expected, control in large measure the local newspapers and periodicals, reign over the church committees, sit on the boards of libraries and universities, dominate the local civic groups, groom the promising young men. Allied to corrupt rule yet immune to the electorate, they would be in a position to prescribe the expectations, shape the ideals and instruct the thinking of their fellow citizens, and, through a thousand social filaments, tincture established society with a uniform and pervasive coloration serviceable to oligarchy.[20]

Bringing the holders of wealth into the political fold requires the use of tactics that range from simple favor trading to the threat of undermining the conditions that produce wealth. Keep in mind that the relationship between government and business is not a relationship between equals: the power that government has to promote or crush business is the carrot and stick that encourage economic support for political objectives. Corporations seek to maximize shareholder value as their legal obligation.[21] And as government has the power to help or hinder that objective, corporations must get in line when those with political power demand it.[22]

So, here is a vision of American politics that goes some distance in explaining why corporations, and corporate media conglomerates in particular, seem to truck in political myths that are unrelated to the corporate pursuit of profit. For if the corporate media are to a large extent dependent for their economic advantage on those who wield political power (as they clearly are, given the dependence of media monopolies on the government's willingness to deregulate the telecommunications industry and relax corporate media ownership rules), then when those powers are interested in promoting a public myth in the interest of political advantage, the media corporations become the natural messengers.

With these reflections in mind, then, the central threat to our freedoms is not corporate power per se but the use of corporations as handmaidens for those with political power. To the powerful, corporate media provide valuable tools for diverting the attention of the public from issues that really matter, issues that relate to our capacity for self rule, our freedom, and our dignity. In the hands of political oligarchs, corporate media become the henchmen that fill the public medium, and the public mind, with half-truths and political noise. They become instruments for dumbing down the public's capacity to think by constantly promoting immediate gratification, anxiety, and a sense of utter futility in reclaiming our lives. In fact—and ironically—the popular myth that corporate power is the source of our ills works well to divert our attention from the very points we've been making here, namely, that politicians are in a position to control and direct corporate power in the interest of meeting their political objectives. In other words, the widespread belief that money controls politics diverts the public's gaze and obscures a perennial truth of politics: *power is more seductive than wealth* (corollary: *money is used in the service of power*).

Let's pause for a moment and catch our breath. We have just presented a hypothetical picture of the relationship between government, corporate America, and the people. The picture is "hypothetical" because we have factored out a widely held but erroneous assumption in presenting our case, namely, that our government reflects the will of the people rather than that of an elite group of rulers. We recognize that many will reject this picture of America as a result of their belief in the power of the electoral process to translate the people's will into policy: if our view is right, then elections would have to be a sham, and as elections are not a sham (runs the conventional wisdom), such a view must be wrong. To reason in this way may make one feel better, but it doesn't reveal the truth. The problem is, election results in America don't actually reflect the will of the people, and this makes the possibility of a ruling elite more than a mere hypothetical.

In the next chapter, we will show that the idea that America is not a democracy is more than just an idea—it is in fact *true*. As you will see, there is very little the Bush administration and its hired henchmen will *not* do in the service of the ideal of a New American Century.

NOTES

1. Howard Zinn, *A People's History of the United States* (New York: New Press, 1997), p. 59.

2. Noam Chomsky, *Hegemony or Survival: America's Quest for Global Dominance* (New York: Metropolitan Books, 2003), pp. 6–7.

3. George Creel, "How We Advertised America," http://www.historytools.org/sources/creel.html (accessed February 14, 2007).

4. Edward Bernays, *Propaganda* (New York: Ig Publishing, 1928), p. 37.

5. Ibid., p. 38.

6. All quotations in this paragraph are cited in Noam Chomsky, *Necessary Illusions: Thought Control in Democratic Societies* (Boston: South End Press, 1989), pp. 16–17.

7. Shadia B. Drury, *Leo Strauss and the American Right* (New York: St. Martin's, 1999), p. 37.

8. Earl Shorris, "Ignoble Liars: Leo Strauss, George Bush, and the Philosophy of Mass Deception," *Harpers*, June 2004, p. 66.

9. Patrick E. Tyler, "U.S. Strategy Plan Calls for Insuring No Rivals Develop a One-Superpower World," *New York Times*, March 8, 2002.

10. Ibid.

11. See Joel Bakan, *The Corporation: The Pathological Pursuit of Profit and Power* (New York: Free Press, 2004), pp. 21–25.

12. "Rebuilding America's Defenses: Strategy, Focus, and Resources for a New Century," http://www.newamericancentury.org/RebuildingAmericasDefenses.pdf (accessed February 14, 2007).

13. Drury, *Leo Strauss and the American Right*, p. 23.

14. Nicholas Confessore, "Welcome to the Machine: How the GOP Disciplined K Street and Made Bush Supreme," *Washington Monthly*, July/August 2003.

15. Ibid.

16. Elizabeth Drew, "Selling Washington," *New York Review of Books* 52, no. 11 (June 23, 2005).

17. Confessore, "Welcome to the Machine."

18. Paul Krugman, "Victors and Spoils," *New York Times*, November 19, 2002.

19. Confessore, "Welcome to the Machine."

20. Walter Karp, *Indispensable Enemies: The Politics of Misrule in America* (New York: Franklin Square Press, 1993), p. 168.

21. *Dodge v. Ford*, cited in Bakan, *The Corporation*.

22. Karp, *Indispensable Enemies*, pp. 173–74.

Chapter 10

DEMOCRACY
IN A BLACK BOX

When historians look back on America at the turn
of the millennium in decades and centuries
hence, one of the biggest stories is sure to be the contentious
presidential election of 2000. Losing the popular vote, the
commander in chief would be ushered in by a controversial
Supreme Court ruling that stopped a recount of ballots in the
hotly contested state of Florida, a state governed by the
brother of the soon-to-be president-elect. This pivotal decision by the Supreme Court would, as it turns out, flout the
will of the people and hand the presidency to George W.
Bush, the prodigal son of the forty-first United States president. Surely these future historians will note the fact that
once the votes in Florida were counted, Al Gore, Bush's
opposition, emerged as the winner (regardless of the criteria
used in the recount), that the exit polls predicting Gore as the
winner—polls used as the basis for the media's initial pro-

jections putting Gore ahead—were accurate, and, despite these facts, the presidency was given to the GOP candidate.[1]

How the rest of the story may go is less clear, however. Future historians might note that in the aftermath of the worst terrorist attack on American soil in 225 years, George W. Bush found his stride, earned the country's respect and admiration, and secured a solid victory in the 2004 presidential race—a victory that secured a political mandate to continue the policies adumbrated in his first four years. Perhaps historians will note the enormous debt Mr. Bush owed to his confidante and political adviser Karl Rove, who helped engineer the social and political climate that would favor the GOP (pitting conservatives against liberals over the issue of family values). Or perhaps history will judge the Bush administration more harshly, noting the cost of a protracted war in the Middle East initiated on the pretext of an imminent threat of weapons of mass destruction in the hands of a brutal dictator. What may not appear in our future textbooks, and what is arguably the most important story of this tumultuous period, is that the US electoral process was hijacked by the GOP in President Bush's first term in office, and that systematic election fraud, not the will of the American people, changed the political landscape in a way that would affect domestic and foreign policy for years to come. Such reflections are unlikely to appear, because political victors write the history books, and this is a piece of American history that the political establishment—Democrats and Republicans—would rather have swept under the rug. The story, legitimate by any rational standard, has been systematically obfuscated by the MSM, even by such "bastions of liberal thought" as the *New York Times*.

THE HELP AMERICA VOTE ACT
(AKA: THE HELP TO END FREE ELECTIONS IN AMERICA ACT)

Unfortunately, one of the great historical ironies will be lost on posterity as a result of an oversight, namely, that it was the election debacle of 2000 that established the conditions that allowed the political establishment to wrest from the hands of the American people what little power remained over those who ruled in their name. In response to the infighting, political maneuvering, and the criminal activity that led to the installation of George W. Bush at the helm of the ship of state, Congress passed the Help America Vote Act (HAVA) in 2002, ostensibly to eliminate the conditions that led to the Florida fiasco.[2] In practice, it was this piece of legislation that effectively turned over the electoral process to the private sector, a move that paved the way for systematic and widespread election fraud in 2004, election fraud that had been piloted in the 2002 midterm elections (see below). As Democrats prepared to combat the forces that had kept them in power in 2000—positioning attorneys at voting precincts across the country, setting up voter hotlines and legal interdiction units—the GOP had already changed the rules of the game. As Rep. Peter King (R-NY) stated at a barbeque at the White House in the summer of 2003, "It's already over [i.e., the 2004 presidential election]. The election's over. We won. . . . It's all over but the counting. And we'll take care of the counting."[3] King's remarks were, he later reflected, merely playful banter, but the events of November 2004 make the remarks appear both ominous and prophetic.

The Help America Vote Act was meant to prevent

another hanging chad from hanging up the election process by allocating money for the use of electronic voting machines across the nation. These machines, designed and manufactured by private corporations with intimate connections to the GOP, replaced difficult paper ballots with touchscreen technology that ostensibly is easy to use. The sleek, clean lines of these voting machines and the appeal of computerized efficiency made for easy sales, and companies like Electronic Systems & Software, Inc. (ES&S), Diebold Inc., and Triton Inc. began supplying Florida, Ohio, and a host of other states with the machines they would need for the elections of the twenty-first century. Americans could feel secure that their votes would not be mishandled by partisan election officials and that the integrity of elections was ensured by the clean, sterile hand of technology.

What Americans did not know, and what should *clearly* have been a topic of inquiry in the press, was that these machines are inauditable: they produce no paper trail, they operate by methods that cannot be observed or verified for accuracy except by inspecting the source code (i.e., the program) that tabulates the votes. What the press failed to reveal while it lauded Congress for redressing the failures of 2000 (and the illegitimate president who signed it into law) was that by using paperless voting machines to tabulate the vote Congress had effectively privatized the electoral process. Without input from the people, without an audible voice of concern from the press (save for an occasional editorial), the GOP saw to it that a handful of American corporations would take over the responsibility of monitoring and managing the process by which Americans choose their leaders, a process that is the very foundation of democracy itself. The press also failed to inform the American people that the same corporations that were managing the vote in half the states of the Union were run by longtime GOP supporters (people like Wally O'Dell, president of Diebold Inc., who at a fundraiser in 2003 pledged his unequivocal support for President Bush and committed himself to the task of giving the state of Ohio to the president in the impending 2004 presidential election).

Had the press been doing its job—serving as the watchdog of democracy—it would have been breaking the news that the software developed by the corporations that design and build electronic voting machines is proprietary, and hence that the contracts between these companies and the states that use their products forbid anyone other than representatives of the companies from examining the source code that tabulates the votes. No election official, no representative from a political party, and no citizens' advocate can examine the program on which our democracy now hinges. Those who know anything about computer programming know how utterly dangerous this is. The source code used in these machines can be written to produce virtually any desired result—a 2 percent redistribution from one candidate to another, a final distribution of 48 percent to 52 percent, or a margin of victory for a candidate specified in terms of the actual number of votes, and so on—*and none of these results can be verified or refuted by observation.*

To put matters plainly, in an environment with no meaningful oversight and no paper trail, vote tampering can occur virtually undetected. As M. K. Dooner, founder of Florida-based Deep Sky Technologies and an expert on the technical aspects of electronic voting puts the point: "There are virtually no limits to the way votes can be distributed. . . . Programmers can write code that is self-erasing and redistributes votes to conform to whatever outside interests are operative, and without any kind of traceability."[4] Dooner's reflections are reinforced by a Johns Hopkins University study in which researchers note that "[s]oftware flaws in a leading US electronic voting system could be used to subvert the outcome of an election."[5] Unwary voters are likely to overlook this point, since computer displays give them a visual confirmation of how they voted; the visual display gives a false sense of security that the vote has been cast for the candidate in question. What people fail to realize is that the name posted on the computer screen *has absolutely nothing to do with how their vote is actually tabulated.* One could use the touch-screen button to vote for Smith, and that vote might actually be recorded as a vote for Jones, even though the computer screen says, "You've voted for Smith." This is what is meant by "Black Box Voting": there simply is no way to know how your vote has been counted.

To make the problems with this current system clear, consider the following thought experiment. Suppose that instead of voting on an electronic machine, you must write your vote down on a slip of paper and hand it over to an election official. In addition, suppose that election official sits alone at a desk in a room with no windows. There is a single door at the front of the room, through which you, the voter, enter when you are ready to cast your vote. Behind the official is an opaque screen suspended between the ceiling and the floor by fixed posts of metallic gray (the screen divides the room in half, but you cannot see what's happening on the other side). On the back of the screen is a chalkboard facing the rear of the room and completely out of view. Now, you've written down your choice for president and hand it to the official; expressionless, the official looks at the card, stands up, and walks behind the screen. There, he puts a single mark in one of two columns set up beforehand to tabulate the vote and then puts the piece of paper you handed him into a shredder. When he's finished, he emerges from behind the screen, sits down at his desk, and hands you a piece of paper with the following inscription: "Your vote has been cast." Secure in the knowledge that you've done your patriotic duty, you get up and leave. The question is, how has your vote been recorded?

The answer is that you have no idea. You don't know whether the official cast your vote for your candidate, the opposing candidate, or whether he simply added it to a "throw away" column that counts for nothing. The integrity of the vote in this scenario depends entirely on the integrity of the election official—on his honesty and willingness to cast the vote as you intended it. At the end of the day, an election official announces the winner and even gives you the percentage by which the victor pulled off his precious victory. But there is no way to verify the accuracy of these numbers, since the slips of paper on which the votes were originally indicated were destroyed. Clearly, a system like this would never be accepted in the real world and yet this is essentially the way our votes are recorded on electronic voting machines. What you see on the actual screen means absolutely nothing; it's like the piece of paper that says, "Your vote has been cast."

In actual fact, the situation with electronic voting machines is considerably worse than this scenario suggests.

Currently there is no governmental oversight of the production of these machines and no background checks are required for employees of the companies that build them. Moreover, the people who manage the vote have very strong political leanings of their own. So, imagine that our election official is also a member of one of the parties represented in the election, that he has given generously to that party, and that he will personally benefit if his candidate wins. With no oversight, no check on his power to adjust the vote, is it plausible that this person will not take advantage of his power? The answer for most of us is that the temptation would be too great. After all, no one is watching. No one is standing over his shoulder to make sure that the votes are being correctly tabulated. Dishonesty in this circumstance not only pays, but there is virtually no danger of being caught.

The only way to tell whether the election is fraudulent is if someone is standing outside and asking voters as they exit, "Who did you vote for?"—that, and records of the party membership for various voting districts, historical trends for those districts, and surveys of candidate popularity. To continue our little thought experiment, we might imagine that you live in a district that has traditionally voted for one of the two parties—call it Party X, that the opposing candidate, a member of Party Y, has a low public approval rating, and that the majority of voters who answered the question "Who did you vote for?" as they left the voting booth indicated that they voted for the favorite son (the Party X candidate). So when the election official comes out at the end of the day and announces that the unpopular candidate Y, against all odds, won the election, you'd be suspicious. But how could you turn mere suspicion into a rational, factually based judgment that election tampering had taken place? The problem is that most people assume that one *can't* make such a judgment, that any claim about tampering is "mere speculation."

In the case of our hypothetical voting room, people might well argue against the results and stand firm on the judgment that it is highly likely that the partisan election official altered the vote (just as the electorate in Ukraine took to the streets in protest after exit polls—funded by the Bush administration—revealed that their presidential election was fraudulent). Election fraud is nothing new, after all, and our intuitive understanding of human nature is a good rule of thumb by which to judge the behavior of others. In such circumstances, it seems pretty clear that charges of election fraud are more than mere speculation, given the way people look out for their own interests and, unfortunately, exploit the ignorance of others. But with electronic voting machines, human nature is at a considerable remove from the voting process, which creates the *illusion* that there is less potential for human intervention and hence that claims about election fraud are illegitimate. Coupled with America's faith in technology and the almost complete suppression of the issue by the MSM, it is hardly surprising that the majority of Americans view claims about election fraud a la electronic voting machines as utterly kooky.

Another contributing factor to the dismissal of the election fraud issue is the lack of context in which to make sense of the stolen 2004 presidential race. Who would do such a thing and why? Who would be able to cover up such widespread election fraud, and why wouldn't some patriotic election official who recognized the terrible disservice to America being perpetrated by such fraud stand up and say something? Without knowing much about politics, corporate America's allegiance to government, and the elitism that has become an integral part of the justification of power, most Americans cannot help but dismiss the election fraud issue as a result of deranged minds. *Liberals* must be behind such ideas, those immoral, godless heathens—the enemy within.

The prior chapters of this book, taken together, can help us make sense of the electronic voting racket currently being run by the Bush administration. The idea that the corporate media are unwilling to jeopardize their financial well-being by reporting on Bush's election antics is certainly a big part of the picture, and we have gone to great lengths to demonstrate the subservience of the corporate media to power. A crucial part of the election fraud story is the way the Republican Party has forced corporate America to fall in line behind the Bush administration and carry out its bidding (recall the K Street Project discussed in the last chapter). Without understanding the political power that directs corporate activity, you might look at the failure of the media as a matter of money alone. From this limited perspective, you might understandably be puzzled by the idea that members of the corporate world aren't standing up for American democracy in the face of the Bush administration's onslaught ("Surely some people in the corporate world must have a conscience.") However, what people overlook is that corporations go along with the Bush administration because not doing so would be the virtual nail on the corporate coffin.

Personal survival is also at stake these days. After 9/11, Americans' civil liberties were seriously curtailed by the PATRIOT Act, by the odd combination of patriotism and fear that led people to voluntarily silence themselves and others, and by the growing realization that Bush & Co. were not all that interested in protecting the Constitution and the Bill of Rights. As you have seen (chapter 7), the Bush administration has threatened to prosecute journalists who publish stories that bear on national security issues, even if those issues are obviously relevant to the public interest. NSA domestic wiretaps, the monitoring of financial transactions of US citizens (monitoring that includes not only what books you purchase online but where your money is, how much you have, and where it is transferred). At the time of this writing, the US Supreme Court has weakened the restrictions on law enforcement to enter a citizen's home by eliminating the "knock and announce rule"—the requirement that officers announce themselves at your door before they enter with a search warrant; it has also eliminated the protections for corporate whistleblowers who reveal the illegal activities of their employers. The holding of prisoners at Guantánamo Bay under the unfortunate denomination "unlawful enemy combatant"; the use of torture and secret prisons; the treasonous act of revealing the identity of a covert CIA agent for political retribution—all of this creates a climate of fear and intimidation that prevents people from standing up and speaking out. Who wants to be the focus of an FBI probe or have their reputation smeared? Who wants to lose their job and the little financial security that comes with it? Americans are currently at the mercy of men who are for all intents and purposes above the law and who have no interest in protecting our rights. Fear is quite rational under these circumstances.

In chapter 9, you have seen the strong, antidemocratic leanings of the neoconservatives, a point that rounds out the election fraud picture. America's most influential political operators don't have moral scruples about stealing elections *because they believe you don't deserve to vote.* Governance is a matter for statesmen, for the übermensch of the American right, for those with genuine virtue—and don't kid yourself, in their eyes you don't have any. Carnes Lord, the Straussian who served on the National Security Council and as Dan Quayle's chief foreign policy adviser, said as much in his book *The Modern Prince: What Leaders Need to Know.* Lord, who in many ways reflects the views of all Straussians in this work, praises the autocrat who acts to control elites (the corporate oligarchs), manages the details of education, and disregards the nation's constitution for the sake of dictatorial power. The Straussian connection to the Bush administration is unquestionable, and the vision of a government run exclusively by the executive branch is the preferred model for the New American Century. The idea that these people are interested in fair elections is absurd, and recognizing this fact fleshes out the context in which the election fraud story must be understood.

So *for us* the context should be clear. Election fraud is not only a possibility in our current political climate but a reality. The idea that the companies that manufacture and monitor the voting machines currently in use are populated with GOP supporters should hardly be surprising in light of the logic of the K Street Project. The idea that ES&S, Diebold, and the handful of other manufacturers are thoroughly dependent on the good graces of the Bush administration should hardly come as a surprise given the GOP's push to privatize public services and make the spoils available only to the party faithful. (In the case of voting machine manufacturers, the dependence on government is all the more striking: the only purchasers of voting machines are governments, and hence government has the power to make or break a company like Diebold with the stroke of a pen. Voting machine manufacturers don't even have a consuming public to fall back on to save the bottom line.) And, finally, the elitism of the neocons who have shaped and controlled the Bush administration should shatter any illusions about the commitment of those in power to free and fair elections.[6]

THE UNIMPEACHABLE EVIDENCE FOR WIDESPREAD, SYSTEMATIC VOTING FRAUD

We have just considered the framework in which the election fraud issue makes more sense, but does this framework justify the assertion that the Republican Party stole the election? Many authors are a little cautious when it comes to saying that the 2004 presidential election was *in fact* fraudulent, because they know that even conditions that make fraud more likely can't guarantee that it actually took place. But to qualify a claim about election fraud with expressions like *possible*, and *could have happened* is to misunderstand the force of the evidence and the standards of reasonableness that allow us to speak more definitively.

Make no mistake about it: *the 2004 presidential election was stolen by the GOP*. That is a *fact*. The evidence for this claim is overwhelming. Take the exit polls. Exit polling is a method by which the outcome of an election is predicted using a variety of well-tested, empirically valid survey instruments. Polling usually takes the form of a brief survey, written or oral, administered by a professional pollster after a voter has already cast her vote (unlike polling before an election, which requires that voters predict how they *will* vote, exit polling focuses on what voters have *actually* done). The methodologies of this science have continually evolved over more than half a century of experience. Making accurate predictions of election results, in fact, involves three steps:

(1) In each state a set of representative precincts is chosen that mirrors the state as a whole in demography and historic voting patterns.
(2) Voters from those precincts are randomly selected for polling as they exit the polling place.
(3) In constructing a prediction for statewide outcomes, algebraic weightings are used to correct for the observed demographic composition of the sample. For example, responders are rebalanced by race and gender in this process to ensure a representative sampling of the state.[7]

Historically, exit polls have been so reliable that they are used in emerging democracies to determine whether or not election fraud has taken place. In the former Soviet Republic of Georgia, for example, the 2004 parliamentary elections were monitored using exit polls sponsored by international foundations. When the official results of that election did not jibe with the exit poll predictions—predictions that indicated the opposition party was victorious—Eduard A. Shevardnadze, the prime minister, was forced to resign under pressure from the US government.[8] The same year, exit polls of voters in Ukraine provided information that motivated

Republican senator Richard Lugar to offer a scathing review of the Ukrainian presidential election: "A concerted and forceful program of election-day fraud and abuse was enacted with either the leadership or cooperation of governmental authorities."[9] Dick Morris, a Republican polling consultant and regular on Fox News, put the reliability of exit polls in perspective immediately following our own 2004 presidential contest: "Exit polls are almost never wrong. . . . To screw up one exit poll is unheard of. To miss six of them is incredible. It boggles the imagination how pollsters could be that incompetent and invites speculation that more than honest error was at play here."[10] District to district, there were far more than six exit polls that diverged significantly from the final tallies in the 2004 presidential election.

Morris's reflections are backed up by Steven F. Freemen of the University of Pennsylvania, who, in a paper released to the public on November 10, 2004, notes that the statistical likelihood of exit polls being as far off the mark as they were on election night in three of the battleground states—Ohio, Pennsylvania, and Florida—is 660,000 to one.[11] (Freemen used polling data that were not adjusted by the networks to fit with the official tally).[12] When you consider that exit polls failed to predict the correct outcome in nine out of the eleven battleground states, and that in every case the error showed that Kerry would be the victor, the statistical likelihood that the exit polls were off by chance becomes a practical impossibility. "When you look at the numbers, there is a tremendous amount of data that supports the supposition of election fraud. . . . The discrepancies are higher in battleground states, higher where there were Republican governors, higher in states with greater proportions of African-American communities and higher in states where there were the most Election Day complaints. All these are strong indicators of fraud—and yet this supposition has been utterly ignored by the press and, oddly, by the Democratic Party."[13] According to Robert F. Kennedy Jr., writing for *Rolling Stone Magazine*, the evidence for fraud was especially strong in Ohio. In nearly half of the precincts polled the results differed widely from the official vote tally and were almost invariably stacked in favor of Bush. In one precinct, Kerry should have received 67 percent of the vote according to the exit polls, yet the official tally gave him only 38 percent. According to Kennedy, "The statistical odds against such a variance are just shy of one in 3 billion."[14]

Well, not knowing anything about the science of polling, you might dismiss such reflections by saying that there is always the possibility that there was some systematic problem with the exit polls, for example, that too many women or not enough Republicans were surveyed, but to attribute this kind of blatant error to polling agencies is itself problematic. Not only are such errors easy to spot and correct, but the corporate bodies that make polling their bread and butter (in this case, Edison Media Research and Mitofsky International) would have filed for bankruptcy long ago as the result of such blatant incompetence. Curiously, two months after the election, and despite the fact that Edison/Mitofsky could find nothing wrong with the methodology employed during the election, pollsters floated a bogus reason for the discrepancy: Bush supporters were apparently reluctant to talk to pollsters after they had voted. But, as Kennedy points out, careful independent examination of the polling data by Steven Freeman and a team of eight researchers showed just the opposite: that it was *Democrats*, not Republicans who were more reluctant to respond to pollsters' questions on Election Day.[15]

Freeman and his research team discovered that 56 percent of the voters in Bush strongholds took the exit surveys provided by pollsters, while only 53 percent of the voters in Kerry country completed the survey, a finding that contradicts the official claim regarding the discrepancy between the exit polls and the official results. Moreover, it was in the Republican districts where the exit polls seemed to go haywire: "In precincts where Bush received at least eighty percent of the vote, the exit polls were off by an average of ten percent. By contrast, in precincts where Kerry dominated by eighty percent or more, the exit polls were accurate to within three tenths of one percent—a pattern that suggests Republican election officials stuffed the ballot box in Bush country."[16]

Given the scientific nature of exit polling, its rigorous methodology and remarkable accuracy, the rational judgment to make is that it was the official vote count that was flawed and that the exit polls got it right. We could go even further and say that, given the fact that no paper trail exists by which to verify the accuracy of the official tally, the only judgment that squares with the evidence is that the exit polls were correct.

Now, something as sensitive as stuffing the ballot box on a national scale shouldn't be attempted cold. The thieves should at least have a *test run* to see if stealing an election with the help of electronic voting machines is really feasible. And, as noted above, the GOP had such a test run in 2002. Faced with an evenly divided Senate (until Jim Jeffords of Vermont changed his allegiance in 2001 to put Republican senators in the minority), the GOP needed a boost in the first midterm election of the Bush presidency to take control of Congress (pushing through unpopular legislation requires strong political allies, after all). Enter Saxby Chambliss and Norm Coleman. Chambliss is the junior senator from Georgia who, despite remarkable odds against him, usurped the Senate seat from Democrat Max Cleland, the Vietnam veteran who lost three limbs fighting for his country (Chambliss apparently couldn't manage service in Vietnam because of a "bad knee"). Coleman is the junior senator from Minnesota who took over after the unexpected death of the popular Democratic senator Paul Wellstone and a highly improbable victory over former presidential candidate Walter Mondale. Needless to say, a lot was riding on these elections, so it was important to ensure a clean contest: Diebold and ES&S machines were used in over 70 percent of the counties in Minnesota, while the midterm election in Georgia used Diebold machines in over 65 percent of its counties.

Saxby Chambliss pulled off a victory over Max Cleland, 51 percent to 46 percent, despite the fact that Chambliss was behind in the polls 49 percent to 44 percent shortly before Election Day.[17] Norm Coleman, who was 5 percentage points behind Walter Mondale prior to the election, pulled off a victory by 2.2 percentage points. Other races were also suspect, including the race for governor in Georgia, where Republican Sunny Purdue beat Gov. Roy Barnes despite being down 9 percentage points prior to the election (the official count in Purdue's favor was a staggering 52 to 45 percent).[18] As Mark Crispin Miller notes in his detailed account of the election fraud issue, "In Colorado, Republican Wayne Allard, a born-again with a 100 percent approval rating from the Christian Coalition, beat Democrat Tom Strickland by nearly five percentage points, although the polls had shown the Democrat ahead by several points. (Diebold touch-screen machines were used in Saguache, Weld and El Paso Counties, collectively accounting for over 750,000 votes. Strickland lost by 70,000 votes)."[19]

The likelihood of these races suddenly flipping in favor of the underdog is slim indeed. You have a better chance of winning the lottery or of being struck by lightning twice in the same week. Yet the GOP would have us believe that the results are a consequence of good political tactics developed by strategists like Karl Rove. Such nonsense is pure propaganda and serves to hide the malfeasance of the Bush administration and its allies.

Then there is the story of Senator Chuck Hagel of Nebraska who, in 1996, pulled out two improbable victories during his meteoric rise to the Senate. Right up until two weeks before he announced his candidacy for the Senate, Hagel had been chairman of American Information Systems (AIS), the company that would become ES&S after merging with Business Records Corporation (which, in turn, was part of Cronus Industries—a holding company controlled by a handful of influential far-right activists).[20] AIS produced the voting machines that calculated as many as 85 percent of the votes cast in the senatorial race, a race in which Hagel defeated a better-known Republican candidate in the primary on his way to a landslide victory over a popular Democratic governor who had led in the polls the entire race.[21] No doubt Hagel's victories in the mid-1990s were the source of exuberance for Karl Rove and the neoconservatives in the GOP.

But it would be misleading to pin all the blame on electronic voting machines and the people who build them. In 2000 America witnessed the bare-knuckle tactics of the GOP firsthand in Florida—tactics that included intimidation of black voters, phony felon lists, hired thugs sent by Tom DeLay to stop the recount, a secretary of state who did all that could be done to push the election in Bush's favor, and so on. The same tactics and more were employed in 2004 (most visibly in Ohio, thanks to the highly partisan and deeply immoral secretary of state Kenneth Blackwell), and the outcome of the election was no doubt swayed by these methods as well. Too few voting machines in Democratic precincts and plenty in Republican; leaving John Kerry's name off some of the paper ballots; discarding registration cards for Democrats over mere technicalities; using machines with a higher failure rate in Democratic districts; throwing out "spoiled" ballots; excluding voters casting their ballots from overseas; telling Democrats in poor areas that they are to vote on November 3 (the day after the election), and a litany of other tactics were employed across the nation that created a cumulative effect that pushed the election in the same general direction. These tactics, coupled with the willful failure to fix well-known problems and discrepancies when they act in one's favor (*strategic neglect*), were widespread and well documented, a fact that itself insinuates an underlying method to the apparent chaos.[22] Electronic voting machines are part of this larger story, though their role was clearly central in stealing the election.

But how could the GOP pull all this off without the voters catching wind of things beforehand? After all, election fraud on a scale such as this would have to involve a lot of money and a lot of people. One must keep in mind that

the central players in the theft of a presidential election are
people with extraordinary financial and political means. For
example, the Bush family has all sorts of interesting connections with foreign investors, offshore corporate entities,
trusts, and bank accounts that could be used to transfer funds
to political operatives for the purpose of financing the theft
of an election. The family's connections with Saudi
investors through the Carlyle Group (Saudi investors owned
a majority share of Election.com—an online voting and
voter registration company involved in the 2004 election)—
as well as the close political association between Bush
senior and Adnan Khashoggi, an arms broker between the
US government and the Saudi government in the 1970s,
raises some interesting possibilities when it comes to understanding the forces that move American government
(Khashoggi was implicated in the Iran-Contra arms-for-
hostages scandal as the middle man between Oliver North
and the Iranian mullahs).[23] One of Khashoggi's business
clients is Lockheed Martin, the defense contractor that
works with NASA and subcontracts work to Yang Enterprises, Inc.; Yang Enterprises is the company that employed
Clint Curtis, the computer programmer who in testimony
before the Conyers hearings on election fraud claimed that
he had been approached by Florida representative Tom
Feeney and asked to write a program to switch votes unde-
tectably to help the GOP.[24] These connections (Khashoggi
—Lockheed Martin—Yang Enterprises, Inc.), as well as
those between the companies that manage the vote and the
GOP, suggest interesting lines of influence, both financial
and political, that could be used for the purposes of stealing
an election. (It is worth noting that Lockheed Martin, as well

as the defense contractor Northrup Grumman, lobbied hard to get HAVA passed, the legislation that paved the way for the use of electronic voting machines. It hardly needs stating that these defense contractors profited handsomely from having the bellicose Bush serve a second term as Commander in Chief.)[25]

One of the companies that helped make Bush president in 2004 was Sproul & Associates, a fledgling company founded by a young warrior of the Right by the name of Nathan Sproul. Sproul & Associates was hired by the GOP to accomplish two tasks: to stem the tide of the considerable effort to register new Democrats to vote in 2004 and to create the appearance that Democrats were jumping ship and reregistering as Republicans. To that end, Sproul operatives destroyed registration cards of Democrats and used fake petitions that tricked young Democrats into inadvertently registering as Republicans.[26] The purpose of suppressing the Democratic vote by eliminating registration cards is obvious; what is not obvious is why getting Democrats to register as Republicans would be an important objective (they could still vote for Kerry, even if they do so as Republicans). The answer is, it creates the appearance of legitimacy for the official vote count after the fact. If it appears that significant numbers of Democrats turned Republican, then one has a cover for how the GOP pulled off such an improbable victory. In any event, Sproul & Associates played a significant role in suppressing the Democratic vote and creating political cover for the Bush administration. The Republican National Committee (RNC) hid the costs of hiring Sproul & Associates under the heading "Political Consulting" in its reports to the Federal Election Commission, the government organization that oversees election spending, as well as under other bogus rubrics. At the end of the day, "all the payments by the RNC to Sproul add up to a whopping $8,359,161—making it the RNC's eighth-largest expenditure of the 2004 campaign, and a major piece of evidence suggesting that the party broke the bank to fix the national vote for president."[27] Yet despite the considerable evidence of an institutional effort to thwart the democratic process, a full investigation was never made, and the corporate media remained mum.

There is also the occasional telltale slip-up by government officials. A recent example of this is the case of Timothy Griffin, Karl Rove's assistant and Bush's pick to replace the US attorney for the Eastern District of Arkansas. (In fact, several federal prosecutors were fired when they refused to cave to heavy-handed and improper political pressure from Republican lawmakers.) In October 2004, in a scheme to divest 70,000 mostly Black and Hispanic voters from Democratic precincts of their voting right, Griffin e-mailed "Caging" lists of voters marked for challenge to the e-mail address GeorgeWBush.org. Only he had intended them for RNC cronies at GeorgeWBush.com. Confusing the "org" with the "com" in these addresses, the e-mail messages instead went to a John Wooden, owner of GeorgeW Bush.org, who in turn forwarded the messages to independent journalist Greg Palast, who analyzed the lists and uncovered the voting fraud scheme. The story was posted to Palast's Web site and progressive media such as Air America played it up, but, not surprisingly, the corporate MSM failed to pick up the story.

We could go on ad nauseam about the evidence—about

the political associations, the business connections, the tactics, and the illegality—but by now some basic principles should be clear. While the corporate media dismiss exit polls as off the mark (a claim that is entirely predictable in light of the connection between government and the press), the truth is that the exit polls got it right and the media simply buried the issue. The claim that exit polls were correct and that John Kerry was the legitimate winner of the 2004 presidential race is as certain as any scientific claim on the books: if you believe in the power of modern medicine to heal, in the reality of space flight, or in the claim that the earth is more than six thousand years old, then you should believe that exit polls are reliable predictors of election results. And when you consider the exit polls in light of the mountains of evidence that point to election fraud, as well as the political context laid out in this book, the level of certainty only increases. The GOP stole the 2004 presidential election, just as they stole crucial senate races in 2002.

But don't the results of the 2006 midterm elections, elections in which the Democrats managed to take back both houses of Congress, show that such claims are overblown or false? Don't those results demonstrate that our election system, though flawed at points, is still responsive to the will of the people? The answer is a resounding "No!" It is true that the election results were a setback for the GOP—clearly, the Republicans wanted to keep control of Congress—but this setback is largely insignificant, for several reasons.

First, to jump from the observation that the Democrats won in 2006 to the idea that the voting machines work properly is a catastrophic failure of reason. The problems with the machines are well established, and where "failures" and "anomalies" appeared in the 2006 election—for example, in Florida'a Thirteenth Congressional District and North Carolina's Eighth Congressional district—the trend favored Republicans over their Democratic challengers.[28] The bottom line is that the machines are still in place, still manufactured by the same companies, and still subject to influence by the same political and financial powers that have thwarted the will of the people in the last three national elections. To find comfort in the 2006 election results is to thoroughly misjudge the scope and nature of the election fraud issue.

Second, Congress is largely irrelevant at this point. Already the newly elected Democratic Congress has betrayed a clear mandate from the American people by struggling lamely to pass a *nonbinding* resolution against escalating the Iraq war while quietly bracing to fund it. The Democrats may make a fuss about this and that over the next few years, but nothing of substance need be done—and Bush knows it. Letting Congress go is already proving to be an empty concession that conveniently helps to lessen public skepticism about the legitimacy of elections and creates the false impression that democracy in America is still working.

Third, we are still in the relatively early stages of the GOP/PNAC's election management project, and as a result certain variables could not be controlled in the 2006 election. For example, the fact that the voting system in America is a chaotic patchwork of state and local guidelines, procedures, and methods—a patchwork that has been exploited in the days of yesteryear to both perpetrate and whitewash election fraud—now works against a systematic, nationalized attempt to skew election results across the board. Without a national system in place that allows political operatives to manage contingencies on the ground close to election day, there is always the chance that one will overestimate the influence of vote tampering or underestimate the ferocity of the political opposition in certain districts. In 2006, the GOP, recognizing that a wide margin of victory would dispel the illusion of election legitimacy in light of Bush's unpopularity, may have sought to maintain power by too slim a margin. Had the will of the people been truly reflected in the outcome, the Democrats might have gained more seats in both the House and the Senate. As public suspicion about the legitimacy of elections grows in coming years, it is likely that a national election system will be seriously considered, a system that would allow for a more seamless management of the vote.

How, then, are we to interpret the 2006 midterm elections? Karl Rove is certainly interpreting the results as an opportunity to consolidate power even further and lay the groundwork for a GOP "victory" in the much more important 2008 presidential race. And he is right to be optimistic. With the Democrats in a nominal position of power in Congress, the next two years can be used to lay the blame for a failed Iraq policy at their feet, to cast them as obstructionist and anti-American, and to use these manufactured failings as a way to lessen the chance of Republicans losing the next presidential election. In addition, as many Americans are likely to look at 2006 as an indication that fears of fraud are unfounded, a stolen election in 2008 will be easier to cover up than if the Republicans had won big in 2006. Karl Rove has built his political career on turning disadvantages into advantages and on using the power of illusions to hide the truth. Our current situation may be no different.

This is why one should be deeply skeptical about the

emerging interest in establishing a paper trail for electronic voting. At the time of this writing, the new Republican governor of Florida, Charlie Crist, is pressing for the establishment of a paper trail in response to public concerns over the integrity of electronic voting machines, and Rep. Rush Holt (D-NJ) has presented a bill in the House that would amend the Help America Vote Act to require paper trails for electronic voting machines.[29] But don't count on such measures, even if passed, to fix our broken election system. Like HAVA, this legislation may still be used to perpetuate the illusion of integrity of while hiding new tactics for undermining our democracy. As Daniel P. Tokaji, an assistant professor of law at Ohio State University, notes in his review of a "voter-verified paper audit trail"(VVPAT) piloted in Ohio in 2006,

> A closer examination of this type of VVPAT system reveals difficulties, both legal and practical, that could arise in the event of a recount. On the practical side, an in-depth study of the equipment used in . . . Ohio's May primary election showed that 10% of the VVPAT records were in some way compromised. Among the problems were blank VVPAT tapes, accordion-style crumpling, destroyed VVPATs, printing anomalies, and missing text.[30]

These practical issues give rise to legal issues about the way the law governing a recount uses VVPATs. A 2004 statute passed by the Ohio state legislature reads:

> For any recount of an election in which ballots are cast using a direct electronic voting machine with a voter verified audit trail, the voter verified paper audit trail shall serve as the official ballot to be recounted. ORC 3506.18.

This statute gives the public a false sense of security, however. This is because Ohio's office of the Secretary of State has issued "standards" for implementing the statute that could in principle be used to undermine the value of the paper trail: "In the case of a difference between the electronic record and the paper record copy, the paper record copy shall govern, *unless there is clear evidence that the paper record is inaccurate, incomplete or unreadable* as defined in the system procedures." While the statute is supposed to trump the guidelines issued by the secretary of state, the potential for legal wrangling and fraud is clearly evident here. One should expect similar problems to arise in Florida if comparable legislation is passed there.

The lifeline of democracy is free elections. If we, as citizens, can vote out a corrupt regime and replace it with a government that truly represents the will of the American people, then there is still hope for the future of democracy in America. Unfortunately, in light of the evidence of widespread and systematic election fraud at the hands of the GOP and the Bush administration, this can no longer be assumed. America is now dominated by a single party bent on bringing the private sector in line politically with its interest in global domination and preventing the American people from interfering with its agenda. America is now a country in which civil liberties are being trammeled by nationalistic fervor and a hyped-up war on terror. America is a country in which its citizens are being conditioned to accept torture, domestic spying, the elimination of free speech, and unprecedented executive power.

The most important question now is what we the American people can do to try to reverse this downward descent into fascism. At best, we are now in the last days of democracy. The window of opportunity is rapidly closing—and it will soon slam shut. Are we going to take it lying down?

NOTES

1. Dennis Loo, "No Paper Trail Left Behind: The Theft of the 2004 Presidential Election," *Project Censored 2006*. See footnote 17 of Loo's paper, http://www.projectcensored.org/newsflash/voter_fraud.html (accessed May 12, 2006).

2. "Preserving Democracy: What Went Wrong in Ohio. Status Report of the House Judiciary Committee Democratic Staff," January 5, 2005, http://www.house.gov/judiciary_democrats/ohiostatusrept1505.pdf (accessed June 15, 2006).

3. Interview with Alexandra Pelosi, quoted in Mark Crispin Miller's "None Dare Call It Stolen: Ohio, the Election, and America's Servile Press," *Harpers*, August 2005, p. 46.

4. Personal correspondence.

5. "E-voting Systems Flaws 'Risk Election Fraud,'" *New Scientist.com*, July 25, 2003.

6. Don't be fooled by recent events: the fact that the 2006 midterm elections gave congress back to the Democrats changes nothing here. As we shall see below, the growing public hostility toward the war in Iraq and President Bush's strident antidemocratic stance was not without its consequences, but the apparent shift in power is, to quote Karl Rove, "only temporary."

7. "US Count Votes," Study of the 2004 Presidential Election Exit Poll Discrepancies, http://www.exit-poll.net/election-night/EvaluationJan192005.pdf, p. 3. (accessed February 16, 2007).

8. Steven F. Freeman, PhD, "The Unexplained Exit Poll Discrepancy," http://www.buzzflash.com/alerts/04/11/The_unexplaind_exitpoll_discrepancy_v00k.pdf (accessed November 26, 2006).

9. "Republican Challenges Presidential Election Based on Exit Polls," *New York Times*, November 23, 2004.

10. Richard Morris, "Those Faulty Exit Polls Were Sabotaged," *The Hill*, November 4, 2004.

11. Freeman, "The Unexplained Exit Poll Discrepancy." Freeman's original paper reported even slimmer odds. These numbers have been adjusted to square with Freeman's later, more detailed analysis.

12. The unadjusted data were posted on CNN's Web site on election night, but were pulled around 1:30 AM and replaced with the data adjusted to fit the vote tallies.

13. Steve Freeman and Joel Bleifuss, *Was the 2004 Presidential Election Stolen? Exit Polls, Election Fraud, and the Official Count* (New York: Seven Stories Press, 2006), p. 128.

14. Robert F. Kennedy Jr., "Was the 2004 Election Stolen? Republicans Prevented More Than 350,000 Voters in Ohio from Casting Ballots or Having Their Votes Counted—Enough to Have Put John Kerry in the White House," *Rolling Stone*, June 2006.

15. Steven Freeman, "Illegitimate Election: A Key Source for Robert F. Kennedy Jr. Responds to Criticism of His Analysis of the 2004 Election," Salon.com, June 12, 2006, http://www.salon.com/opinion/feature/2006/06/12/freeman/ (accessed February 16, 2007).

16. Freeman and Bleifuss, quoted in Kennedy, "Was the 2004 Election Stolen?" p. 130.

17. *USA Today*, November 3, 2004.

18. Thom Hartmann, "The Theft of Your Vote Is Just a Chip Away," Alternet, posted July 30, 2003.

19. Mark Crispin Miller, *Fooled Again: How the Right Stole the 2004 Election & Why They'll Steal the Next One Too (Unless We Stop Them)* (New York: Basic Books, 2005), p. 94.

20. Ibid., p. 195.

21. Beverly Harris and David Allen, *Black Box Voting: Ballot*

Tampering in the 21st Century (Renton, WA: Talion Publishing, 2004); "Chuck Hegal . . . Landslide Upset," *Business Week*, July 10, 2000.

22. Greg Palast, *Armed Madhouse* (New York: Dutton, 2006), p. 234.

23. Miller, *Fooled Again*, pp. 216 ff.; Seymour Hersh, "Lunch with Chairman," *New Yorker*, March 2003.

24. "Feeney Implicated in Vote Fraud," *Seminole Chronicle*, December 6, 2004.

25. Jim Hightower and Phillip Fraser, eds., "Who's Counting Our Votes? Bushite Corporate Bosses," *Hightower Lowdown* 5, no. 10 (October 2003), http://www.hightowerlowdown.org/node/810 (accessed February 6, 2007).

26. See Miller, *Fooled Again*, pp. 154–70.

27. Ibid., p. 168.

28. See, for example, Michael Collins, "Wrong Winner Chosen Twice by Same Voting Maching," *The Scoop* (http://www.scoop.co.nz/stories/HL0701/S—173.htm [accessed February 7, 2007]), and Jim Stratton's piece in the *Orlando Sentinal*, November 22, 2006, "Florida: Elections 2006—Sarasota Recount 'Analysis: Ballots favored Dems.'"

29. http://www.josephhall.org/tmp/HOLT_2-5-07.pdf (accessed February 16, 2007).

30. D. Tokaji, "Recount Redux? What Might Happen in a Close Election," October 31, 2006, *Election Law @ Moritz*, http://moritzlaw.osu.edu/electionlaw/comments/articles.php?ID=17 (accessed February 12, 2007).

Chapter 11

WHAT NOW, COMPATRIOTS?

The Declaration of Independence opens with an affirmation of the equality of men and the natural right of the people to dissolve a government that no longer serves the public good. Our government no longer serves the public, at least not in the sense envisioned by the Founding Fathers. Moreover, those who run the government have embraced a view of humanity that runs entirely counter to the principle of equality evidenced in that profound document. *We the People* have been shut out. *We the People* have been shut off. And *We the People* are being forced into servitude by those who believe they are entitled to lord over us. The truth is uncomfortable because it pulls away the veil of ignorance that deludes us into thinking our leaders are shepherds rather than wolves in sheep's clothing. But we dare not delude ourselves any longer, for the hour is late and our democracy is in peril. It is time to wake up and take up the task of restoring the power of all Americans to govern themselves and to pursue their happiness unencumbered by the tyranny of the small-minded. It is time to recommit to the principles on which this country was founded and restore our quickly vanishing freedoms. The future of our country depends on our efforts and our children deserve no less.

THE TIMELY LESSON OF NAZI GERMANY

It is very easy to sit on the sidelines and watch as the final nails are driven into the coffin of freedom and our fate is forever sealed. It has happened before in history, and it is happening right now, here in America. We should not allow the lesson of Nazi Germany to escape us. "It could never happen here" is pure arrogance—as though the average German were somehow morally inferior to the average American.

To the contrary, the similarities between Nazi Germany and America today are incredibly striking. Like the present American regime, the Third Reich ruled by fear and hate mongering. For Nazi Germany, the common enemy was not liberals or Arabs (equated to terrorists); instead it was Jews. But the strategy was exactly the same: invent a common foe that threatens the very survival of the state, declare war on that foe, and then use all imaginable powers of government—whatever it takes—to eradicate it.

In Nazi Germany, there was also a systematic program of indoctrination and brainwashing in place. Radio, newspapers, movies, music, and all other forms of media were carefully monitored by the government to make sure that the German people read, saw, and listened to only what the Nazis wanted the people to read, see, and hear. There was also an officer of disinformation (a "minister of propaganda")—not unlike our own Karl Rove—whose job it was to make sure journalists toed the Nazi line.

The Nazi regime discouraged independent thinking and demanded lockstep conformity instead. The politico-corporate media establishment in America operates on the identical principle. As you have seen, in America the politico-corporate media matrix serves the same tactical function.

The Nazi government also operated in secrecy, and it made law as it went along, defending its abuses of power in the name of national security—that is, in the name of protecting the state against its common enemy. The systematic violations of law and civil liberties in America—the operation of secret prison camps; the president's claimed right to torture prisoners of war (as against the Geneva Conventions); the warrantless eavesdropping on phone conversations and e-mail messages; the assumed power of the president to declare martial law and turn America into a police state; the claim that the entire nation is a "battlefield in the war on terror" so that ordinary legal protections don't apply; the president's use of signing statements to nullify legislative constraints on executive power; the threat to prosecute journalists for treason if they report information that endangers "national security" (as determined exclusively by the president and company); the canceling of habeas corpus; the labeling as "unlawful enemy combatants" anyone the president deems "hostile" to the interests of the United States; the suspension of legal protections for whistleblowers who expose government corruption; the attempt to control judicial outcomes (from firing federal prosecutors and intimidating state and federal judges to stocking the Supreme Court with right-wing conservatives)—these and many other antidemocratic, authoritarian activities make the analogy with Nazi Germany not only fitting but compelling.

And things keep getting progressively worse. Keep in mind that Nazi Germany also grew progressively worse over time. That regime did not begin with the same grotesque violations with which it ended. In these last days of what remains of our democracy, there may still be some hope of taking back America, but these glimmerings are steadily fading into oblivion.

It takes both insight and strength of will to do something about the current American crisis. First we must realize what's happening in and to America. This book has attempted to provide you with an enlightened perspective. It tells the morose tale of how the quest for money and power has created a dangerous, unholy alliance between big business and government, crushing the American dream, snuffing out civil liberties, and leaving us stranded in a media sea of propaganda and lies. It is a story of how we—the American people—have been shocked and awed into submitting to a megalomaniac government that has made the war on terror a pretext for keeping us all on a short leash. This is a story about the abominable degeneration of a robust America, a land of opportunity; a land where poor immigrants who had left their oppressive homelands in search of hope and promise could find a permanent home; a land where people could vote their consciences and have their vote count; a land where there were checks and balances on government power including a functional Fourth Estate; a land where we were free to express our political views without fear of government reprisal; a land where our home was secure from unlawful search and seizure. It is a story about the degeneration of a land where our heroes used to be genuine champions of democracy and not charlatans, thieves, and sociopaths.

It is a story about how the corporate media, including its marketers, advertisers, and TV/radio pundits and news personalities, have collectively helped an oppressive government regime propagate government lies and propaganda while masquerading as trustworthy representatives of public welfare. The sad truth is that this is also a media with incredible power to stop the spread of totalitarianism instead of fostering it.

What do you think would happen if the media suddenly told the true story about what has happened in and to America? What would happen if instead of concealing and deceiving Americans about the present government incursion into our democratic way of life, it spoke with blunt candor: "Wake up, America before it's too late! You are now in the last days of democracy. You are systematically being controlled and manipulated by a fascist regime that doesn't give a damn about the will of Americans (at least not as long as it doesn't mindlessly reflect its own political agenda). You have been stripped of your protected right to vote for the candidate of your choice; the Constitution and the rule of law no longer apply in this national "battlefield in the war on terror"; and your civil liberties are now at the discretion of the president who may decide at his whim to eavesdrop on you, confiscate your personal records, put you on an enemies list, arrest you for protesting against the government, and even brand you an "unlawful enemy combatant" and send you away to a detention camp at an undisclosed location.

Would this message resonate with most of us if it were heralded unrelentingly and consistently across all commercial mass media—from broadcast and cable TV to newspapers, radio, and Internet? How compliant with this oppressive government regime would most of us be if this message were driven home in earnest even by right-wing conservatives like Bill O'Reilly and Rush Limbaugh? Would this unified voice of Truth sweeping across America like a whirlwind, from sea to shining sea, awaken us from our trance and stir us to do something about the current crisis in America?

The media has incredible power to unite this nation against a common foe: it has already proven this by doing such an effective job in helping government to frighten us into submission. Why not use this extraordinary media power to unite us against the forces of totalitarianism that are now stealing our nation right under our noses?

Unfortunately, the MSM is now part of the problem, not the solution, and it is unlikely that it will provide such a consistent, blunt voice of Truth aimed at blowing the whistle on a formidable totalitarian government. The truth is that celebrities like O'Reilly and Limbaugh will continue to prostitute themselves to a fascist regime and cowardly pundits like Chris Matthews will continue to obey their corporate masters.

But what if the American people begin to see through this? What if we begin to fight back by refusing to go along with the charade? What if we begin to find alternative exits out of the Platonic cavern in which we are now enslaved?

What if we begin to look for Truth elsewhere, beyond the bogus shadows cast before us on the cave wall? What if we Americans escape the manipulative media matrix that constrains and keeps us in the dark? To do so, we must first realize that what we think of as democracy is really only bogus shadows, an empty illusion put before us for the sake of keeping us in chains.

We hope this book has helped to expose this ominous illusion. A well-informed public is to a dictatorship like garlic is to a vampire. Why else would the government have taken such pains to control the media and to use it to spread its propaganda? So here is rule number one of a dictatorship: keep the public uninformed—and even better, misinformed. The opposite rule—keep the people informed—is therefore a cardinal rule for fighting off dictatorship.

We have not claimed that the MSM is *totally* nonfunctional. As you have seen, corporate media is driven by an insatiable appetite for profit. It is not inherently interested in politics and, if it were not for its financial interest in satisfying government, it would have good reason to avoid taking *any* political stance (since getting political has potential to alienate consumers who disagree with the stance taken). Thus, even gigantic conglomerates like General Electric and News Corp can at least occasionally (unfortunately, not consistently) provide credible programming. Moreover, as discussed in chapter 2, if a media company is relatively small, focused primarily on news reporting, and has as its primary mission a clear commitment to quality journalism, it is more likely to take its job as Fourth Estate seriously than the giant conglomerates where the newsroom is just another division of the larger corporate culture. The appendix to this book lists some of the more credible MSM news sources.

In fact, the less popular a government administration becomes among the American people, the less vigilant the MSM is likely to be in touting its agenda. As you have seen, giant corporations are fair-weather friends and will take the path that offers the least resistance to making a profit. If Americans begin to see through the façade that the government is truly democratic—"by and for the people"—the MSM will have good reason to take a more critical look at government in reporting the news. Otherwise it stands to alienate too much of its audience—which turns away advertisers and decreases corporate revenues from advertising. The media will do its job of keeping us adequately informed only if we hold its feet to the fire, but we can do so only if the media does its job in the first place. So we appear to be stuck in a vicious cycle. What is needed to break this cycle is an independent source of news.

After September 11, 2001, corporate media devoted its energies to creating the image of America under siege and a valiant Bush administration bent on saving us from the terrorists—who hated us "because we are free." As a result of this portrayal, the corporate media got their pound of flesh, and the Bush administration grew abundantly more powerful. Most Americans were intimidated into surrendering their civil liberties—in the name of protecting "freedom"—and they rallied around the flag to strike back at "the enemy." The slogan "Freedom is not free" became the spur to sacrificing the very freedom we were supposed to be defending. Unfortunately, what we lost in the undertaking was not offset by any gains. To the contrary, our borders remain just as vulnerable as ever to terrorist attacks; terrorism in Iraq is now rampant unlike prior to the US invasion; and the biggest threat to American freedom—the Bush administration—now poses an even bigger threat.

Since 9/11, the corporate media has for the most part kept up the façade, and it is evident that it will continue to do so unless we Americans begin to see through it. However, this is unlikely unless we start relying less on the corporate media to keep us informed. Paradoxically, we must cease to take the corporate media seriously before it will *become* serious. In this schizophrenic context, it is obvious why an independent news source is now more vital than ever to the preservation of democracy in America. By turning away from the mainstream to *alternative* media, we Americans can help to bring the MSM to its knees begging us for our attention. The corporate media can only exist if people tune in, and people will be less inclined to tune in if they know they can keep themselves better informed by going elsewhere.

KEEPING INFORMED WITH INDIE MEDIA

This is why independent ("indie") media present a threat to the Bush administration. Indie media have the potential to undermine the corporate media matrix that government relies on to spread its propaganda. In chapter 8, you have seen how PNAC includes the PNAN plan to establish government dominance and control over Internet content. This control is sought largely because the Internet is presently a rich source of independent media. This is why it must be kept alive and why Americans owe it to their nation as well as to themselves as Americans to go online to keep informed. In the appendix of this book, we have listed some trustworthy online news sources to which you can turn—at least for now.

In these last days of democracy, it is crucial for us to keep ourselves as informed as possible. This means going online to get our news. It also means being very selective about what we watch and listen to in the mainstream media. That is why we entreat you to turn off the MSM. Yes, that's right, boycott it; bring it to its knees. Save democracy; shut off Chris Matthews, Bill O'Reilly, Rush Limbaugh, and company. Instead of permitting the corporate media matrix to control you, you can in this way begin to control it, and to take back America.

Democracy is founded on the collective will of the people. This collective will is hard to ignore for long. So the objective is to enlist others, as many as you can, in this effort to take back America. Urge your compatriots to join you in the boycotting of the corporate media matrix. Send e-mail messages, even chains of them. Spread the word far and wide that we shall not be denied the heritage of our Founding Fathers.

Of course, it's much easier to take no such initiative. It's also easier to sit back and watch Fox or CNN if this is what you have grown accustomed to doing. It takes willpower to make a new, special effort to look elsewhere for your information. But this extra effort is just what we should be making if we are true to our desire to live as a free people. Freedom does not exist unless you exercise it. It is not freedom to sit back and enjoy the show while you are being pumped full of propaganda and sanitized information.

There are a significant number of Americans who neither tune into the MSM nor seek out any alternative news sources. Such willful ignorance offers no antidote to the growth of fascism in America. On the contrary, this helps it to fester and grow. The less we know, the more emboldened the government will be to steal off with our freedoms. Choosing to remain ignorant simply feeds into the hands of a megalomaniacal, self-aggrandizing fascist regime.

SAVING THE FREE INTERNET

We have emphasized the need to keep the free Internet alive in order to reap the full benefits of an independent source of information. Unfortunately, as you have seen (chapter 8), giant telecom companies like Verizon and Comcast have taken control of the Internet cable and phone lines, and it is a matter of months before they institute a "pay for play" system that will end Net neutrality across these pipes.

As you have also seen, these companies have now set their sights on taking control of newer technologies such as Wi-Fi Internet and want nothing more than to put an end to community-controlled wireless Internet. However, these companies must have the approval of cities in order to build their infrastructures on public property. This approval to exploit public right-of-way should be refused by community leaders on the grounds that it is not in the best interest of the public.

As members of our respective communities, and as caring Americans, we should advocate instead for building community Wi-Fi systems. We can do this by bringing proposals to the floors of our respective city halls. The pressure to create such systems must come from us—the residents of these communities. Local pressure can in turn create a domino effect. If the communities speak in unison, the state representatives might listen, which might, in turn, kindle a fire in Washington.

There are also nonprofit organizations such as the National League of Cities (NLC), which advocate for cities at both state and federal levels. The NLC is in the trenches giving a legal voice to the concerns of local governments. These governments can and should avail themselves of the aid offered by the NLC. In addition, media activist groups such as the Free Press (see appendix) have launched campaigns in the form of letters to Congress opposing persistent attempts by the giant telecoms to pass legislation outlawing community Internet. We can and should support such grassroots efforts with our John Hancock.

The collective American voice can be a powerful one. There can be great strength in numbers. Stand up and be counted! The impending alternative is far less palatable. The PNAN plan will ripen, and all of us will soon inhabit a world in which our "choice" of Web sites will depend largely on what the politico-corporate media establishment determines. Empty rhetoric about Internet freedom and democracy will likely prevail behind a great American firewall while political reality will be just as the government says it is. The annals of Soviet history are filled with examples of this sort of oppression even in a much less technical age. In this Stepford universe, anyone who stands in opposition to the dominant powers will be branded an enemy of state or worse, insane—and therefore in need of "therapy." Unfortunately, from inside the walls of this dark, Platonic cyber cave, cut off from the light of truth, there will be little point in trying to prove otherwise.

What else can we the people do to reclaim America?

PEACEFUL ASSEMBLY AND CIVIL DISOBEDIENCE

The First Amendment says that Congress shall make no law abridging "the right of the people peaceably to assemble." Our great nation was founded on peaceful demonstration, but at this time in our history we are systematically being discouraged from questioning government authority. For example, on numerous occasions, Americans have been arrested or forced to leave Bush rallies and events just for holding signs or wearing clothing that expressed opposition to the war and administration policies. Under our system of government, people have a right to freedom of speech, especially political speech. This is the cornerstone of our democracy.

A few of these protesters who were arrested have filed lawsuits against state, local, and federal government agencies and officers for violating their rights to free speech and equal protection under the law. These individuals have set clear examples of what it means to be an American. They realize that being free is more than hollow words uttered by a president in a State of the Union address. A right to free speech does not exist unless one is allowed to *exercise* it, and these noble Americans are attempting to use the system of justice established by our Constitution to protect this right.

There is nothing more American than standing up for the rights granted and protected by our Constitution. We have an obligation to defend these rights against anyone who seeks to nullify them. Presently, the executive branch of the government is such a one. The right to peaceful assembly and demonstration is an essential part of the corpus of American democracy. It is now more urgent than ever that we take this right seriously and exercise it—especially since expressing our will through the vote is now also on the line.

In the summer of 1846, Henry David Thoreau spent a night in prison for refusing to pay his poll taxes, which he declined in order to protest the government's waging of a bloody war against Mexico and its support of slavery. Thoreau intended to remain in prison, but when someone paid his taxes for him, he was forced to leave. Thoreau's act of "civil disobedience" aimed at setting an example for others to follow. He believed that if others followed his example, then the jails and courts would become clogged with dissenters, and the government would be forced to repeal its evil laws. Thoreau also believed that there was a higher law of conscience than the civil laws imposed by a tyrannical government, and that when this law of conscience conflicted with the latter civil law, the former must take precedence.

There is no better time than the present to reflect on the moral ideals that motivated Thoreau to stand up against the oppressive government policies of his day. When Nazi war criminals were brought to justice at Nuremberg, after World War II, many of those accused of heinous acts claimed to be following the laws laid down by Hitler. This excuse for engaging in barbaric acts of inhumanity did not bode well with the Court. Rather, these individuals were charged with defying a higher *moral* law that binds in conscience and trumps the commands of a tyrant.

This is an important lesson we can learn from history. We must remain true to our consciences and not allow ourselves to be intimidated or frightened into going along with an oppressive regime. We must not stand on the sidelines and allow our Constitution to be desecrated. As Thoreau entreated, we must collectively be guided by our consciences rather than blindly submitting to tyranny. With the

Bill of Rights as our guiding light, together we can wield incredible power to stop oppression. Wars cannot be waged without citizens to pay taxes to support them and soldiers to fight them. Government lies and propaganda cannot be disseminated without the cooperation of people willing to disseminate and believe them. Media companies cannot exist without people willing to watch or listen to their programs.

Thoreau did not think that patriotism was a mere matter of displaying a popular bumper sticker or waving an American flag. Quite the contrary, such blind conformity, he believed, was responsible for helping to sustain iniquitous government policies and actions. For Thoreau, patriotism involved deep personal resolve to do what was right for one's nation and its citizens regardless of personal sacrifice. So he was willing to pay the price of going to prison in order to follow his conscience and to help affect constructive change in the law. He and his family were also abolitionists and were actively involved in the Underground Railroad, which helped runaway slaves to attain their freedom. These were acts of conscience involving personal risk. They give meaning and substance to patriotism.

This does not mean that you must engage in civil disobedience to be patriotic. It does mean, however, that you must be true to your conscience. Does it offend your conscience to know that your government has been torturing detainees at Abu Ghraib, Guantánamo, and at a number of secret prison camps—raping, sodomizing, chemically burning, electrically shocking, stamping, punching, kicking, depriving of food and sleep, humiliating religiously and sexually, and in some cases even killing detainees? The Geneva Conventions were established after World War II in response to Nazi atrocities in order to prevent cruel and inhumane treatment of prisoners. The US War Crimes Act of 1996 made the Geneva Conventions proscription against deliberate "killing, torture or inhumane treatment of detainees" the law of the land. So, the acts of torture committed by the US government are not only unconscionable and in violation of international law, they also violate US federal law.

Do you believe that the more than three thousand American youths who lost their lives in Iraq and the many thousands who have lost their limbs or who now suffer from other serious physical and psychological disabilities as a result of their service deserved to be told the truth about why they were risking their lives? Do you believe that all Americans are entitled to due process and the right to trial by jury, to have free elections, and to be protected against unlawful searches and seizures?

When you remain silent while the government engages in unconscionable violations of fundamental human rights, you are not being patriotic. If you want to stand up for your nation, then you must stand up against such violations. This might take the form of educating others about these abominations of human rights, by denouncing them and by attempting to convince others to do the same—whether in the workplace, at a social gathering, in a public forum, at a political rally, or in the classroom. To sit back and do absolutely nothing is to give tacit approval to what no person in good conscience can rightly accept. Nor will it do to claim faith that your government—including Congress, whether Democratic or Republican—knows what it is doing. This is to forget that democracy is *by the people and for the people*. To place blind trust in a government authority is already to give up on democracy!

EDUCATORS ARE VANGUARDS OF DEMOCRACY

We the people should also be keeping a close eye on our educational institutions. As the earlier analogy with Nazi Germany suggests, you can expect the public schools supported by your tax dollars to become factories for programming children to support government policies. There have already been attempts to silence teachers who speak out against government policies. In one case, an elementary school music teacher lost her job when she refused to stop encouraging her students to sing songs about love and peace.[1] In another case, a high school teacher was fired because he refused to censor a student's poetry that criticized the war in Iraq and Bush's "No Child Left Behind" educational policy.[2] In another case, a community college English teacher lost her job for making antiwar comments.[3] Examples of such cases can be given ad nauseam. In addition, as discussed in chapter 6, attempts have already been made by Bush cronies at the state level to pass laws that intimidate "leftist" professors against expressing their views in class by giving students the right to sue them for expressing their views.[4]

The teachers of America need to stand firm against attempts by government to censor free speech and to stifle the creative spirit of self-expression. Those who clam up and will not speak their consciences because they are afraid of losing their jobs have already given up on the democratizing power of education.

It is incumbent on college and university teachers, especially those who teach in the liberal arts and social sciences, to enlighten their students about the erosion of democracy in

America.[5] Academia, by its very nature, flourishes in a free-thinking, democratic environment and wilts on the vine in a sterile, controlled one. Awareness of what is now happening to America is therefore monumentally important for the survival of the American academy. Any professor who fails to address the decline of democracy in America is therefore remiss in his or her pedagogic duty.

As should now be evident, this can hardly be emphasized enough in the case of teachers who teach in schools of journalism. These teachers, who teach the prospective purveyors of democracy, must drive home the inestimable importance of their role as Fourth Estate. Emphasis on teaching the technical skills of editing, reporting, copyediting, and the like is pointless unless these skills are seen in their *moral* context. Ethics should not be an adjunct to instruction as this artificially separates morality from competence. Instead, the moral quality of technical competence should be stressed and the skills viewed as empty corpses until the democratic spirit of the press breathes life into them.

Officers and members of journalism associations should be vigilantly vocal about the current state of American journalism. For example, the Society of Professional Journalists has recognized "a special obligation to ensure that the public's business is conducted in the open and that government records are open to inspection."[6] In this regard, it publishes a list of "red flags" on its Web site that indicate when such freedom of information is in danger of being violated (for example, "Government files, which had been available, suddenly become unavailable").[7] But, these associations should make abundantly clear that the news organizations, under political pressures, are *themselves* active participants in undermining public welfare. This requires the generation of a new set of "red flags" that should send signals to individual journalists that organizational self-censorship, playing down of stories, and promulgation of government propaganda are now undermining the role of the press as Fourth Estate. Journalists need to be encouraged by journalism associations to resist the politico-corporate pressures that lead to this surrender of their obligation to the American people.

To ease these pressures, journalists should also band together to form unions whose primary purpose is to preserve journalistic integrity in the corporate work environment. So long as journalists confront the politico-corporate establishment as individuals, they will remain weak and vulnerable. On the other hand, if the corporate media had to contend with well-organized, powerful independent unions in setting the conditions of hiring and keeping competent journalists under their employ, then we might well see some improvement in MSM news coverage. Journalism schools should also work cooperatively with such unions to encourage their graduates to become union members as a matter of professional obligation.

Teachers and practitioners of law in America are also in a unique position to defend democracy against tyranny. Given lawyers' special fund of knowledge and training, they have an unparalleled capacity to expose breaches of law by government. A useful example is the American Bar Association's recent denouncement of President Bush's uses of "signing statements" (see also chapter 1). An eleven-member, bipartisan panel of the ABA concluded that, in claiming the power to disregard selected provisions of the bills he signs, Bush is eroding the Constitution and the rule of law. Such use of signing statements, said the panel, is "contrary to the rule of law and our constitutional system of separation of powers."[8] Not surprisingly, with the exception of CNN's Lou Dobbs, the other major television networks failed to mention the ABA report.[9]

In the end, all Americans have a vital role to play in the effort to restore democracy to America. To a large extent, it is knowledge that can set us free. The answer does not lie in falling for the titillating and seductive allure of an extreme corporate media makeover. The answer cannot be found in the fashion tabloids or in following the heated exploits of desperate housewives, or in the digitized slaying of monsters. Nor will it be found in the dogmatic spinnings of a Bill O'Reilly—no matter how entertaining you may find him, or in the "hardball" antics of a charlatan like Chris Matthews. This is all for show—and the show will eventually become your life if you let it.

To the contrary, the answer lies in keeping before us the American dream, the vision of ourselves as free agents capable of autonomously shaping our own destinies according to our own spiritual, moral, social, and political lights. The America that is great is a land of the free—a potpourri of diverse peoples living tolerantly under one national roof, all pursuing the American dream in their own special ways. It is not a land where one religion, one political party, and one set of morals fits all. Such an artificial hothouse climate is one where dictatorship will thrive and democracy will shrivel up and die. Unfortunately, this is the course that has been chartered for America by its current regime.

You will not likely wake up one day to find that democracy in America has finally come to an end. There will not be any breaking news to this effect. More than likely, you will still hear the usual regurgitations coming across the MSM (which will come in many different flavors of vanilla) and you may even hear an occasional report that seems critical of a government policy. But you will not likely find out how *un-free* you really are unless you step out of line and challenge the politico-corporate puppeteers who pull the strings. For the majority of Americans who never realize that they are at the other end of those strings, life will seem pretty much the same as ever. That, we think, would be the biggest tragedy.

NOTES

1. Robert L. Jamieson Jr., "Anti-war Teacher Quits Her Job Rather Than Principles," Seattlepi.com, September 24, 2003, http://seattlepi.nwsource.com/jamieson/141016_roberto24.html (accessed February 12, 2007).

2. Bill Hill, "Teacher Fired over Student's Anti-war Poetry," *Daytona Beach News Journal*, May 22, 2004, http://www.rense .com/general53/teacher.htm (accessed February 12, 2007).

3. "Teacher Fired for Anti-war Remarks to Appear before FTTC Trustees," Common Dreams, December 12, 2003, http:// www.commondreams.org/scriptfiles/news2003/1212-05.htm (accessed February 12, 2007).

4. Robert L. Rexroad, "The Foxification of Education," TVNewsLies.org, April 16, 2005, http://www.tvnewslies.org/ phpbb/viewtopic.php?t=1248&sid=db15781951c420e272620c5 dbc8b3593 (accessed February 12, 2007).

5. While this may be more the case for professors of political science than professors of mathematics, even the latter do not entirely escape the obligation to point out the importance of crit-

ical thinking in mathematics and the threat to such thinking from a totalitarian state that demands blind conformity. The same can also be said of the natural sciences.

6. Society of Professional Journalists, Code of Ethics, http://www.spj.org/ethics_code.asp (accessed February 11, 2007).

7. Society of Professional Journalists, "Red Flags" to Violation of Freedom of Information (FOI), http://www.spj.org/foia _opendoors_flags.asp (accessed February 12, 2007).

8. Robert Pear, "Legal Group Says Bush Undermines Law by Ignoring Selected Parts of Bills," *New York Times*, July 24, 2006, http://www.nytimes.com/2006/07/24/washington/24prexy.html ?ei=5090&en=b748a5a2247f3591&ex=1311393600&partner =rssuserland&emc=rss&pagewanted=print (accessed February 12, 2007).

9. "*LA Times*, Networks, Fox News Ignored ABA Conclusion That Bush Signing Statements 'Weaken Our Cherished System of Checks and Balances and Separation of Powers,'" Media Matters, July 27, 2006, http://www.mediamatters.org/ items/200607270005 (accessed February 12, 2007).

Appendix
SELECTED MEDIA

T he entries on this list that have been marked with an asterisk may be especially vulnerable to politico-corporate pressures.

INDEPENDENT ONLINE NEWS SOURCES

Alternet.org http://www.alternet.org/
Buzzflash.org http://www.buzzflash.com/
CommonDreams.org http://www.commondreams.org/
Counterpunch http://www.counterpunch.org/
Daily Kos http://www.dailykos.com/
DemocraticUnderground.com http://www.democraticunderground
   .com/
Greg Palast http://www.gregpalast.com/
Herald Globe http://www.heraldglobe.com/

Huffington Post http://www.huffingtonpost.com/
Jim Hightower http://www.jimhightower.com/
Media Channel.org http://www.mediachannel.org/
Moveon.org http://www.moveon.org/
Raw Story http://www.rawstory.com/
Salon.com http://www.salon.com/
Sky Reporter (Arthur Kent) http://www.skyreporter.com/
TomPaine.com http://www.tompaine.com/
TruthOut.org http://www.truthout.org/

ONLINE MEDIA AND GOVERNMENT WATCHDOG ORGANIZATIONS

American Civil Liberties Union http://www.aclu.org/
Center for Digital Democracy http://www.democraticmedia.org/
Center for Media and Democracy http://www.prwatch.org/
Center for Public Integrity http://www.publicintegrity.org/
    default.aspx
CorpWatch http://www.corpwatch.org/
Electronic Frontier Foundation http://www.eff.org/
Fairness and Accuracy in Reporting (FAIR) http://www.fair.org
Free Press http://www.freepress.net/
Institute for Public Integrity http://www.publicintegrity.org/
Media Access Project http://www.mediaaccess.org/
Media Alliance http://www.media-alliance.org/
Media Matters for America http://mediamatters.org/
Prometheus Radio Project http://www.prometheusradio.org/

RADIO

Democracy Now http://www.democracynow.org/

Pacifica Radio http://www.pacifica.org/
Air America Radio http://www.airamerica.com/

MAGAZINES AND PUBLICATIONS

In These Times http://www.inthesetimes.com/
MotherJones http://www.motherjones.com/
The Nation http://www.thenation.com/
The Progressive http://www.progressive.org/
Project Censored http://www.projectcensored.org/
Z Magazine http://www.zmag.org/weluser.htm

NEWSPAPERS

Guardian Unlimited http://www.guardian.co.uk/
*Los Angeles Times** http://www.latimes.com/
*New York Times** http://www.nytimes.com/
*Washington Post** http://www.washingtonpost.com/

BROADCAST AND CABLE TELEVISION

CSPAN http://www.c-span.org/
MSNBC Countdown with Keith Olbermann* http://www.msnbc
    .msn.com/id/3036677/
PBS, NOW with David Brancaccio* http://www.pbs.org/now/

DOCUMENTARIES

Fahrenheit 9/11 http://www.fahrenheit911.com/

An Inconvenient Truth http://www.climatecrisis.net/

Iraq for Sale http://iraqforsale.org/

Outfoxed: Rupert Murdoch's War on Journalism http://www.out-foxed.org/

The U.S. vs. John Lennon http://www.buzzflash.com/store/reviews/470

SELECTED BIBLIOGRAPHY

Bakan, Joel. *The Corporation: The Pathological Pursuit of Profit and Power.* New York: Free Press, 2004.

Barstow, David, and Robin Stein. "Under Bush a New Age of Prepackaged TV News." *New York Times*, March 13, 2005.

Bernays, E. *Propaganda.* New York: Ig Publishing, 2005.

Bohlert, Eric. *Lap Dogs: How the Press Rolled Over for Bush.* New York: Free Press, 2006.

Borjesson, Kristina. *Feet to the Fire: The Media after 9/11, Top Journalists Speak Out.* Amherst, NY: Prometheus Books, 2005.

Brock, David. *The Republican Noise Machine: Right Wing Media and How It Corrupts Democracy.* New York: Crown, 2004.

Chatterjee, Pratap. *Iraq, Inc.: A Profitable Occupation.* New York: Seven Stories Press, 2004.

Chomsky, Noam. *Hegemony or Survival: America's Quest for Global Dominance.* New York: Metropolitan Books, 2003.

Cohen, Elliot D. *News Incorporated: Corporate Media Ownership and Its Threat to Democracy.* Amherst, NY: Prometheus Books, 2005.

————. "Web of Deceit: How Internet Freedom Got the Federal Ax, and Why Corporate News Censored the Story." Buzzflash, July 18, 2005. http://www.buzzflash.com/contributors/05/07/con05238.html.

Confessore, Nicholas. "Welcome to the Machine: How the GOP Disciplined K Street and Made Bush Supreme." *Washington Monthly*, July/August 2003.

Conyers Report. "The Constitution in Crises: The Downing Street Minutes and Deception, Manipulation, Torture, Retribution, and Cover-Ups in the Iraq War." Prepared by Representative Conyers's staff and available on the Conyers Web site.

————. *Preserving Democracy: What Went Wrong in Ohio. Status Report of the House Judiciary Committee Democratic Staff*, Janurary 5, 2005. http://www.house.gov/judiciary_democrats/ohiostatusrept1505.pdf.

Crispin Miller, Mark. *Fooled Again: How the Right Stole the 2004 Election & Why They'll Steal the Next One Too (Unless We Stop Them)*. New York: Basic Books, 2005.

————. "None Dare Call It Stolen: Ohio, the Election, and America's Servile Press." *Harpers*, August 2005.

Dawson, Michael. *The Consumer Trap: Big Business Marketing in American Life*. Chicago: University of Illinois Press, 2003.

Dean, John W. *Conservatives without Conscience*. New York: Viking, 2006.

Drew, Elizabeth. "Selling Washington." *New York Review of Books* 52, no. 11 (June 23, 2005).

Drumheller, Tyler. *On the Brink: An Insider's Account of How the White House Compromised American Intelligence*. New York: Caroll & Graf, 2006.

Drury, Shadia B. *Leo Strauss and the American Right*. New York: St. Martin's, 1999.

Freeman, S., and J. Bleifuss. *Was the 2004 Presidential Election Stolen? Exit Polls, Election Fraud, and the Official Count*. New York: Seven Stories Press, 2006.

Fritz, Ben, Brian Keefer, and Brendan Nyhan. *All the President's Spin: George W. Bush, the Media, and the Truth.* New York: Simon & Schuster, 2004.

Healy, G., and T. Lynch. "Power Surge: The Constitutional Record of George W. Bush." Cato Institute, 2006.

Hersh, Seymour. "Lunch with Chairman." *New Yorker,* March 2003.

Karp, Walter. *Indispensable Enemies: The Politics of Misrule in America.* New York: Franklin Square Press, 1993.

Kennedy, Robert F., Jr., "Was the 2004 Election Stolen? Republicans Prevented More Than 350,000 Voters in Ohio from Casting Ballots or Having Their Votes Counted—Enough to Have Put John Kerry in the White House." *Rolling Stone,* June 2006.

Krugman, Paul. "Victors and Spoils." *New York Times,* November 19, 2002.

Kull, Steven, et al. "Misperceptions, the Media, and the Iraq War." Program on International Policy Attitudes, October 2, 2003. http://www.americanassembler.com/issues/media/docs/Media _10_02_03_Report.pdf.

Linn, Susan. *Consuming Kids: The Hostile Takeover of Childhood.* New York: New Press, 2004.

McChesney, Robert, and John Nichols. *Tragedy & Farce: How the American Media Sell Wars, Spin Elections, and Destroy Democracy.* New York: New Press, 2006.

Norton, Anne. *Leo Strauss and the Politics of American Empire.* New Haven, CT: Yale University Press, 2004.

Ott, Richard. *Creating Demand: Powerful Tips and Tactics for Marketing Your Product or Service.* Burr Ridge, IL: Irwin, 1992.

Palast, Greg. *Armed Madhouse.* New York: Dutton, 2006.

Phillips, Peter. *Impeach the President: The Case against Bush and Cheney.* New York: Seven Stories Press, 2006.

Pratkanis, A., and E. Aronson. *Age of Propaganda: The Everyday Use and Abuse of Persuasion*. New York: Owl Books, 2001.

Project for the New American Century. "Rebuilding America's Defenses: Strategy, Focus, and Resources for a New Century." http://www.newamericancentury.org/publicationsreports.htm.

Risen, James, and Eric Lichtblau. "Bush Lets U.S. Spy on Callers without Courts." *New York Times*, December 16, 2005.

Rycroft, Matthew. "The Secret Downing Street Memo." *Sunday Times*, May 1, 2005. http://www.timesonline.co.uk/tol/news/uk/article387374.ece.

Shorris, Earl. "Ignoble Liars: Leo Strauss, George Bush, and the Philosophy of Mass Deception." *Harpers*, June 2004.

INDEX